ALL NEW 100 MATHS LESSONS

YEAR 1

Ann Montague-Smith

Contents

Published by
Scholastic Ltd
Villiers House
Clarendon Avenue
Leamington Spa
Warks. CV32 5PR

© **Scholastic Ltd, 2005**
Text © Ann Montague-Smith, 2005
Printed by Bell & Bain
23456789   5678901234

Series Consultant
Ann Montague-Smith

Author
Ann Montague-Smith

Editors
Joel Lane and Gaynor Spry

Assistant Editor
Aileen Lalor

Series Designer
Joy Monkhouse

Designers
Allison Parry, Micky Pledge
and Andrea Lewis

Illustrations
Jim Peacock and
Dorian Spencer Davies
(Beehive Illustration)

CD development
CD developed in association
with Footmark Media Ltd

Visit our website at
www.scholastic.co.uk

Acknowledgements
Extracts from the National Numeracy Strategy Framework for Teaching Mathematics © Crown copyright. Reproduced under the terms of HMSO Guidance Note 8

Designed using Adobe Inc. InDesign™ v2.0.1

British Library Cataloguing-in-Publication Data
A catalogue record for this book is available from the British Library.
ISBN 0-439-98467-X
ISBN 978-0439-98467-6
The right of Ann Montague-Smith to be identified as the Author of this work has been asserted by her in accordance with the Copyright, Designs and Patents Act 1988.

Every effort has been made to trace copyright holders for the works reproduced in this book and the publishers apologise for any inadvertent omissions.

About the series

100 Maths Lessons is designed to enable you to provide clear teaching, with follow-up activities that are, in the main, practical activities for pairs of children to work on together. These activities are designed to encourage the children to use the mental strategies that they are learning and to check each other's calculations. Many of the activities are games that they will enjoy playing, and that encourage learning.

About the book

This book is divided into three termly sections. Each term begins with a **Medium-term plan** ('Termly planning grid') based on the National Numeracy Strategy's *Medium-term plans* and *Framework for teaching mathematics*. Each term's work is divided into a number of units of differentiated lessons on a specific subject.

Note: Because the units in this book follow the structure of the National Numeracy Strategy's *Framework for teaching mathematics*, the units in each term jump from Unit 6 to Unit 8. The Strategy suggests you put aside the time for Unit 7 for Assess and review.

Finding your way around the lesson units

Each term is comprised of 11 to 12 units. Each unit contains:
- a short-term planning grid
- three to five lesson plans
- photocopiable activity sheets.

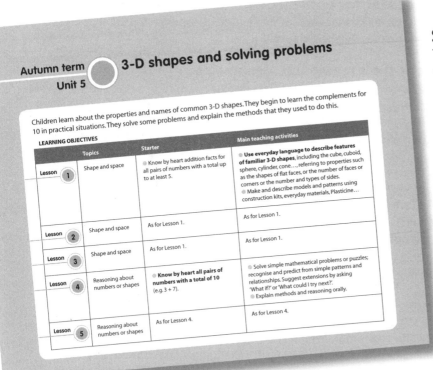

Short-term planning grids

The short-term planning grids ('Learning objectives') provide an overview of the objectives for each unit. The objectives come from the Medium-term plan and support clear progression through the year. Key objectives are shown in bold, as in the Yearly Teaching Programme in the NNS *Framework for teaching mathematics*.

Lesson plans

The lessons are structured on the basis of a daily maths lesson following the NNS's three-part lesson format: a ten-minute **Starter** of oral work and mental maths, a **Main teaching activities** session with interactive teaching time and/or group/individual work and a **Plenary** round-up including **Assessment** opportunities. In some lessons, differentiated tasks are supplied for more able and less able pupils.

However, this structure has not been rigidly applied. Where it is appropriate to concentrate on whole-class teaching, for example, the lesson plan may not include a group-work session at all. The overall organisation of the lesson plan varies from unit to unit depending on the lesson content. In some units all the plans are separate, though they provide different levels of detail. Elsewhere you may find a bank of activities that you can set up as a 'circus', or instruction and support for an extended investigation, either of which the children will work through over the course of several days.

Most units of work are supported with activity pages provided in the book, which can also be found on the accompanying CD. In addition to these core activity sheets, the CD contains differentiated versions for less able and more able ability levels. Some are available as blank templates, to allow you to make your own further differentiated versions.

How ICT is used

Ideas for using ICT are suggested wherever appropriate in *100 Maths Lessons*. We have assumed that you will have access to basic office applications, such as word-processing, and can email and research using the Internet. The QCA's *ICT Scheme of Work for Key Stages 1 and 2* has been used as an indicator of the skills the children will be developing formally from Year 1 and their progression in the primary years.

While some lessons use dataloggers or floor robots, we have avoided suggesting specific software, except for the games and interactive teaching programs (ITPs) provided by the NNS. If you do not already have them, these can be downloaded from the NNS website at: http://www.standards.dfes.gov.uk/numeracy

How to use the CD-ROM

System requirements
Minimum specification:
- PC with a CD-ROM drive and at least 32 MB RAM
- Pentium 166 MHz processor
- Microsoft Windows 98, NT, 2000 or XP
- SVGA screen display with at least 64K colours at a screen resolution of 800 x 600 pixels

100 Maths Lessons CD-ROMs are for PC use only.

Setting up your computer for optimal use
On opening, the CD will alert you if changes are needed in order to operate the CD at its optimal use. There are two changes you may be advised to make:

Viewing resources at their maximum screen size
To see images at their maximum screen size, your screen display needs to be set to 800 x 600 pixels. In order to adjust your screen size you will first need to **Quit** the program.

If using a PC, select **Settings**, then **Control Panel** from the **Start** menu. Next, double click on the **Display** icon and then click on the **Settings** tab. Finally, adjust the **Screen area** scroll bar to 800 x 600 pixels. Click **OK** and then restart the program.

Adobe® Acrobat® Reader®
Acrobat® Reader® is required to view Portable Document Format (PDF) files. All of the unit resources are PDF files. It is not necessary to install Acrobat Reader on your PC. If you do not have it installed, the application will use a 'run-time' version for the CD, i.e. one which only works with the 100 Maths Lessons application.
However if you would like to install **Acrobat® Reader®**, the latest version (6) can be downloaded from the CD-ROM. To do this, right-click on the **Start** menu on your desktop and choose **Explore**. Click on the + sign to the left of the CD drive entitled '100 Maths Lessons' and open the folder called **Acrobat Reader Installer.** Run the program contained in this folder to install **Acrobat® Reader®.** If you experience any difficulties viewing the PDF files, try changing your **Acrobat® Reader®** preferences. Select **Edit**, then **Preferences**, within **Acrobat® Reader®**. You will then be able to change your viewing options. For further information about **Adobe® Acrobat® Reader®**, visit the **Adobe®** website at www.adobe.com.

Getting started
The *100 Maths Lessons CD-ROM* program should auto run when you insert the CD-ROM into your CD drive. If it does not, use **My Computer** to browse the contents of the CD-ROM and click on the '100 Maths Lessons' icon.
From the start up screen there are three options: Click on **Credits** to view a list of acknowledgements. You must then read the **Terms and conditions**. If you agree to these terms then click **Next** to continue. **Continue** on the start up screen allows you to move to the Main menu.

Main menu

Each *100 Maths Lessons* CD contains:

- core activity sheets – with answers, where appropriate, that can be toggled by pressing the 'on' and 'off' buttons on the left of the screen
- differentiated activity sheets for more and less able pupils (though not necessarily both more and less able sheets in every instance)
- blank core activity sheets for selected core activity sheets – these allow you to make your own differentiated sheets by printing and annotating.
- general resource sheets designed to support a number of activities.

You can access the printable pages on the CD by clicking:

- the chosen term ('Autumn','Spring' or 'Summer')
- the unit required (for example,'Unit 2: Place value and ordering)
- the requisite activity page (for example,'Numbers to 10';'Less able').

To help you manage the vast bank of printable pages on each CD, there is also a 'Practical assessment record sheet' provided on the CD that you can use to record which children have tackled which pages. This could be particularly useful if you would like less able children to work through two or three of the differentiated pages for a lesson or topic.

CD navigation

Back: click to return to the previous screen. Continue to move to the **Menu** or start up screens.

Quit: click **Quit** to close the menu program. You are then provided with options to return to the start up menu or to exit the CD.

Help: provides general background information and basic technical support. Click on the **Help** button to access. Click **Back** to return to the previous screen.

Alternative levels: after you have accessed a CD page, you will see a small menu screen on the left-hand side of the screen. This allows you to access differentiated or template versions of the same activity.

Printing

There are two print options:

- The **Print** button on the bottom left of each activity screen allows you to print directly from the CD program.
- If you press the **View** button above the **Print** option, the sheet will open as a read-only page in **Acrobat® Reader®**. To print the selected resource from **Acrobat® Reader®**, select **File** and then **Print**. Once you have printed the resource, minimise or close the **Adobe®** screen using _ or **x** in the top right-hand corner of the screen.

Viewing on an interactive whiteboard or data projector

The sheets can be viewed directly from the CD. To make viewing easier for a whole class, use a large monitor, data projector or interactive whiteboard.

About Year 1

Year 1 is the first year when a formally-structured daily maths lesson is expected. Children will start the year learning to count from 1 to 20 and beyond, and to count on and back from any small number in ones and tens,from and back to zero. They say the numbers that are 1 or 10 more or less than a given number. They develop mental strategies for addition and subtraction (as 'take away', 'difference' and 'how many more') and write number sentences in horizontal format. They learn by heart all pairs of numbers with a total of 10. They solve number and measures problems. They make direct comparisons of measures, then choose appropriate units to make estimates and measures. They use everyday language to describe familiar 3-D and 2-D shapes. These will be the key concepts learned this year.

EVERY DAY: Practise and develop oral and mental skills (e.g. counting, mental strategies, rapid recall of + and – facts)

- Know the number names and recite them in order to at least 20.
- **Count reliably at least 20 objects.**
- Describe and extend number sequences: **count on in ones from any small number.**
- **Read and write numerals from 0 to at least 20.**
- **Know by heart all pairs of numbers with a total of 10** (e.g. 3 + 7).
- Know by heart addition facts for all pairs of numbers with a total up to at least 5, and the corresponding subtraction facts.
- Know by heart addition doubles of all numbers to at least 5 (e.g. 4 + 4).

Units	Days	Topics	Objectives
1	3	Counting, properties of numbers and number sequences	Know the number names and recite them in order to at least 20, from and back to zero. **Count reliably at least 20 objects.** Describe and extend number sequences: **count on in ones from any small number, and in tens from and back to zero.**
2–4	15	Place value and ordering	**Read and write numerals from 0 to at least 20.** **Within the range of 0 to 30, say the number that is 1 or 10 more or less than any given number.** Begin to know what each digit in a two-digit number represents. Partition a 'teens' number into a multiple of 10 and ones (TU).
		Understanding addition and subtraction	**Understand the operation of addition, and of subtraction (as 'take away', 'difference' and 'how many more make'), and use the related vocabulary.** Begin to recognise that addition can be done in any order. Begin to use +, – and = signs to record mental calculations in a number sentence, and to recognise the use of symbols such as □ or △ to stand for an unknown number.
		Mental calculation strategies (+ and –)	Use knowledge that addition can be done in any order to do mental calculations more efficiently. For example: put the larger number first and count on in ones, including beyond 10 (e.g. 7 + 5).
		Problems involving 'real life', money or measures	Recognise coins of different values. Find totals and change from up to 20p.
		Making decisions	Choose and use appropriate number operations and mental strategies to solve problems.
5–6	8	Shape and space	**Use everyday language to describe features of familiar 3-D and 2-D shapes,** including the cube, cuboid, sphere, cylinder, cone, circle, triangle, square, rectangle, referring to properties such as the shapes of flat faces, or the number of faces or corners or the number and types of sides. Make and describe models, patterns and pictures using construction kits, everyday materials, Plasticine…
		Reasoning about numbers or shapes	Solve simple mathematical problems or puzzles; recognise and predict from simple patterns and relationships. Suggest extensions by asking 'What if?' or 'What could I try next?'. Explain methods and reasoning orally.
		Measures	Understand and use the vocabulary related to length, mass and capacity. **Compare two lengths by direct comparison**; extend to more than two. Measure using uniform non-standard units (e.g. straws, wooden cubes, plastic weights), or standard units (e.g. metre sticks, litre jugs).

EVERY DAY: Practise and develop oral and mental skills (e.g. counting, mental strategies, rapid recall of + and – facts)

- **Count reliably at least 20 objects.**
- Describe and extend number sequences: **count on and back in ones from any small number, and in tens from and back to zero.**
- **Read and write numerals from 0 to at least 10.**
- **Order numbers to at least 10**, and position them on a number track.
- Know by heart addition doubles of all numbers to at least 5 (e.g. 4 + 4).
- Begin to know addition facts for all pairs of numbers with a total up to at least 10, and the corresponding subtraction facts.

Units	Days	Topics	Objectives
8	5	Counting, properties of numbers and number sequences	Know the number names and recite them in order to at least 20, from and back to zero. Describe and extend number sequences: **count on and back in ones from any small number, and in tens from and back to zero.**
		Reasoning about numbers or shapes	Solve simple mathematical problems or puzzles; recognise and predict from simple patterns and relationships. Suggest extensions by asking 'What if?' or 'What could I try next?'.
9–11	15	Place value and ordering	**Read and write numerals from 0 to at least 20.** Begin to know what each digit in a two-digit number represents. Partition a 'teens' number and begin to partition larger two-digit numbers into a multiple of 10 and ones (TU). **Understand the vocabulary of comparing and ordering numbers,** including ordinal numbers to at least 20. Use the = sign to represent equality.
		Estimating	Understand and use the vocabulary of estimation. Give a sensible estimate of a number of objects that can be checked by counting (e.g. up to about 30 objects).
		Understanding addition and subtraction	**Understand the operation of addition, and of subtraction (as 'take away'), and use the related vocabulary.**
		Mental calculation strategies (+ and –)	Use patterns of similar calculations (e.g. 10 – 0 = 10, 10 – 1 = 9, 10 – 2 = 8).
		Problems involving 'real life', money or measures	**Use mental strategies to solve simple problems** set in 'real life', money or measurement contexts, **using counting, addition, subtraction, doubling and halving, explaining methods and reasoning orally.**
		Making decisions	Choose and use appropriate number operations and mental strategies to solve problems.
12–13	10	Organising and using data	Solve a given problem by sorting, classifying and organising information in simple ways, such as: using objects or pictures; in a list or simple table. Discuss and explain results.
		Measures	Understand and use the vocabulary related to length, mass and capacity. **Compare two lengths, masses or capacities by direct comparison**; extend to more than two. Measure using uniform non-standard units (e.g. straws, wooden cubes, plastic weights, yogurt pots) or standard units (e.g. metre sticks, litre jugs). **Suggest suitable standard or uniform non-standard units and measuring equipment to estimate, then measure, a length, mass or capacity,** recording estimates and measurements as 'about 3 beakers full' or 'about as heavy as 20 cubes'. Understand and use the vocabulary related to time. Order familiar events in time. Know the days of the week and the seasons of the year. Read the time to the hour or half hour on analogue clocks.
Total	56		

Counting to 10 then to 20

Children are encouraged to count to 10, and to extend the count up to 20 as they become more confident in their counting. They learn to count on from any small number. They practise counting out a given quantity of objects, again, up to 10.

LEARNING OBJECTIVES

	Topics	Starter	Main teaching activities
Lesson 1	Counting, properties of numbers and number sequences	● Know the number names and recite them in order to at least 10.	● Know the number names and recite them in order to at least 20. ● Describe and extend number sequences: **count on in ones from any small number.**
Lesson 2	Counting, properties of numbers and number sequences	● Know the number names and recite them in order to at least 10. ● Describe and extend number sequences: **count on in ones from any small number.**	● As for Lesson 1.
Lesson 3	Counting, properties of numbers and number sequences	● As for Lesson 1.	● **Count reliably at least 10 objects.**

Lessons   overview

Preparation
Photocopy 'Numeral cards 0–9' onto thin card and cut out the cards.

Learning objectives
Starter
● Know the number names and recite them in order to at least 10.
● Describe and extend number sequences: **count on in ones from any small number.**
Main teaching activities
● Know the number names and recite them in order to at least 20.
● Describe and extend number sequences: **count on in ones from any small number.**

Vocabulary
number, zero, one, two, three… to twenty, count, count (up) to, count back (from, to), count in ones

You will need:
CD pages
'Numeral cards 0–9', one set for each group of four children (see General Resources).

Lesson

Starter
Ask the children to count together with you from zero to 10 and back again. When they are confident with this, count again – but this time each child takes a turn to say the next number. Carry on up to 10, then back to zero, back up to 10 and so on until everyone has had a turn. Keep the pace sharp.

Main teaching activities

Whole class: Tell the children that you would like them to take turns to say the next number in the count. Start with zero and count all together to 20, then back again. Keep the count going at a good pace and with a steady rhythm. If the count falters, say the number for the children in order to keep up the pace. When the children are confident with this, repeat the activity, this time starting with any small number. Ask questions such as:

- *What comes after 6? Before 9?…*
- *Count back 5 from 15. What number will you get to?*

Group work: Ask the children to work in groups of four. They take turns to pick up a card from the shuffled pack, which is placed face down on the table. The child who picks up the card says the number. They then count individually around the table from that number to 20 and back to zero. The next child turns over a card, and the activity is repeated.

Differentiation

Less able: Limit the starting numbers to 0, 1, 2 and 3. Decide whether the children should count up to 10, 15 or 20, depending on their confidence with these counting numbers.

More able: Decide whether the children should extend the count beyond 20 to 25 or 30 and back to zero.

Plenary & assessment

Ask the children to count together from 0 to 20 and back again. Keep the pace sharp, again providing the next number if a child falters. Ask probing questions such as:

- *What number comes before/after…?*
- *Count on 6 from 11. What number will you get to? Who would like to count that aloud?*

Lesson

Repeat the Starter from Lesson 1. Repeat the whole-class activity from Lesson 1, this time counting individually around the class. Repeat the group work activity, this time asking the children to count back from their starting number to zero, then up to 20 or beyond, then back to their starting number. During the plenary, invite the children to count around the class from a starting number to 20 and back again.

Lesson overview

Learning objectives

Starter
- Know the number names and recite them in order to at least 10.
- Describe and extend number sequences: **count on in ones from any small number.**

Main teaching activities
- **Count reliably at least 10 objects.**

Vocabulary
Number, zero, one, two, three… to twenty, count, none, how many…?

You will need:

Equipment
Materials for counting, such as counters, cubes and small counting toys; containers to hold the counting resources; larger items for counting.

Lesson ③

Starter

Repeat from Lesson 1. This time, put the children into two groups, counting alternate numbers: *1*, *2*, *3*, *4*....

Main teaching activities

Whole class: Put out six items (such as cubes) on a table, counting them aloud as you place them. Invite a child to count them, touching and moving each item as he or she counts it. This will partition the set, so that the children can see clearly which items have been counted and which are still to be counted. Repeat this for quantities from about five to about ten. Ask questions such as:

- *What was the last number in the count? So how many toys are there?*
- *There are five here. If I put one more with them, how many will there be? Someone count to check.*
- *What if I take one away? Now how many are there?*

Group work: Ask the children to work in pairs. They take turns to take a small handful of counting toys from the container and count them. Their partner checks to make sure that the count is correct. Encourage the children to touch and move an item as they say each counting number.

Differentiation

Less able: Limit the size of the count to up to about six by providing larger items to be counted. Check that the children count carefully and co-ordinate the 'touch, move and count' process.

More able: Decide whether to provide smaller items, so the children can pick up more of them.

Plenary & assessment

Invite various children to put out some items and to count them using the 'touch, move and count' method (check that they do this in a co-ordinated way). The other children can join in the count by pointing and saying the numbers. Ask probing questions:

- *What was the last number we said? How many are there here? How do you know that?*
- *What if I put out one more/one fewer? How many would there be then? Someone show me.*

Place value and ordering

This unit includes reading and writing numerals up to 20 and ordering these on a number line. Children respond to 'one more than' and 'one less than my number' questions. They use apparatus to explore place value for the teen numbers.

LEARNING OBJECTIVES

		Topics	Starter	Main teaching activities
Lesson	**1**	Place value and ordering	● Know the number names and recite them in order to at least 20.	● **Read and write numerals from 0 to at least 20.** ● **Within the range of 0 to 20, say the number that is 1 more or less than any given number.**
Lesson	**2**	Place value and ordering	As for Lesson 1.	As for Lesson 1.
Lesson	**3**	Place value and ordering	● **Read and write numerals from 0 to at least 20.**	● Begin to know what each digit in a two-digit number represents. ● Partition a 'teens' number into a multiple of 10 and ones (TU).
Lesson	**4**	Place value and ordering	As for Lesson 3.	As for Lesson 3.
Lesson	**5**	Place value and ordering	As for Lesson 3.	As for Lesson 3.

Lessons overview

Preparation
Copy 'Numeral cards 0–9' and 'Numeral cards 10–20' to A3 size, cut each A3 sheet in half, then enlarge each half onto thin A3 card. Cut out the cards. Copy the relevant 'Numbers to 10' and 'Butterfly numbers' sheets according to ability. Hang up the washing line.

Learning objectives
Starter
● Know the number names and recite them in order to at least 20.
Main teaching activities
● **Read and write numerals from 0 to at least 20.**
● **Within the range of 0 to 20, say the number that is 1 more or less than any given number.**

Vocabulary
one more, one less, compare, number, zero, one, two, three… to twenty and beyond

You will need:
Photocopiable pages
'Numbers to 10' (see page 16) and 'Butterfly numbers' (see page 17) for each child.

CD pages
'Numbers to 10' and 'Butterfly numbers', less able, more able and template versions for both (see Autumn term, Unit 2); 'Numeral cards 0–9' and 'Numeral cards 10–20' (one set of enlarged cards) (see General Resources).

Equipment
A washing line, pegs.

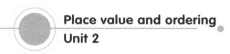

Lesson ①

Starter

Tell the children that you would like them to count from zero to 20 and back quickly together. They may find it helpful to slap alternate knees as they count in order to keep the rhythm going. When they are confident with this, ask them to begin from any small number, counting up to 20 and back to the small number.

Main teaching activities

Whole class: Show the children the large numeral cards. Explain that you would like them to read the number on each card with you, and then you will ask someone to peg the card onto the washing line so that all the cards go onto the line in order. Begin with 0, 1, 2 and so on. When all the numbers are on the line, invite individual children to remove the cards – saying, for example:
- *Jon, take the card that has the number one more than 5… 9… 13…*
- *Salma, find the number that is one less than 8… 1… 14….*
- *Which number is one before 1… 3… 12… 20…?*

When the children are confident with this, remove all the cards from the line and give them out to the children. Ask those holding a card to peg their cards back on the line in the correct order, starting with 0.

Individual work: Ask the children to complete the 'Numbers to 10' activity sheet. They have to trace a set of numerals, then fill in the missing numerals on simple number tracks. Check that they trace and write in the writing direction: from left to right.

Differentiation

Less able: You may prefer these children to attempt the simplified version of 'Numbers to 10' initially; this involves writing only the numerals to 10. If the children find these difficult, encourage them to recite the numbers from zero or any small number to 10, forwards and backwards.
More able: These children could try the more difficult version of 'Numbers to 10', which has number tracks to be completed with numbers to 20.

Plenary & assessment

Invite 21 children each to hold one of the set of large numeral cards (0–20). Ask them to take turns to peg their card onto the washing line, until all of the cards are in order. Say:
- *Which number is one more/one less than…?*
- *Mei Mei, point to the number that is one more/one less than…*

Point to the numbers in order, asking the children to say each number as you point to it.

Lesson ②

Starter

Repeat the Starter from Lesson 1. This time suggest that the children count around the class, up to a number of your choice and back to zero.

Main teaching activities

Whole class: Repeat the activity from Lesson 1. This time, count around the class individually as well as all together.
Individual work: Ask the children to complete the 'Butterfly numbers' activity sheet. This involves writing the numbers that are one more and one less than some given numbers to 20. The core version of the sheet has two pages, the differentiated versions one page each.

Differentiation

Less able: Offer these children the version of the activity sheet that uses only the numbers to 10.
More able: Offer these children the version that uses numbers to 30.

Plenary & assessment

For the plenary, write table headings on the board or flip chart as shown below. Write a number in the 'My number' column and invite a child to write in the other two numbers. Repeat this for different numbers, taking account of the range of abilities within the class. Ask questions such as:

- *Which number is one more/one less than…?*
- *How do you know that?*
- *Choose your own number. Now, what is one more/one less than that?*
- *How did you work that out?*

One less than	My number	One more than

Lessons   overview

Preparation

Make some ten rods with the interlocking cubes, using alternate colours to aid counting. Enlarge a copy of 'Two-spike abacus' to A3 size and pin it to the flip chart. Print the numeral cards onto thin card and cut them out.

Learning objectives

Starter
- **Read and write numerals from 0 to at least 20.**

Main teaching activities
- Begin to know what each digit in a two-digit number represents.
- Partition a 'teens' number into a multiple of 10 and ones (TU).

Vocabulary

units, ones, tens, digit, 'teens' number, zero, one, two, three… to twenty

You will need:

CD pages
'Numeral cards 0–9', 'Numeral cards 10–20' and 'Numeral cards 21–30' per pair of children; 'Arrow cards' and 'Two-spike abacus' for each child, plus an A3 copy of 'Two-spike abacus' (see General Resources).

Equipment

Individual whiteboards and pens; interlocking cubes; counters; Blu-Tack; paper and pencils.

Lesson

Starter

Explain that when you say a number, you would like the children to write it on their whiteboards. When you say *Show me*, the children should hold up their boards to show you their written number. Say:

- *Write 3… 8… 10… 15… Show me.*
- *Write the number that is one more than… Show me.*
- *Write the number that is one less than… Show me.*

Main teaching activities

Whole class: Show the children a ten rod that you have made, and ask them to count with you as you point to each cube. Agree that there are ten cubes in the rod. Now show the children the ten rod and a separate cube, and ask: *How many are there now? Yes, there are 11. 11 is the same as 10 and 1.* Ask the children to write the number 11 on their whiteboards, and to hold them up to show you.

Repeat this, demonstrating with cubes and asking the children to write the number, for 12, 13, 14…
up to 20.

Group work: Ask the children to work in pairs. They shuffle the 10–20 numeral cards and place
them in a stack face down. They take turns: one child turns over a card and the other makes the
number (as ten and ones) with interlocking cubes.

Differentiation

Less able: Decide whether the children should make the numbers 10–20, or whether they need
further work on the numbers 1–10. They can use numeral cards 1–10 and show the numbers with
interlocking cubes.

More able: Decide whether to extend the activity to numbers to 30 by including numeral cards
21–30.

Plenary & assessment

Write a number from 10–20 on the flip chart and ask the children to say this number together. Invite
a child to demonstrate the number using interlocking cubes. For example, 15 would be shown as
a ten rod and five ones. Repeat this for other numbers, extending to 30 for more able children (if
appropriate) and including the numbers 1–9 for less able children. Ask questions such as:

- (Hold up a ten rod and three ones.) *How many tens does this number have? How many ones?*
- *How do you know that?*
- *Look at the number 18 on the flip chart. How many tens are there? How many ones?*
- *How do you know?*

Lesson ④

Starter

Repeat the Starter from Lesson 3, focusing on 'teens' numbers. Check that the children have understood how
to write a 'teens' number as one 10 and some units.

Main teaching activities

Whole class: Provide each child with arrow cards to make the numbers to 20. Show the children
how to make a TU number by placing the units arrow card on top of the tens card so that the
arrows match (see below).

Explain that you will say some numbers. Ask the
children to make these numbers with their arrow
cards and hold up the cards to show you. Use
numbers such as 12, 19, 20, 17…

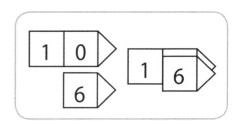

Group work: Ask the children to work in pairs
with the arrow cards for 10 and 1–9. They should
take turns to choose a units card and place it
onto the 10 card. The other child should say
the number that has been made, then use the
interlocking cubes to make that number.

Differentiation

Less able: Work with this group and check that the children can say the TU numbers and model
them with the cubes.

More able: Provide further tens cards, such as 20 and 30, and challenge the children to make
numbers to 39. They should show each ten rod separately – for example, making 25 as two ten rods
and five units.

Plenary & assessment

Repeat the whole-class activity. Ask questions such as:

- *What number is this? How do you know?*
- *How many tens are there in this number? How many units? How can you tell?*

Lesson

Starter

Repeat the Starter from Lesson 3. Say, for example: *Write the number that is one more than 16…, two less than 20….* Keep the pace sharp.

Main teaching activities

Whole class: Each child will need a set of arrow cards. Look at the enlarged 'Two-spike abacus' sheet together. Put six display counters onto the units spike, fixing these with Blu-Tack. Ask: *What number does this represent? Show me that number with your arrow cards.* Put one counter onto the tens spike and repeat the questions. Repeat this for other numbers.

Group work: Ask the children to work in pairs. They should take turns: one child makes a number from 10 to 30 with the arrow cards, the other child makes the same number on the 'Two-spike abacus' sheet with counters. They should record each number and arrangement of counters in this form (see right):

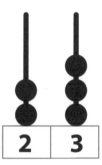

Differentiation

Less able: Decide whether to limit the children to making just the numbers 10–15 with the arrow cards. Alternatively, an adult could work with this group to help them complete the task together, using just the 'Two-spike abacus' sheet and no recording sheet.

More able: Decide whether to extend the range of numbers to up to 39.

Plenary & assessment

Invite some children to demonstrate different numbers by placing counters onto the displayed abacus sheet. Include larger numbers for more able children. Ask questions such as:

- *What number have you made?*
- *How many tens/units are there? How do you know?*
- *What if I put one more/one fewer counters on this spike? What number would it be then?*

Name	Date

Numbers to 10

Trace over these numbers with your pencil.

Write the missing numbers on these number tracks.

Name

Date

Butterfly numbers

Write the missing numbers on the wings.

Write the number that is one less in the □ .

Write the number that is one more in the ○ .

2

3

6

5

10

8

13

19

14

Understanding addition and mental strategies

Children develop their mental calculation strategies for addition of small numbers. They are introduced to the operation symbols + and = , their meanings and how to read an addition sentence using these symbols. They explore different ways of making a given total.

LEARNING OBJECTIVES

	Topics	Starter	Main teaching activities
Lesson **1**	Understanding addition and subtraction Mental calculation strategies (+)	● **Count reliably at least 10 objects.**	● **Understand the operation of addition, and use the related vocabulary.** ● Begin to recognise that addition can be done in any order. ● Begin to use + and = signs to record mental calculations in a number sentence. ● Use knowledge that addition can be done in any order to do mental calculations more efficiently. For example: put the larger number first and count on in ones.
Lesson **2**	Understanding addition and subtraction Mental calculation strategies (+)	As for Lesson 1.	As for Lesson 1.
Lesson **3**	Understanding addition and subtraction Mental calculation strategies (+)	● **Know by heart addition facts for all pairs of numbers with a total up to at least 5.**	As for Lesson 1.
Lesson **4**	Understanding addition and subtraction Mental calculation strategies (+)	As for Lesson 3.	As for Lesson 1.
Lesson **5**	Understanding addition and subtraction Mental calculation strategies (+)	As for Lesson 3.	As for Lesson 1.

Lessons  overview

Preparation
Ask the children to colour in their 'Work mat' sheet, then laminate them.

Learning objectives
Starter
● **Count reliably at least 10 objects.**
Main teaching activities
● **Understand the operation of addition, and use the related vocabulary.**
● Begin to recognise that addition can be done in any order.
● Begin to use + and = signs to record mental calculations in a number sentence.
● Use knowledge that addition can be done in any order to do mental calculations more efficiently. For example: put the larger number first and count on in ones.

Vocabulary
add, more, plus, make, sum, total, altogether, one more, two more, is the same as, equals, sign

You will need:
Photocopiable pages
'Add it up' (see page 22) for each child.

CD pages
'Add it up', less able, more able and template versions (see Autumn term, Unit 3); 'Work mat' for each child (see General Resources).

Equipment
Interlocking cubes, containers for cubes; two blank dice marked 1, 1, 2, 2, 3, 3 and 2, 2, 3, 3, 4, 4 for each pair; some 1–6 dice marked with numerals; flip chart or board; paper and pencils.

Lesson ①

Starter

Give each child a laminated work mat, and place containers with cubes inside (enough for ten cubes per child) on each table. Say the following:

- *Count out five cubes onto your mat. Check that there are five by counting again.*
- *Put one back into the pot. Count how many are on your mat now.*
- *Put two more onto the mat. How many are there now?*
- *What if you put a cube back into the pot – how many would be on the mat then?*

Repeat this for different starting numbers, keeping the quantity of cubes between 3 and 10. Invite various children to answer your questions. Check that the children count using the 'touch, move and count' process in a co-ordinated way.

Main teaching activities

Whole class: Explain that in today's lesson, the children will be learning a new way to add small numbers mentally. Write on the flip chart: 2 + 3 = and ask the children to read this number sentence to you.

Check that they can read the signs + and =. Ask: *How could we work out this sum?* Children may suggest: counting out two and then three cubes, then counting them all; counting on fingers; and so on. *What if we put the larger number first, then count on? Do you think that would work? Let's try it.* Rewrite the sum as 3 + 2 = .

Ask the children to put the 3 in their heads, and count on two: 3, 4 and 5. So 3 add 2 is 5. Write 5 after the = sign. Use cubes to demonstrate that this is the correct answer: combine a three-rod with a two-rod and count all the cubes.

Repeat this for other sums, such as 2 + 4 and 1 + 3.

Group work: Ask the children to work in pairs. They roll two dice each time (a 1, 1, 2, 2, 3, 3 dice and a 2, 2, 3, 3, 4, 4 dice) to generate a sum. Remind them to put the larger number first and count on. They can record their sums in the form: 1 + 3 = 4, and so on.

Differentiation

Less able: Provide two 1, 1, 2, 2, 3, 3 dice so the totals are smaller. Make sure the children are clear about what is meant by 'larger' and 'smaller' numbers, so they count on from the larger number each time.

More able: Decide whether to replace one or both dice with 1–6 dice. This will give totals up to 12. Encourage the children to devise their own method of recording.

Plenary & assessment

Invite some children from each ability group to write one of their sums on the flip chart. Ask the other children to work out the answer, counting on from the larger number. Ask questions such as:

- *Which is the larger number?*
- *How do you know that?*
- *What if you counted on from the smaller number – would you get the same answer?*

Lesson ②

Repeat the Starter and the whole-class activity from Lesson 1. For individual work, provide appropriate differentiated copies of the 'Add it up' activity sheet for each group (one sheet per child). For the plenary session, choose some of the sums from each group and ask individual children to explain how they worked out the answer. Check that the children are using effective mental strategies.

Lessons   overview

Preparation
Enlarge a copy of the 'Work mat' sheet to A3 and pin it to the flip chart. Make a class set of number fans from the resource sheet. Copy the 'Dog show sums' activity sheet, differentiated for ability range.

Learning objectives
Starter
- **Know by heart addition facts for all pairs of numbers with a total up to at least 5.**

Main teaching activities
- **Understand the operation of addition, and use the related vocabulary.**
- Begin to recognise that addition can be done in any order.
- Begin to use + and = signs to record mental calculations in a number sentence.
- Use knowledge that addition can be done in any order to do mental calculations more efficiently. For example: put the larger number first and count on in ones.

Vocabulary
add, more, plus, make, sum, total, altogether, one more, two more, is the same as, equals, sign

You will need:
Photocopiable pages
'Dog show sums', one for each child (see page 23).

CD pages
'Dog show sums', less able, more able and template versions (see Autumn term, Unit 3); 'Work mat' and 'Number fan' for each child, and an A3 version of 'Work mat' (see General Resources).

Equipment
Some counters; Blu-Tack; interlocking cubes for each group; flip chart or board.

Lesson

Starter
Explain to the children that you will say some additions, and you would like them to show you the answer each time by holding up fingers. Say:
- *What is 1 add 1? Show me!*
- *What is 2 add 1? Show me!*
- *What is 3 add 2?*
- *What is 4 added to 1? And 2 added to 3?*
- *How many is 1 and 3? And 2 and 2?*

Allow time between the questions for the children to work out the answers. At this stage, some of them may have rapid recall of some addition facts. Ask *How did you work that out?* where a child has worked very quickly. Praise those who take longer and have the correct answer.

Main teaching activities
Whole class: Use Blu-Tack to stick five counters onto the enlarged work mat. Say: *We are going to make some additions with these counters. Can anyone suggest an addition sentence we could make with this total?* The children may suggest 1 + 4 or 2 + 3. Ask them to check that each sum is correct by keeping the larger number in their heads and counting on in ones. Invite a child to demonstrate with the counters by separating the full set to show the two amounts, and by writing the sum on the flip chart. Repeat for other small totals, such as 6 and 7.

Group work: Provide pairs with eight interlocking cubes. They should agree on a sum with a total of 8. While one child uses the cubes to make the sum, the other child (without looking at the cubes) works out the same sum by counting on mentally in ones from the larger number and states the total. Repeat for other sums, taking turns to use the cubes and recording their sums on paper.

Differentiation
Less able: Decide whether to limit the sum total to 4, then 5. Check that the children find the total by counting on in ones from the larger number, and demonstrate using your fingers.
More able: If the children are confident, ask them to make larger totals, such as 10 to 12.

Plenary & assessment

Invite various children to write a sum from their recording on the flip chart. Each time, ask: *What is the total? How did you work that out?* Repeat this for other sums, checking that the children are confident with the strategy of 'keeping the larger number in their head and counting on in ones'.

Lesson

Starter

Explain that you are going to continue the work from the previous lesson on making sums. Repeat the Starter from Lesson 3.

Main teaching activities

Repeat the group activity from Lesson 3, but increase the size of the total for each pair. Most of the class should be able to partition a set of 9 or 10 cubes and make the corresponding sums.

Differentiation

Less able: Ask these children to make totals of 6 and 7.
More able: These children could go on to make totals of 12–15.

Plenary & assessment

Encourage the children to explain their strategies for making the sums. Review how the children have recorded their sums. Praise effective, efficient and neat recording.

Lesson

Starter

Repeat the Starter from Lesson 3, this time asking the children to show the answer using their number fans.

Main teaching activities

Whole class: Repeat the whole-class activity from Lesson 3 to revise the strategy of counting on in ones from the larger number.
Individual work: Provide copies of the 'Dog show sums' activity sheet. The core version (for most of the class) requires the child to match sums to answers where the totals go up to 10.

Differentiation

Versions of the 'Dog show sums' sheet are available on the CD as follows:
Less able: Match sums to answers going up to 6.
More able: Match sums to answers going up to 13.

Plenary & assessment

Choose some of the sums from the activity sheets, making sure that there are questions for each ability group, and write them on the board without the answers. Ask:
- *What is the total of…?*
- *How did you work it out?*
- *Who did this a different way? What did you do?*
- *Which way do you think is easier? Why is that?*

Name	Date

Add it up

Write the answers to these sums.

1 + 3 = ☐   4 + 2 = ☐

2 + 4 = ☐   4 + 4 = ☐

3 + 3 = ☐   5 + 3 = ☐

2 + 1 = ☐   6 + 2 = ☐

3 + 4 = ☐   3 + 5 = ☐

5 + 1 = ☐   6 + 4 = ☐

Name   Date

Dog show sums

Join each dog to its bone.

2 + 4 =

3 + 6 =

5 + 2 =

9

7

10

3 + 4 =

1 + 8 =

5 + 5 =

6

7

7

9

2 + 7 =

6 + 3 =

4 + 4 =

10

9

2 + 5 =

3 + 1 =

4 + 6 =

4

8

Solving money problems

Recognition of the coins and their equivalences is covered in this unit. Children total amounts and write these as addition sentences. They solve money problems, then invent their own money problems for a spend of up to 10p.

LEARNING OBJECTIVES

		Topics	Starter	Main teaching activities
Lesson	1	Problems involving 'real life', money or measures	● Know by heart addition facts for all pairs of numbers with a total up to at least 5, and the corresponding subtraction facts.	● Recognise coins of different values. ● Find totals from up to 10p.
Lesson	2	Problems involving 'real life', money or measures	As for Lesson 1.	As for Lesson 1.
Lesson	3	Problems involving 'real life', money or measures	As for Lesson 1.	As for Lesson 1.
Lesson	4	Problems involving 'real life', money or measures Making decisions	● **Know by heart all pairs of numbers with a total of 10 (e.g. 3 + 7).**	● Recognise coins of different values. ● Find totals from up to 10p. ● Choose and use appropriate number operations and mental strategies to solve problems.
Lesson	5	Problems involving 'real life', money or measures Making decisions	As for Lesson 4.	As for Lesson 4.

Lessons   overview

Preparation
Fold 'Add facts to 5' and copy each half to A4 size, then copy each sheet onto A3 card. Cut out a teaching set of cards. Photocopy 'Price labels' onto card and cut out a set of labels for each child; enlarge 'Price labels' to A3 to make a teaching set.

Learning objectives
Starter
● Know by heart addition facts for all pairs of numbers with a total up to at least 5, and the corresponding subtraction facts.
Main teaching activities
● Recognise coins of different values.
● Find totals from up to 10p.

Vocabulary
money, coin, penny, pence, pound, price, cost, buy, sell, spend, spent, pay, how much…?, total

You will need:
CD Pages
A 'Number fan' and a set of 'Price labels 1p–10p' for each child, teaching sets of 'Add facts to 5' cards and 'Price labels 1p–10p' (see General Resources).

Equipment
Coins of all values, containers for coins and Blu-Tack; paper and pencils.

Lesson

Starter

Provide each child with a number fan. Say that you will hold up a sum card, and the children should hold up the answer using a number fan. Work through the 'Add facts to 5' cards, asking individuals *How did you work that out?* Where there is no rapid recall, encourage the children to count on in ones from the larger number.

Main teaching activities

Whole class: Set the context by discussing how we use money when we go shopping. Provide each group with some coins in a container. Ask the children to work together to sort the coins by their value. Check that they know the names of the different coins. Say:

- *Hold up a penny.*
- *Now show me a 2… 5… 10… 20… 50 pence coin.*
- *Show me a £1… £2 coin.*

Discuss how every coin has a value. Concentrate on 1p, 2p, 5p and 10p coins. Explain that two 1p coins are worth the same as a 2p coin. Now consider the 5p coin: *How many penny coins are worth the same as a 5p coin?* Attach a 5p coin to the flip chart with Blu-Tack, and ask a child to attach sufficient pennies to make 5p.

Now ask: *Which 2p and 1p coins are worth the same as a 5p coin?* Again, invite children to demonstrate their answers by attaching coins to the flip chart. Their responses should include 2p + 2p + 1p and 2p + 1p + 1p +1p. Write these as sums, as well as showing the coins. Explain that 'p' stands for pence. Repeat this for the 10p coin.

Now put up a 2p and a 5p. *How much is this?* Encourage the children to count on in ones from the 5p: *5p and 6p and 7p. 5p and 2p is 7p.* Repeat for other combinations of two coins, counting on from the larger number each time.

Individual work: Provide each child with some 1p, 2p and 5p coins and paper. The children choose two coins and draw them, then add them and write the total.

Differentiation

Less able: Work with the children. It may be necessary to reinforce the equivalent values of the coins if they do not understand that a 2p coin is worth two 1p coins, and instead count it as 'one'.
More able: Challenge the children to choose three coins each time, and to write out the sum with the answer.

Plenary & assessment

Invite various children to write a money sum on the board and challenge the others to work out the total mentally. Include examples suitable for each ability group. Ask questions such as:

- *How much is 5p and 2p?*
- *How did you work that out?*
- *What other way could we make 7p using coins?*

Lesson

Starter

Repeat the Starter from Lesson 1. Keep the pace sharp. Encourage the children to use rapid recall, where possible.

Main teaching activities

Whole class: Provide containers of coins for each pair of children to use. Show the children the teaching set of price labels. Explain that you will hold up a price label, and the children should work with a partner to count out enough coins to make that amount. Begin with, say, 3p. Ask:

- *Which coins did you choose?*
- *Is there another way?*

Invite children to write number sentences on the board that show the coin sums: 2p + 1p = 3p and 1p + 1p + 1p = 3p. Repeat this for other values, until the children understand that coins can be combined to make a range of total values.

Group work: The children work in pairs with their own set of price labels. They should take turns to count out an appropriate set of coins for each price, then record their money sums on a sheet of paper.

Differentiation

Less able: Check that the children understand that each coin has a specific value, and that they do not count every coin as being worth '1p'. Limit the labels to prices to 5p.

More able: When the children have completed the group activity, challenge them to use coins to make the values 11p to 15p.

Plenary & assessment

Invite some children from each ability group to demonstrate how they made particular values. Ask them to write their sums on the board. Ask key questions as in Lesson 1.

Lesson ③

Starter

Repeat the Starter from Lesson 1. Most of the children should have rapid recall of these facts by now.

Main teaching activities

Whole class: Explain that you would like the children to combine two price labels to make a new total, then show this amount in coins. Hold up pairs from the teaching set of price labels, using the labels 1p to 5p. Encourage the children to 'put the larger number in your head and count on in ones' to find the total, then put out coins to represent the total. Check that they use a range of coins to do this, not just 1p coins.

Group work: Each pair will need two sets of price labels 1p to 5p. The children should combine pairs of price labels to make as many different totals as possible. Ask them to write each sum on paper, then draw coins to make the same total. Encourage them to use the smallest possible number of coins.

Differentiation

Less able: Decide whether to limit the activity to using the labels for 1p to 3p.
More able: These children can combine the price labels for 1p to 7p.

Plenary & assessment

Review the children's work, asking questions such as:

- *How did you work that out?*
- *Is there another way of making that amount?*
- *How could you do that using fewer coins?*

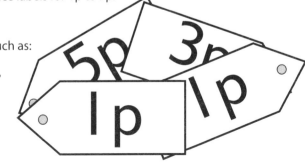

Lessons   overview

Preparation
Make three money word problem cards (see Lesson 4).

Learning objectives
Starter
- **Know by heart all pairs of numbers with a total of 10 (e.g. 3 + 7).**

Main teaching activities
- Recognise coins of different values.
- Find totals from up to 10p.
- Choose and use appropriate number operations and mental strategies to solve problems.

Vocabulary
money, coin, penny, pence, pound, price, cost, buy, sell, spend, spent, pay, how much…?, total, answer, right, wrong, number sentence, sign, operation

You will need:
Equipment
1p, 2p and 5p coins for each pair of children; containers for coins; prepared money word problem cards; flip chart or board; paper and pencils.

Lesson

Starter
Say, for example:
- *What do I need to add to 7 to make 10?*
- *Double which number makes 10?*
- *What must be added to 4 to make 10?*

Ask the children to hold up fingers to show the 'missing number' needed to make a total of 10.

Main teaching activities
Whole class: Explain that the children will be asked to solve some problems involving money. Ask them to solve the following problem, working mentally: *James paid exactly 4p for some sweets. Which coins could he have used?* Encourage the children to explain how they worked out the answer. Write their solutions on the flip chart, and demonstrate with coins that each solution is correct. Repeat this problem using a different amount, such as 5p.

Group work: Provide the children with three cards, each containing a money word problem. For example:
- *John buys an apple for 3p and an orange for 4p. How much does he spend altogether?*
- *I pay 6p for some chews. Write three ways of making 6p.*
- *Jill bought a lolly for 4p and a cone for 6p. How much did she spend?*

The children should write the problems and answers as addition sentences.

Differentiation
Less able: Provide simpler versions of the money problems, which should involve calculating totals to 5p. Provide coins for the children to model the problem and its solution.

More able: Provide more demanding versions of the money problems, which should involve calculating totals to 15p. Challenge the children to find the solutions by working mentally.

Plenary & assessment
Choose one problem from the cards for each ability group and invite some children to explain how they solved it. Ask questions such as:
- *How did you work that out?*
- *Who found a different solution?*
- *What if the total was … instead? Can you solve that too? How did you work it out?*

Lesson ⑤

Starter
Use the Starter from Lesson 4, this time asking the children to put up their hands to respond.

Main teaching activities
Whole class: Set the children some more money word problems. Ask individuals to answer and to explain how they worked it out. For example:

- *Anna buys a toffee for 3p and a chew for 2p. How much does she pay? Which coins would you use to pay this?*
- *Tom buys two mystery bags at the fair. He pays 4p each for them. How much does he pay in total? What coins would you use to pay this amount? What other ways could you use?*
- *The shopkeeper sells Sam a marble for 6p and a marble bag for 3p. How much does Sam pay altogether? Which coins do you think he used to pay that amount? How else could he pay it?*

Group work: The children should work in pairs. Ask them to invent their own word problems involving money, for a total spend of up to 10p. Challenge them to write at least three different problems. Set a tight deadline of about 10 minutes for this.

Differentiation
Less able: These children may benefit from working as a group, with an adult to help them write out their word problems.
More able: Challenge these children to invent word problems for totals up to 15p.

Plenary & assessment
Invite some pairs of children to read out a problem for the others to solve. Ask questions such as: *How did you solve this problem? What strategy did you use?* Talk about the vocabulary the children have used, such as *total* and *altogether*. Ask the children to suggest how each problem could be reworded using a different word for 'total'.

3-D shapes and solving problems

Children learn about the properties and names of common 3-D shapes. They begin to learn the complements for 10 in practical situations. They solve some problems and explain the methods that they used to do this.

LEARNING OBJECTIVES

		Topics	Starter	Main teaching activities
Lesson	**1**	Shape and space	● Know by heart addition facts for all pairs of numbers with a total up to at least 5.	● **Use everyday language to describe features of familiar 3-D shapes**, including the cube, cuboid, sphere, cylinder, cone…, referring to properties such as the shapes of flat faces, or the number of faces or corners or the number and types of sides. ● Make and describe models and patterns using construction kits, everyday materials, Plasticine…
Lesson	**2**	Shape and space	As for Lesson 1.	As for Lesson 1.
Lesson	**3**	Shape and space	As for Lesson 1.	As for Lesson 1.
Lesson	**4**	Reasoning about numbers or shapes	● **Know by heart all pairs of numbers with a total of 10** (e.g. 3 + 7).	● Solve simple mathematical problems or puzzles; recognise and predict from simple patterns and relationships. Suggest extensions by asking 'What if?' or 'What could I try next?'. ● Explain methods and reasoning orally.
Lesson	**5**	Reasoning about numbers or shapes	As for Lesson 4.	As for Lesson 4.

Lessons   overview

Preparation
Make sure there are things visible in the classroom that have the shapes of cubes, cuboids, pyramids (such as chocolate containers), spheres, cones (such as pointed hats) and cylinders. Fold 'Add facts to 5' and copy each half to A4 size, then copy each sheet onto A3 card. Cut out a teaching set of cards.

Learning objectives
Starter
● Know by heart addition facts for all pairs of numbers with a total up to at least 5.
Main teaching activities
● **Use everyday language to describe features of familiar 3-D shapes**, including the cube, cuboid, sphere, cylinder, cone…, referring to properties such as the shapes of flat faces, or the number of faces or corners or the number and types of sides.
● Make and describe models and patterns using construction kits, everyday materials, Plasticine…

Vocabulary
shape, flat, curved, straight, round, hollow, solid, corner, point, pointed, face, side, edge, end, sort, make, build, draw, cube, cuboid, pyramid, sphere, cone, cylinder

You will need:
CD pages
'Add facts to 5' cards (enlarged teaching set) (see General Resources.)

Equipment
A set of 3-D shapes (cube, cuboid, pyramid, sphere, cone, cylinder) for each group; containers for the shapes; feely bags; Plasticine; everyday materials (for model-making); glue; construction kits; individual whiteboards and pens; paper and pencils.

Lesson ①

Starter

Use the enlarged teaching set of 'Add facts to 5' cards. Explain to the children that you will hold up a card with a number fact on. Ask them to write the answer on their whiteboard and hold it up when you say *Show me!*

Main teaching activities

Whole class: Hold up a cube and ask: *What is this shape called? What can you tell me about this shape?* Encourage the children to describe its properties, such as: *It has square faces; all the faces are the same size…* Repeat this for other 3-D shapes, including a sphere, cone and cylinder.

Now introduce the cuboid and its name. Invite the children to tell you what they notice about its properties (such as its flat faces). Discuss how it is similar to, and how it is different from, a cube.
Group work: Provide each group with a set of 3-D shapes. Ask the children to look carefully around the classroom and find something in the room that has the same shape as one of the 3-D shapes. They should repeat this for each shape, drawing the correct objects under the headings 'cube', 'cuboid', 'cone', 'cylinder' and 'sphere'.

Differentiation

Less able: Decide whether to limit the range of shapes for the children to find to a cube, cuboid, sphere and cone. Encourage the children to name and describe each shape.
More able: Encourage the children to write about the properties of a cube, cuboid, pyramid, sphere, cone and cylinder.

Plenary & assessment

Review the shapes that the children drew, asking for examples from the classroom of cubes, cuboids, pyramids, spheres, cones and cylinders. Ask the children to explain how they recognise the items as having those specific shapes. Ask questions such as:
- *What shape is that? How do you know?*
- *What else did you find that was the same shape?*
- *What do you know about shapes like this?*

Lessons ② ③

Starter

Repeat the Starter from Lesson 1 in both lessons. By Lesson 3, the children should know most of these addition facts.

Main teaching activities

Whole class: Provide each group with a set of 3-D shapes. Explain that you are thinking of a shape, and will say some properties of it. You would like them to sort the shapes as you say each property, putting any shapes that do not fit the description back into the container. Say, for example:
- *My shape has no curved faces.*
- *All its faces are the same shape.*
- *All its faces are the same size.*

Repeat this for other shapes.
Group work: Choose from this range of activities. You may wish to use them as a circus of activities for all the children to attempt.
- Sort sets of shapes by given properties such as 'Has a curved face' and 'Has six faces'. Record by placing the shapes inside labelled circles.

- Choose a 3-D shape and either describe it orally or write a description of its properties.
- Place some shapes inside a feely bag. In groups of about four, the children take turns to feel for a shape inside the bag and describe what they feel to the group, who then have to guess the shape.
- Each child in a group has a feely bag containing a set of shapes. They take turns to feel inside their bag and name a shape by touch. The others have to find that shape by touch. When everyone is ready, they bring out their shapes to check that they were correct.
- Use a variety of construction kits to make specific 3-D shapes.
- Use Plasticine to model specific 3-D shapes.
- Use everyday materials to build models of their own design, then use the vocabulary of 3-D shape to describe what shapes they have used.

Differentiation
Less able: Decide whether to limit the range of shapes that the children use to a cube, cuboid, sphere and cone.
More able: Challenge the children to make a model using at least one each of a cube, cuboid, pyramid, sphere, cone and cylinder. They will need to make decisions based on the properties of the shapes, such as which shapes make good bases for models and which do not. Encourage them to justify the decisions that they make.

Plenary & assessment
Ask the children to describe the properties of the shapes they have been using. Ask individuals questions such as:
- *Which shapes have flat/curved faces?*
- *Which shapes have flat and curved faces?*
- *Which shapes are good for making models? Why is that?*

Lessons   overview

Preparation
Fold 'Complements of 10' in half and enlarge each half to A4 size, then enlarge each sheet onto A3 card and cut out a teaching set of cards. Enlarge copies of 'Get to 10' and 'Stickers' to A3 size.

Learning objectives
Starter
- **Know by heart all pairs of numbers with a total of 10** (e.g. 3 + 7).

Main teaching activities
- Solve simple mathematical problems or puzzles; recognise and predict from simple patterns and relationships. Suggest extensions by asking 'What if?' or 'What could I try next?'.
- Explain methods and reasoning orally.

Vocabulary
pattern, puzzle, answer, right, wrong, what could we try next?, how did you work it out?, count, add, number sentence, sign, operation

You will need:
Photocopiable pages
'Get to 10', (see page 34) for each pair, and 'Stickers' (see page 35) for each pair, plus A3 copies of both.

CD pages
'Number fan' for each child, 'Complements of 10' teaching set of cards (see General Resources).

Equipment
A large teaching dice;
a 1–6 dice and two counters for each pair;
red, blue and green crayons and marker pens;
interlocking cubes.

Lesson

Starter

Use the teaching set of 'Complements of 10' cards. Explain that you will hold up a card with a sum written on it. Ask the children to find the missing number on their number fans and hold it up when you say *Show me*. Where they do not have rapid recall, encourage them to count on in ones from the larger number. Ask questions such as: *How did you work that out? Is there another way?*

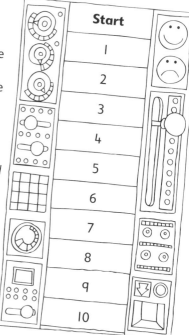

Main teaching activities

Whole class: This activity follows on from the Starter, since it requires knowledge of the complements to 10. Pin the enlarged copy of 'Get to 10' on the flip chart. Invite the class to play a game in two teams. Choose two team leaders to take turns to roll a large dice, count down the track and mark their position. Play the game a couple of times, so the children are sure of how it works.

Group work: Now ask the children to work in pairs to solve this problem: *Tom and Sunita are playing this game with a dice. They roll the dice and move their counter along the track. Tom wins the game with just two dice rolls. Work out what the two dice rolls could be.*

Provide a copy of 'Get to 10' for each pair, and ask them to look at the game. Check that they understand how it is played. They may like to play it for themselves before they solve the problem. Tell the children that you are really interested in how they go about solving the problem. They can record their work on paper. Challenge them to find as many solutions as possible.

Differentiation

This is by outcome.

Less able: The children may make random attempts at finding solutions. They may find it helpful to have ten interlocking cubes, make a tower with them and then find different ways of partitioning the tower.

More able: The problem could be extended so that Tom wins the game with three rolls of the dice.

Plenary & assessment

Ask the children how they solved the problem. Invite solutions from each ability group, and ask questions such as:

- How did you work it out?
- Who found a different solution?
- Is the solution '4 then 6' the same as the solution '6 then 4'? Why do you think that?

The range of solutions is: 4 then 6; 5 then 5; 6 then 4. The two dice rolls are independent events, so '4 then 6' can be considered a different solution from '6 then 4'.

If the more able children undertook the challenge described above, invite them to explain to the others what they did and their results. Discuss with all of the children how working systematically can help them to spot more solutions, because they will see a number pattern in their results. There are 27 solutions for three dice rolls: 1 then 3 then 6; 1 then 4 then 5; 1 then 5 then 4; 1 then 6 then 3; 2 then 2 then 6; and so on.

Lesson (5)

Starter

Repeat the Starter from Lesson 4. It is important to encourage the children to begin to use rapid recall where they can.

Main teaching activities

Whole class: Tell the children that you would like them to work in pairs to solve a puzzle. Say: *Jane decided to put three coloured stickers onto her pencil case. Each sticker can be either red, blue or green. How many different ways can Jane use her coloured stickers?*

Show the children the enlarged copy of 'Stickers'. Ask individuals to show you, using coloured pens, how Jane might colour the three stickers. Make it clear that for each sticker, there is a choice of red, blue and green.

Group work: Provide each pair with a copy of 'Stickers'. Ask the children to find as many different ways of colouring the stickers as they can, recording on the activity sheet. Tell them that you will be interested in how they solved the problem.

Differentiation
Differentiation is by outcome.
Less able: Decide whether to work with this group, finding one solution by colouring, then finding another, and so on. Each time, encourage the children to say how the new solution is different from the others.
More able: Challenge these children to find at least ten solutions. Tell them that you will want them to explain how they solved the problem to the other children.

Plenary & assessment
With the children's help, build up a full set of solutions on the flip chart using coloured marker pens. The solutions are shown right (R for red, B for blue, G for green).

The 'answers' version of the sheet shows ten of these solutions, ordered in a systematic way. Look for a systematic approach of this kind.

Ask some children to explain how they solved the problem. Say:
● *How did you work that out?*
● *Are all of these different ways? Are you sure?*
● *How could you check?*
Ask the children to suggest how they might change the puzzle to make a new one – for example, having four stickers and a choice of four colours.

R	R	R
R	R	B
R	R	G
R	B	R
R	B	B
R	B	G
B	R	R
B	R	B
B	R	G
B	B	B
B	B	R
B	B	G
G	G	G
G	G	R
G	G	B
G	R	G
G	R	B
G	B	G

R	G	R
R	G	B
R	G	G

B	G	R
B	G	G
B	G	B

G	B	R
G	R	R
G	B	B

Name   Date

Get to 10

Play this game with a partner.

You will need a dice and two counters.

Take turns to roll the dice and move your counter.

The first player to reach 10 wins.

Start

1

2

3

4

5

6

7

8

9

10

Name	Date

Stickers

Jane put three stickers onto her pencil case.
Each sticker can be either red, blue or green.

Find some different ways of colouring the stickers.

Children make direct comparisons of two, then more than two, lengths and use the appropriate vocabulary. Then they estimate and measure, using uniform non-standard units of length, and record their estimates and results. They are encouraged to explain which units they chose, and why these were suitable for the measuring task.

LEARNING OBJECTIVES

	Topics	Starter	Main teaching activities
Lesson 1	Measures	● Know by heart addition doubles of all numbers to at least 5 (e.g. 4 + 4).	● Understand and use the vocabulary related to length. ● **Compare two lengths by direct comparison**; extend to more than two. ● Measure using uniform non-standard units (e.g. straws, wooden cubes), or standard units (e.g. metre sticks).
Lesson 2	Measures	As for Lesson 1.	As for Lesson 1.
Lesson 3	Measures	As for Lesson 1.	As for Lesson 1.

Lessons   overview

Preparation
Copy 'Double facts to 5 + 5' onto two A4 sheets, then copy each sheet onto thin A3 card and cut out a teaching set of cards. Find items for comparing for length: two of each item, one longer or wider than the other, ideally in different colours. Also prepare some sets of three items to be compared. Items could include scarves, gloves and shoes, or a range of teddies or other toys. Cut some strips of paper 10cm long.

Learning objectives
Starter
● Know by heart addition doubles of all numbers to at least 5 (e.g. 4 + 4).
Main teaching activities
● Understand and use the vocabulary related to length.
● **Compare two lengths by direct comparison**; extend to more than two.
● Measure using uniform non-standard units (e.g. straws, wooden cubes), or standard units (e.g. metre sticks).

Vocabulary
measure, size, compare, guess, estimate, enough, not enough, too much, too little, too many, too few, nearly, roughly, close to, about the same as, just over, just under, length, width, height, depth, long, short, tall, high, low, wide, narrow, deep, shallow, thick, thin, longer, shorter, taller, higher…, longest, shortest, tallest, highest…, far, near, close, metre, ruler, metre stick

You will need:
CD pages
Set of 'Double facts to 5 + 5' cards; 'Number fan', 'Measures chart 1', 'Measures chart 2' (see General Resources).

Equipment
Trays of items to be compared for length or width, such as pencils, paintbrushes and scissors; items to be compared such as scarves, gloves and shoes; items to be used for measuring, such as wooden cubes or straws; several 10cm strips of paper; a Valiant Roamer; a metre stick; flip chart or board.

Lesson

Starter

Hold up the 'Double facts to 5 + 5' cards. Ask the children to use their fingers to show the answers. Ask: *How did you work that out?* If they count on their fingers, check that they are counting on in ones.

Main teaching activities

Whole class: Show the children two scarves. Ask: *Are these the same length, or is one longer than the other? How can we find out?* Invite two children to hold the scarves with the end of each scarf just touching the floor, so that a direct comparison can be made. Point out that both scarves start at the same point so that we can compare them. Say: *The blue scarf is longer than the red scarf. So the red scarf is shorter than the blue scarf.* Repeat this for other items, making comparisons of length and width. Mention which item is shorter or narrower, as well as which is longer or wider.

Longer	Shorter

When the children are confident with this, introduce a third item of different length, and ask: *Which is the longest? Which is the shortest? How can we find out? Can you help to put these in order, starting with the shortest?* Invite children to compare them. They should make sure that one end of each of the three items is level. Invite children to describe the comparisons, using sentences such as: *The red scarf is longest, the blue scarf is shortest. The yellow scarf is longer than the red scarf and shorter than the blue scarf.* Repeat this for other items, making comparisons of length and width.

Group work: Provide each group of four to six children with a tray of items to compare. They should choose two items to compare and record the outcome in a table (see left). Then they compare three items for length which they can record by drawing them in order.

Differentiation

Less able: Decide whether to ask the children just to make comparisons of two items, using the language of *longer/shorter* and *wider/narrower*.

More able: When the children are confident with making comparisons (such as *longest/widest*), ask them to find their own sets of three objects and record them on the back of the sheet.

Plenary & assessment

Ask some children to show the class what they have compared. Invite them to use comparative language, and for each pair of items to use sentences with both *longer/shorter* and *wider/narrower*. Repeat for the superlatives *longest/shortest* and *widest/narrowest*. Ask:

● *Which is longer… shorter… wider… narrower? How can you tell?*
● *Which is the longest… shortest… widest… narrowest? How can you tell?*
● *What else is longer… shorter… wider… narrower than this?*
● *Look at these three things. Just by looking, estimate which is longest… shortest… widest… narrowest. Now let's check by comparing them side by side. Did you make a good guess?*

Lessons

Main teaching activities
Whole class: Provide some 10cm strips of paper, and explain that these can be used for measuring. Ask: *Can you guess how many lengths of paper will be about the same as the width of this cupboard?* Record the children's suggestions on the flip chart. Now invite two children to measure the cupboard. Check that they match the strips end to end, then count how many have been used. Ask: *Did the strips fit exactly? No, so we can say that the cupboard is just over/under four strips long.*
    Repeat this in Lesson 3 to measure other items in the room.

Group work: Choose from these activities for both lessons. You may wish to set up a circus of activities for all the children to use.
- Use items of the same length, such as rods, cubes or paintbrushes, to measure one item such as a book. Record estimates and then measures on 'Measures chart 1'.
- Choose different items to measure using the same unit. Record estimates and measures on 'Measures chart 2'.
- Estimate how far it is between two points in the classroom, then check by programming a Roamer. Record by drawing a sketch and writing estimates and measures.
- Estimate which items in the classroom are about a metre long (or high), then check using a metre stick. Record this on 'Measures chart 2'.

Differentiation
Less able: Choose an activity that the children will enjoy. Limit the range of items available. If possible, ask an adult to work with this group, encouraging them to use the vocabulary of length in sentences. Encourage them to make estimates and compare these with the measures.
More able: Use the Roamer, programmed for the default distance of 30cm as 1 unit. Tell the children that the Roamer has to make two or three stops on the way from A to B. Encourage them to estimate the distance, then program the Roamer for the whole journey. The children should assess their decisions and reprogram the Roamer, trying to become more accurate each time.

Plenary & assessment
Discuss the activities that each group has undertaken, asking key questions such as:
- *Which units did you choose to measure that? Was that a good choice? Why?*
- *What can you tell me about your estimate and your measure? Were they about the same?*
- *What else could you measure with that unit? Why do you think that?*

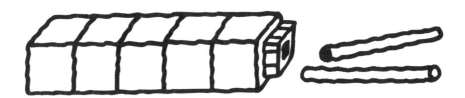

Counting to 20, counting in 10s and solving problems

Children count to 20 from 0 and back again. They count on and back from any small number. Next the children count in tens from 0 to 100 and back again, then counting on and back in a given number of tens from any decade number. They are introduced to the hundred square as a counting aid. They solve problems related to addition.

LEARNING OBJECTIVES

		Topics	Starter	Main teaching activities
Lesson	1	Counting, properties of numbers and number sequences	● **Count reliably at least 20 objects.**	● Know the number names and recite them in order to at least 20, from and back to zero. ● Describe and extend number sequences: **count on and back in ones from any small number.**
Lesson	2	Counting, properties of numbers and number sequences	As for Lesson 1.	● Know the number names and recite them in order to at least 20, from and back to zero. ● Describe and extend number sequences: **count on and back in ones from any small number, and in tens from and back to zero.**
Lesson	3	Counting, properties of numbers and number sequences	As for Lesson 1.	As for Lesson 2.
Lesson	4	Reasoning about numbers or shapes	As for Lesson 1.	● Solve simple mathematical problems or puzzles; recognise and predict from simple patterns and relationships. Suggest extensions by asking 'What if?' or 'What could I try next?'.
Lesson	5	Reasoning about numbers or shapes	As for Lesson 1.	As for Lesson 4.

Lessons   overview

Preparation
Make A3-sized copies of 'Blank number tracks' and 'Hundred square' resource.

Learning objectives
Starter
● **Count reliably at least 20 objects.**
Main teaching activities
● Know the number names and recite them in order to at least 20, from and back to zero.
● Describe and extend number sequences: **count on and back in ones from any small number, and in tens from and back to zero.**

Vocabulary
number, zero, one, two, three… to twenty and beyond, zero, ten, twenty… one hundred, none, how many…?, count, count (up) to, count on (from, to), count back (from, to), count in ones, tens…, above, below

You will need:
Photocopiable pages
'Spin a ten' (see page 44) and 'Counting patterns' (see page 45) for each child.

CD pages
'Numeral cards 0–9', 'Numeral cards 10–20' and a 'Work mat' for each pair; 'Numeral cards 21–30' for each more able pair; 'Blank number tracks' and 'Hundred square' copied to A3 size and A4 size copies of the latter for each child (see General Resources for all these sheets).

Equipment
A set of objects for counting, such as cubes or counters, for each group; paperclips.

Lesson ①

Starter
Ask the children to work in pairs at their tables. Say: *One of you take 10 cubes and put them on the work mat. Now the other one counts the cubes by touching them, but not moving them. Are there really 10 cubes?* Ask the children to swap roles, so that they each have a turn at counting out a specific number of cubes and at checking in this way. Include quantities of cubes from 8 to 20.

Main teaching activities
Whole class: Ask the children to count with you from 0 to 20, and back again. Keep a sharp pace to the counting. Repeat, this time starting from any small number such as 3, 4 or 5. Pin the A3 copy of the 'Blank number tracks' sheet to the board, and write the numbers 12, 11, 10, 9 in the middle of the first track. Ask:
- *What number comes next? How did you work that out? And the next number?*
- *What number would come before 12?*
  Repeat this for other starting numbers, counting in ones each time. Write blanks as well as numerals and ask the children to tell you the missing numbers. For example:
- _ _ _ 10 11 12 _ .
- 18 17 16 15 _ .
Group work: Ask the children to work in pairs with a set of 0–20 numeral cards between them. They shuffle the cards, then turn over the top card and place it on the table in front of them. Now they take turns to take the next card and place it in order to complete the number sequence 0–20. Explain that they should leave spaces between the cards for those they know are still to come.

Differentiation
Less able: Decide whether to limit the number range to 0–10, and to ask the children to find the zero card and place this first so that they have a starting point for the sequencing of the numerals.
More able: Decide whether to extend the number range to 30, using the numeral cards 21–30.

Plenary & assessment
Using the A3 copy of 'Blank number tracks', write in a blank track: _ _ _ 14 15 16 _ _ Ask:
- *What number comes before 14? How did you work that out?*
- *What comes after 16?*
- *Who can write in the missing numbers?*
Repeat this for other number sequences. If more able children used the extended number range to 30, include a couple of examples of this so that all of the children hear and see the numbers 21–30.

Lesson ②

Starter
Repeat the Starter from Lesson 1, this time asking the children to point to the cubes but not touch them. They will thus be starting to remember, during the count, which cubes have been counted and which are still to be counted.

Main teaching activities
Whole class: Ask the children to count in tens with you, going from zero to 100 and back again. Repeat this, keeping the pace sharp. Now ask the children to keep a count of the tens that they say on their fingers: as they count 0, 10, 20 and so on, they show each ten by holding up a finger. Stop the count at, say, 70 and ask: *How many tens have you counted?* Repeat this for other counts from zero.

Pin the A3 'Hundred square' sheet to the board. Point to zero, then 10, 20 and so on, inviting the children to say the number names. Ask questions such as:

- *What is ten more… less than 20? How did you work that out?*
- *Count on three tens from 10. What number do you reach?*
- *Count back two tens from 40. What number do you reach?*

Group work: Ask the children to work in pairs to play 'Spin a ten', filling in individual copies of the sheet. They need to write in each count in tens on a snake.

Differentiation

Less able: Decide whether to work with the children as a group and complete the 'Spin a ten' sheet together. Encourage the children to say each count of tens aloud.

More able: When the children have completed the sheet, they can use the spinner together with a dice. The dice generates a starting number, they then use the spinner to tell them how many tens to count on. For example, dice number 2, spinner number 6: 2… 12… 22… up to 52.

Plenary & assessment

Ask the children to count together, in tens, from zero to 100 and back again. Repeat this, keeping a count of the tens on your fingers. Say 'Stop' and ask: *What was the last ten that you said? How many tens was that? How do you know?* Repeat this for different tens numbers.

Lesson

Starter

Repeat the Starter from Lesson 2. Emphasise the importance of remembering, during the count, which cubes have been counted and which are still to be counted.

Main teaching activities

Whole class: Repeat the counting in ones activity from Lesson 1, and the counting in tens activity from Lesson 2. Check that the children are confident in counting forwards and back in ones and tens.

Using the A3 'Hundred square' sheet, point to 1, then ask the children to count forward in tens with you as you point to 11, 21 and so on. Repeat this for other counts in tens, both forwards and back.

Individual work: Provide copies of 'Counting patterns' for the children to complete. They may find it helpful to have a copy of the 'Hundred square' sheet to refer to.

Differentiation

Less able: These children will benefit from completing the activity sheet as a group, with adult input. Check that they can say the number names for these counting patterns.

More able: Challenge the children to complete the activity sheet without using the 'Hundred square' sheet as an aid.

Plenary & assessment

Review 'Counting patterns' together. Invite various children to complete the number sequences. Ask questions such as:

- *How did you work that out?*
- *What would the ten before/after that one be? How do you know that?*

Lessons   overview

Learning objectives
Starter
- **Count reliably at least 20 objects.**

Main teaching activities
- Solve simple mathematical problems or puzzles; recognise and predict from simple patterns and relationships. Suggest extensions by asking 'What if?' or 'What could I try next?'.

Vocabulary
pattern, puzzle, answer, right, wrong, what could we try next?, how did you work it out?, number sentence, sign, operation

You will need:

Equipment
A picture from a Big Book or poster showing objects that can be counted; three boxes or paper plates for each pair of children; interlocking cubes; a tambourine; a box of 'double 9' dominoes for each group; flip chart or board; paper and pencils.

Lesson

Starter

Ask the children to sit so they can all see the large picture. Explain that you would like them to count things in the picture by pointing, but not touching. Remind them to remember, during the count, which items they have already counted and which they still have to count. Say:
- *How many… did you count?*
- *How can you be sure that you counted them all?*
- *How many would there be if there were one more/one less?*
- *Now count the…*

Main teaching activities

Whole class: Explain that you want the children to solve a problem about numbers. Display ten cubes and three boxes, and say: *Here are ten cubes and three boxes. How many different ways can you put the cubes into the boxes?* Invite a child to demonstrate one way of doing this and to write the number sentence on the board, for example: 3 + 4 + 3 = 10.

Group work: Provide each pair with ten cubes and three boxes (or paper plates). Ask the children to work in pairs to find as many different ways as possible, and to record their answers on paper.

Differentiation

Less able: Decide whether to give the children just two boxes (or paper plates) for their ten cubes.
More able: Encourage the children to look for a pattern, and to explain why they think that they have found all the possible solutions.

Plenary & assessment

Invite various children to give their responses to the problem. Ask questions such as:
- *What would happen if you moved one cube from this box to that one? What number sentence would that make?*
- *Can you see a pattern in your results?*

Encourage more able children to describe any patterns they have found, such as:

10 + 0 + 0 = 10
9 + 1 + 0 = 10
8 + 1 + 1 = 10 and so on.

Lesson ⑤

Starter

Sit or stand so that you can hide a tambourine, perhaps behind a Big Book propped up. Explain that you will tap the hidden tambourine, and you would like the children to count the taps. They may find this quite difficult, as it involves counting events that cannot be seen. Begin with small numbers of taps, such as 3 and 4, then increase to numbers up to 10. If the children are confident with this, increase to 15 and then to 20. If the children find the counting difficult, suggest that they shut their eyes while they listen.

Main teaching activity

Whole class: Explain that you would like the children to solve a problem. Give each group a set of 'double 9' dominoes and explain the problem: *Look at the set of dominoes. Your task is to find all the dominoes that have a total of 9 spots. Record what you find.*
Group work: Encourage the children to decide for themselves how they will record their answers.

Differentiation

Less able: The children may need adult help to record their answers.
More able: Challenge the children to find all the dominoes with a total of 12 spots.

Plenary & assessment

Ask some children to explain how they solved the problem. On the flip chart, write each domino as a number sentence (for example, 5 + 4 = 9). Ask the children to help you order the dominoes and number sentences, so that they can see a pattern: 9 + 0 = 9, 8 + 1 = 9 and so on.

Discuss how, for example, 9 + 0 = 9 and 0 + 9 = 9 are the same domino. Model this with a domino, demonstrating both number sentences by turning the domino around.

Discuss how the children recorded their results. Ask them which were the best ways of recording, and why. Some children may have ordered their responses and then checked whether any were missing: 0 + 9; 1 + 8; 2 + 7; 3 + 6; 4 + 5.

Name   Date

Spin a ten

Work with a partner.

Spin a paperclip around a pencil on the spinner.

Where it stops will tell you how many tens to write.

Write the tens in the snake, like this:

| 10 | 20 | 30 | 40 | 50 |

Name	Date

Counting patterns

These number patterns go forward or back in tens.

Write in the missing numbers.

10	20	30			
70	60	50			
100	90				
30	40				80
			50	60	
				50	40
40				80	
			40	30	

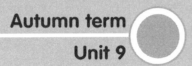
Place value, ordering and estimating

The children build TU numbers up to 20, then extend this beyond 20. They use money as an aid to understanding exchange. Ordinal number is explored for numbers to 10, then extended up to 20. They estimate how many for handfuls of apparatus, keeping the count to within 20.

LEARNING OBJECTIVES

		Topics	Starter	Main teaching activity
Lesson	1	Place value and ordering	● Describe and extend number sequences: **count on and back in ones from any small number.**	● **Read and write numerals from 0 to at least 20.** ● Begin to know what each digit in a two-digit number represents. ● Partition a 'teens' number and begin to partition larger two-digit numbers into a multiple of ten and ones (TU).
Lesson	2	Place value and ordering	As for Lesson 1.	As for Lesson 1, plus: ● Use the = sign to represent equality.
Lesson	3	Place value and ordering	● **Read and write numerals to at least 10.**	● **Understand the vocabulary of comparing and ordering numbers**, including ordinal numbers to at least 20.
Lesson	4	Place value and ordering	As for Lesson 3.	As for Lesson 3.
Lesson	5	Estimating	● **Count reliably at least 20 objects.**	● Understand and use the vocabulary of estimation. ● Give a sensible estimate of a number of objects that can be checked by counting (e.g. up to about 20 objects).

Lessons   overview

Learning objectives
Starter
● Describe and extend number sequences: **count on and back in ones from any small number.**
Main teaching activities
● **Read and write numerals from 0 to at least 20.**
● Begin to know what each digit in a two-digit number represents.
● Partition a 'teens' number and begin to partition larger two-digit numbers into a multiple of ten and ones (TU).
● Use the = sign to represent equality.

Vocabulary
units, ones, tens, exchange, digit, 'teens' number, the same number as, as many as, equal to

You will need:
Photocopiable pages
'Penny exchange' (see page 51) for each child.

CD pages
'Penny exchange', less able, more able and template versions (see Autumn term, Unit 9); 'Arrow cards' and 'Work mat' for each child (see General Resources).

Equipment
Twenty 1p coins and up to four 10p coins for each child; more able children will need forty 1p coins each; flip chart or board.

Lesson ①

Starter

Ask the children to sit in a circle and count together from zero to at least 20 and back again. Now ask them to count around the circle, starting from zero. If a child falters, say the number yourself to keep the counting pace sharp. Ask: *If Paul says five, who will say ten?* Now, starting with any small number, ask the children to count around the circle from that number to at least 20 and back. Ask questions such as:

- *If I count on five from seven, what numbers will I say?*
- *If I count on six from nine, what number will I stop on?*

Main teaching activities

Whole class: Provide each child with a set of arrow cards. Recap on how to use them. Explain that you will say a number, and you would like them to show you that number with their cards. Say:

- *Show me ten. Now show me four. Use the cards to show 14.*
- *Show me 15, 2, 11, 9, 19…*
- *Show me the number that is 1 ten and 6 units, 1 ten and 2 units… 2 tens.*

Now ask the children to show you numbers from 21 to 30 in the same way.

Group work: Ask the children to work in pairs with a set of arrow cards, using the 10 and 20 cards and the 1–9 unit cards. They should take turns to show their partner a tens and units number and ask their partner to say this number in two ways: as how many tens and units, and as a composite number. For example, for 15, the child would say: *One ten and five units; the number is fifteen.*

Differentiation

Less able: Decide whether to limit the number range to the 'teens' numbers, with the children using the 10 card and the 1–9 unit cards.

More able: Decide whether to extend the number range by including the 30 and 40 cards.

Plenary & assessment

On the board, write a TU number such as 17. Ask: *What is this number? How many tens are there? How many units?* Repeat for other numbers, extending the range into the twenties. Then extend into the range covered by the more able children, so that all of the class see and hear these numbers.

Now write 12 and 21 on the board. Point to 12 and ask: *What is this number?* Do the same for 21. Invite the children to explain how these numbers are different. Say: *But both numbers have a 2 and a 1. How can you tell which is which?* Repeat this for 23 and 32.

Lesson ②

Starter

Repeat the Starter from Lesson 1. If the children are confident with counting to 20, extend to 25 or 30.

Main teaching activities

Whole class: Show the children some 1p and 10p coins. Ask: *How many pennies is a 10p coin worth?* Ask a child to count out ten 1p coins and exchange them for one 10p coin. Ask the children to work in pairs: one child counts out 15 pennies and puts them onto the work mat, then the other child exchanges ten of these for a 10p coin. Ask: *How many 10p coins do you have now? How many pennies?* On the board, write: *15p is the same as 10p and 5p*, and: *15p = 10p + 5p*. Repeat this for other amounts, recording on the flip chart each time.

Group work: Provide copies of the activity sheet 'Penny exchange'. The core version of this sheet requires the children to make amounts to 20p. Explain that the children will find it helpful to use the coins on their work mats to help them complete this sheet.

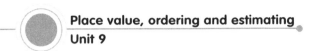
Differentiation
Less able: Decide whether to provide the version of the sheet with a maximum value of 15p.
More able: Decide whether to provide the version that extends the maximum value to 40p.

Plenary & assessment
On the flip chart, write '17p'. Ask: *How much is this? How many penny coins do I need to make it? If I used 10p coins too, how many tens and how many penny coins would I need?* Repeat this for other amounts, extending to amounts with two 10p coins, then three and four 10p coins for more able children.

Lessons   overview

Preparation
Pin an A3 copy of the 'Ordering' sheet to the flip chart.

Learning objectives
Starter
- **Read and write numerals to at least 10.**

Main teaching activities
- **Understand the vocabulary of comparing and ordering numbers,** including ordinal numbers to at least 20.

Vocabulary
first, second, third… tenth, eleventh… twentieth, last, last but one, before, after, next, between, halfway between

You will need:
Photocopiable pages
'Ordering' (see page 52) for each child, plus an A3 copy to pin up.

CD pages
'Work mat' (see General Resources).

Equipment
A Big Book; a reading book for each pair of children; interlocking cubes in various colours for each group; a whiteboard and pen for each child; flip chart or board; paper and pencils.

Lesson

Starter
Provide each child with a whiteboard and pen. Explain that you will say a number and you would like them to write it down, then hold up their board when you say *Show me.* Say: *Write down 8, 10, 17… Write down the number that is one more/one less than 6, 1, 14… Write down the number that has 1 ten and 3 units…* Repeat this for different numbers.

Main teaching activities
Whole class: Ask five children to stand at the front of the class, in a line. Invite the other children to count them, going from left to right. Now ask: *Who is first? Who is second? Who is last in the line? Who is between the third and the fifth…?*

Repeat this with a line of ten children. Say: *Sangeeta, change places with the fifth person; Tom, change places with the person between the sixth and the eighth…*

On the board, show the children how to record using numerals: 1st, 2nd, 3rd, 4th…

Group work: Ask the children to work in pairs. They will need a reading book and some paper for recording. Ask them to find the tenth page in the book and then to record the tenth letter on that page and the tenth word on that page. They can repeat this for eighth and twelfth.

Differentiation
This activity can be tackled by all of the children.
Less able: Decide whether to work with these children as a group, using a Big Book that they can all see.

More able: Decide whether to challenge these children to find, for example, the pages, words and letters between the eighth and the twelfth.

Plenary & assessment

Using a Big Book that all of the children can see, invite individuals to help you find the fifth page, word and letter. Repeat with, for example, the sixth, ninth, eleventh… Each time, ask a child to write the ordinal number on the board: 5th, 6th, 9th, 11th…

Lesson 4

Starter

Repeat the Starter from Lesson 3. If appropriate, extend the range of numbers to 30, so that the more able children can become confident with these numbers.

Main teaching activities

Whole class: Provide each group with some coloured interlocking cubes and each child with a work mat. Explain that you will ask them to put out a line of cubes. Say: *Put out ten cubes in a straight line, all the same colour. Now take a different-coloured cube and swap it with the 6th cube. Now do the same with the 9th cube.*

Repeat this, extending the number of cubes to up to 20.

Group work: Provide copies of 'Ordering'. The children work individually to complete the sheet.

Differentiation

Less able: Decide whether to work with these children as a group and complete the activity together. Encourage the children to use positional vocabulary.

More able: When the children have completed the activity sheet, they can put some different-coloured cubes in a line and ask each other questions about the positions of the cubes.

Plenary & assessment

Use the A3 version of 'Ordering' on the flip chart to review the activity. Ask questions such as:
- *Who is one place before/after sixth?*
- *Who is last?*
- *Who is first?*
- *Who is in between fifth place and eighth place?*

Lesson 5 overview

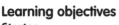

Learning objectives

Starter
- **Count reliably at least 20 objects.**

Main teaching activities
- Understand and use the vocabulary of estimation.
- Give a sensible estimate of a number of objects that can be checked by counting (e.g. up to about 20 objects).

Vocabulary

guess how many, estimate, nearly, roughly, close to, about the same as, just over, just under, too many, too few, enough, not enough

You will need:

CD pages
'Work mat' for each child (see General Resources).

Equipment
A set of counting objects, such as cubes, counters, shells, conkers or marbles, for each group; transparent containers; paper and pencils.

Lesson ⑤

Starter

The children will need a work mat and some counting objects. Ask them to count out 12 objects. Now ask them to check by counting again, touching the objects but not moving them. Repeat this for other amounts between 8 and 20.

Main teaching activities

Whole class: Ask the children to take a handful of about 15 counting objects, without counting them, then put them onto their work mat and count them. Ask: *Did you make a good guess? Try this again. Put the objects back and take another handful of about 15, then check by counting.* Repeat this for other numbers up to about 20 objects.

Now ask the children to work in pairs. One child takes a handful of objects and makes a guess at how many there are. The other child checks by counting. Allow sufficient time for each child both to make an estimate and to check the other child's estimates.

Discuss how accurate the children's estimates were, using the vocabulary listed above.

Group work: Provide each pair with counting objects and their work mats. They should take turns to pick up a handful of counting objects, both estimate how many there are and then check. They should record the results in the form:

_____'s estimate	Number counted	_____'s estimate	Number counted

Differentiation

Less able: Decide whether to provide larger objects, so that the size of the estimate and count is limited by how many the children can hold. Discuss with the children how close their estimates were, using the vocabulary listed above.

More able: The children could move on and fill transparent containers with objects and challenge each other to estimate how many, then check by counting. This prevents them from spreading the objects out, so they will need to take into account those objects in the tub that are hidden by other objects.

Plenary & assessment

Show the children one of the transparent tubs, and pour into it enough of some larger counting objects to fill it. Ask: *How many do you estimate are in here?* Invite a child to count the objects while the others watch. Discuss with the children how accurate their estimates were. Repeat this for another set of counting objects.

Name	Date

Penny exchange

Write how many 10p coins and how many pennies make these amounts.

Amount	10p coins	Penny coins
15p		
11p		
19p		
20p		
16p		
14p		
18p		
17p		

Now work out these amounts.

10p coins	Pennies	Amount
2	0	
1	3	
1	9	
1	7	
1	1	
1	0	
1	8	
1	4	

Name	Date

Ordering

Read the questions about the children in this race.

Write your answers.

Use these words to help you:

first   last   next to   before   after

Who is first?

Who is last?

Who is next to last?

Who is between Meera and Kul?

Who is just in front of Anna?

What place is Paul in?

Understanding addition and subtraction

The children use the mental strategy of counting on from the larger number for addition. They begin to understand that addition is commutative, that is 5 + 3 = 3 + 5. They count back in ones in order to subtract.

LEARNING OBJECTIVES

		Topics	Starter	Main teaching activities
Lesson	1	Understanding addition and subtraction	● Begin to know addition facts for all pairs of numbers with a total up to at least 5.	● **Understand the operation of addition, and use the related vocabulary.**
Lesson	2	Understanding addition and subtraction	As for Lesson 1.	As for Lesson 1.
Lesson	3	Understanding addition and subtraction	● Know by heart addition doubles of all numbers to at least 5 (e.g. 4 + 4).	● **Understand the operation of addition, and of subtraction (as 'take away'), and use the related vocabulary.**
Lesson	4	Understanding addition and subtraction	As for Lesson 3.	As for Lesson 3.
Lesson	5	Understanding addition and subtraction	As for Lesson 3.	As for Lesson 3.

Lessons   overview

Preparation
If you do not already have these cards, fold 'Add facts to 5' in half and copy each half to A4 size, then copy each A4 sheet to A3 size. Cut out a set of large cards.

Learning objectives
Starter
●　Begin to know addition facts for all pairs of numbers with a total up to at least 5.
Main teaching activities
●　**Understand the operation of addition, and use the related vocabulary.**

Vocabulary
add, more, plus, make, sum, total, altogether, score, subtract, take (away), minus, leave, how many are left/left over?, how many are gone?, one less, two less, ten less…

You will need:
Photocopiable pages 'Missing numbers', (see page 58), one for each child.

CD pages
'Missing numbers', less able, more able and template versions (see Autumn term, Unit 10); 'Numeral cards 0–9' for each pair of children and a teaching set of 'Add facts to 5' cards (see General Resources).

Equipment
An individual whiteboard and marker pen for each child; interlocking cubes; flip chart or board; paper and pencils.

Lesson ①

Starter

Use the 'Add facts to 5' cards. Explain that you will hold up a card and would like the children to show you the answer using their fingers. Encourage the children to respond quickly, so that they can demonstrate that they are beginning to recall these facts.

Main teaching activities

Whole class: Remind the children of the addition strategy 'put the larger number in your heads and count on in ones'. Ask them to use this to calculate $6 + 3$. Explain that you will now ask them some addition questions. Use a range of vocabulary, for example: *Add 3 to 5. What is 6 plus 2? What is 5 add 1? What is the sum of 2 and 7? How many are 4 and 6 altogether?* After each example, encourage the children to explain how they worked out the answer, so that those who are not yet confident can hear explanations of the strategies used.

Now ask: *Which two numbers could total 9?* On the board, write $\diamond + \square = 9$. Invite the children to suggest different possible answers. Record these on the board, then write them so that a pattern emerges (see illustration). Encourage the children to talk about any patterns that they see.

Individual work: Ask the children to complete the 'Missing numbers' activity sheet, working individually. The core version of this sheet involves completing addition statements to 10.

$$0 + 9 = 9$$
$$1 + 8 = 9$$
$$2 + 7 = 9$$
$$3 + 6 = 9$$
$$4 + 5 = 9$$
$$5 + 4 = 9$$
$$6 + 3 = 9$$
$$7 + 2 = 9$$
$$8 + 1 = 9$$
$$9 + 0 = 9$$

Differentiation

Less able: Decide whether to provide the version of 'Missing numbers' with addition statements to 6. The children may benefit from using interlocking cubes, partitioning them in different ways to find solutions.

More able: Decide whether to provide the version of the sheet with addition statements to 15. At this stage, the children should be confident with using the 'count on in ones' strategy.

Plenary & assessment

Discuss the strategies the children used to complete their activity sheets. Ask questions such as:
- *How did you work that out? Who had a different way?*
- *Who can remember some addition facts?*

On the board, write: $\diamond + \square = 11$. Ask the children to suggest how they might complete this. Remind them of the pattern that they saw for $\diamond + \square = 9$. Ask: *How did you find the right sums?*

Lesson ②

Starter

Repeat the starter from Lesson 1, this time with the children writing their responses on a whiteboard and holding it up when you say *Show me.*

Main teaching activity

Whole class: Write these sums on the flip chart and invite the children to give the answers.

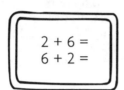

Ask: *What do you notice about these sums?* Encourage the children to say that the numbers added are the same, but in a different order, and that the answer to both sums is the same. Repeat this for other examples, such as: 4 + 3 and 3 + 4; 8 + 2 and 2 + 8.

Group work: Provide each pair of children with a set of numeral cards 0–9. Ask the children to sort the cards into two piles: 0–5 in one pile and 6–9 in the other. They should take turns to take the top card from each pile and make an addition sentence with the two cards; then their partner should make another addition sentence with the same cards. For example, with the cards 3 and 6 they would make 3 + 6 = 9 and 6 + 3 = 9. Ask them to record both addition sentences each time.

Differentiation

Less able: Decide whether to use two sets of 0–5 cards for each pair of children.
More able: Decide whether to let the children shuffle the 0–9 cards and take any two from the top each time. This will produce additions of numbers up to 9 + 8.

Plenary & assessment

Invite pairs of children to write one of their sum pairs on the flip chart. Discuss the fact that it does not matter in addition which order the numbers are added in, and suggest that this can be very useful when we are adding numbers together. Remind them that if they know, say, 6 + 3 = 9, then they can also work out that 3 + 6 = 9. So if they know the one number fact, they can work out the other one.

Lessons   overview

Learning objectives
Starter
- Know by heart addition doubles of all numbers to at least 5 (e.g. 4 + 4).

Main teaching activity
- **Understand the operation of addition, and of subtraction (as 'take away'), and use the related vocabulary.**

Vocabulary
add, more, plus, make, sum, total, altogether, score, double

You will need:
Photocopiable pages
'Take it away' (see page 59) for each pair.

CD pages
'Take it away', less able, more able and template versions (see Autumn term, Unit 10).

Equipment
Interlocking cubes and a blank dice marked 1, 1, 2, 2, 3, 3 for each pair; some 1–6 dice; two different-coloured sets of 12 counters for each pair.

Lesson

Starter
Ask the children to work out some sums involving doubles. Suggest that if they are not sure of the answer, they could use their fingers to show the doubles, one number on each hand, then count on in ones from one of these. Ask, for example:
- *What is double 2? Double 5?*
- *How many is 3 add 3?*

Main teaching activities
Whole class: Make a tower of six interlocking cubes and say: *How many will be left if I take away 2? How can we work this out?* Invite the children to suggest ways of finding the answer, such as taking away two cubes and counting what is left. More able children may suggest counting back 2 from 6.

Remove two cubes from the tower, and count with the children what is left. Say the sentence together: *6 take away 2 leaves 4.* Now ask them to put 6 'in their heads' and count back 2: *6, 5, 4. So 6 take away 2 leaves 4.* Write this on the board as a number sentence: 6 – 2 = 4. Explain that the '–' sign means 'take away'.

Repeat this for other subtractions within 10, this time asking the children to work mentally, saying the subtraction sentence together, then demonstrating with cubes to confirm the answer.

Group work: Provide each pair with a 1, 1, 2, 2, 3, 3 dice. Ask them to roll the dice and subtract the score from 6 each time. They should write a number sentence for each subtraction. They can repeat this for subtractions from 7.

Differentiation
Less able: Decide whether to ask these children to subtract the dice score from 4, then 5, each time.
More able: Decide whether to provide a 1–6 dice and ask the children to subtract from 8, then 9.

Plenary & assessment
Invite some pairs of children to write one of their subtraction sentences on the board, without the answer. Invite the others to find the answer mentally. Ask: *How did you work that out?* Include examples from less able and from more able children so that everyone's work is valued, and so that all the children can hear any strategies that the more able children have adopted.

Lesson

Starter

Repeat the Starter from Lesson 3, this time encouraging all the children to recall as many double facts as they can. Give a slightly longer pause time after posing the question, so that everyone has time to try to respond.

Main teaching activities

Whole class: Explain that today's lesson continues from the day before. Use cubes to review the strategy of taking away by counting back.

Group work: Ask the children to work in pairs. They take turns to take up to eight interlocking cubes and make a tower, hiding it from their partner. They tell their partner how many cubes there are, then take away some cubes and say how many have been taken away. The other child writes a number sentence for this subtraction and works out how many are left, then checks by looking at the tower.

Differentiation

Less able: Decide whether to limit the tower size to six cubes.
More able: Decide whether to extend the cube limit to 12.

Plenary & assessment

Repeat the plenary session from Lesson 3. Ask:
- *What is 8 take away 3? What is 3 add 5?*
- *What do you notice about these two number sentences?*

Explain that if the children know an addition fact, this can help them to find a subtraction fact.

Lesson

Starter

Repeat the Starter from Lesson 3, this time increasing the pace to see who has recall of these facts.

Main teaching activities

Whole class: Review with the children the strategy of taking away by counting back.

Group work: Provide each child with a copy of the 'Take it away' activity sheet. Ask them to work in pairs, and to use mental strategies to find the answers. Each pair will need two different-coloured sets of 12 counters.

Differentiation

There are versions of the sheet differentiated for less able children and more able children. Decide whether to work with less able children to encourage them to work mentally, rather than using their fingers or cubes.

Plenary & assessment

Ask some oral subtraction questions, encouraging all the children to work mentally. For example:
- *What is 4 take away 2? How did you work that out?*
- *Take 2 away from 8.*
- *Subtract 3 from 7.*

Name	Date

Missing numbers

Write in the missing numbers.

3 + 6 =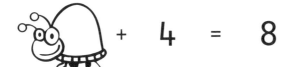

5 + 🐛 = 7

🐞 + 4 = 8

9 + 1 = 🕷

🐞 + 2 = 5

3 + 🐛 = 8

2 + 8 = 🕷

7 + 🐛 = 9

3 + 🐛 = 6

2 + 🐛 = 8

Now write sums for these answers.

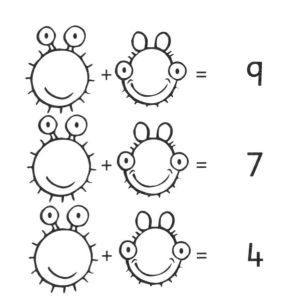

⬡ + ⬡ = 5

⬡ + ⬡ = 8

⬡ + ⬡ = 6

⬡ + ⬡ = 9

⬡ + ⬡ = 7

⬡ + ⬡ = 4

Name	Date

Take it away

Work with a partner.

You will need some counters in two colours.

Choose a take away question from the grid.

Tell your partner the answer.

If your partner agrees with you, cover the
question with a counter.

Carry on until all the questions have been covered.

The winner is the one with the most counters on the grid at the end.

6 – 4 = ☐	5 – 2 = ☐	9 – 5= ☐
7 – 3 = ☐	3 – 3 = ☐	8 – 2 = ☐
5 – 0 = ☐	10 – 7 = ☐	8 – 6 = ☐
7 – 5 = ☐	9 – 4 = ☐	10 – 1= ☐

Mental calculations for addition, solving problems and making decisions

The children explore subtraction patterns, such as 9 – 0, 9 – 1… They solve number and money problems which involve addition and subtraction and are encouraged to make decisions about which operations and mental strategies to use to find the solutions.

LEARNING OBJECTIVES

	Topics	Starter	Main teaching activities
Lesson 1	Understanding addition and subtraction Mental calculation strategies (+ and –)	● Begin to know addition facts for all pairs of numbers with a total up to at least 10.	● **Understand the operation of addition, and of subtraction (as 'take away'), and use the related vocabulary.** ● Use patterns of similar calculations (e.g. 10 – 0 = 10, 10 – 1 = 9, 10 – 2 = 8).
Lesson 2	Understanding addition and subtraction Mental calculation strategies (+ and –)	As for Lesson 1.	As for Lesson 1.
Lesson 3	Problems involving 'real life', money or measures Making decisions	● Know by heart addition doubles of all numbers to at least 5 (e.g. 4 + 4).	● **Use mental strategies to solve simple problems** set in 'real life', money or measurement contexts, **using counting, addition, subtraction and doubling, explaining methods and reasoning orally.** ● Choose and use appropriate number operations and mental strategies to solve problems.
Lesson 4	Problems involving 'real life', money or measures Making decisions	As for Lesson 3.	As for Lesson 3.
Lesson 5	Problems involving 'real life', money or measures Making decisions	As for Lesson 3.	As for Lesson 3.

Lessons   overview

Preparation
Make a teaching set of large 'Complements of 10' cards by enlarging the sheet onto two A4 sheets and then onto two sheets of A3 card.

Learning objectives
Starter
● Begin to know addition facts for all pairs of numbers with a total up to at least 10.
Main teaching activities
● **Understand the operation of addition, and of subtraction (as 'take away'), and use the related vocabulary.**
● Use patterns of similar calculations (e.g. 10 – 0 = 10, 10 – 1 = 9, 10 – 2 = 8).

Vocabulary
add, more, plus, make, sum, total, altogether, score, double, subtract, take (away), minus, leave, how many are left/left over?, how many are gone?, one less, two less, ten less…

You will need:
Photocopiable pages
'Take it away', (see page 59) for each pair.

CD pages
'Take it away', less able, more able and template versions (see Autumn term, Unit 10); 'Complements of 10' teaching cards (see General Resources).

Equipment
Interlocking cubes; two different-coloured sets of 12 counters for each pair.

Lesson ①

Starter

Using the teaching set of the 'Complements of 10' cards, explain that you will hold up a card and you would like the children to show you the answer with their fingers. For example, for the card $4 + \square = 10$, they would hold up six fingers.

Main teaching activities

Whole class: Remind the children of the addition pattern they considered for 9: $0 + 9$, $1 + 8$, $2 + 7$... Explain that, in this lesson, they will look at some subtraction patterns. Start by writing '5 – 0 =' on the board and asking the children to discuss what the answer is. Talk about how taking away zero leaves a number unchanged. Continue the pattern (see right).

Ask: *What do you notice about this pattern?* Encourage the children to discuss what they see: what the number after the take away sign goes up by each time, and what the number in the answer goes down by each time.

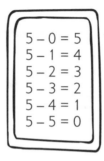

$$5 - 0 = 5$$
$$5 - 1 = 4$$
$$5 - 2 = 3$$
$$5 - 3 = 2$$
$$5 - 4 = 1$$
$$5 - 5 = 0$$

Group work: Ask the children to work in pairs, writing out the subtraction patterns for 6, 7 and 8.

Differentiation

Less able: Decide whether to simplify the task and ask these children to write out the subtraction patterns for 3 and 4. They may benefit from using interlocking cubes to observe what happens as a tower of cubes is partitioned. If a new tower is used for each subtraction, the pattern can be shown visually.

More able: Decide whether to ask these children to write the patterns for 9 and 10.

Plenary & assessment

Ask the children to help you write part of the subtraction pattern for 6 on the board. Go as far as $6 - 3 = 3$. Now ask the children to tell you what is written there, and then to finish the pattern orally. Suggest to them that this pattern is very useful: they can use it to work out subtraction facts that they do not know from facts that they *do* know. Finish by asking questions such as:

● *What is 7 take away 1? So 7 take away 3 would be…?*
● *How did you work that out? Did you use the subtraction pattern?*

Lesson ②

Repeat the Starter from Lesson 1, encouraging the children to use rapid recall. Use the whole-class teaching activity to review a subtraction pattern, such as that for 8. Now ask the children to play the subtraction game on the 'Take it away' sheet in pairs (this activity is repeated from Unit 10, Lesson 5). This sheet is differentiated for the core ability level, less able children and more able children.

In the plenary session, play the game with the children. Divide the class into two teams, with team captains who decide which team member will answer each question. This will give you an opportunity to assess how confident the children are with recall of subtraction facts.

Lessons overview

Preparation
If necessary, make a teaching set of cards from the 'Double facts to 5 + 5' sheet: copy it onto two A4 sheets and copy each sheet onto A3 card, then cut out the cards. Write four number problems on the flip chart (see Lesson 5).

Learning objectives
Starter
● Know by heart addition doubles of all numbers to at least 5 (e.g. 4 + 4).
Main teaching activities
● **Use mental strategies to solve simple problems** set in 'real life', money or measurement contexts, **using counting, addition, subtraction and doubling, explaining methods and reasoning orally.**
● Choose and use appropriate number operations and mental strategies to solve problems.

Vocabulary
pattern, puzzle, answer, right, wrong, what could we try next?, how did you work it out?, number sentence, sign, operation

You will need:
CD pages
A set of 'Double facts to 5 + 5' teaching cards, a set of 'Price labels' for each child (see General Resources).

Equipment
A collection of coins (several each of 1p, 2p, 5p and 10p) for each group; flip chart or board; paper and pencils.

Lesson

Starter
Use the 'Double facts to 5 + 5' cards. Ask the children to read the question on the card, then respond by showing the double fact on their fingers. Ask individual children: *What is double...? What is ... add ...?*

Main teaching activities
Whole class: Explain that you will ask the children to solve some number problems. Start with: *I think of a number, then add 3. The answer is 8. What was my number?* Invite the children to give the answer and tell you how they worked out the problem. For those who are not sure about this, go through the steps of solving this problem. Ask: *What do we know? What are we trying to work out?* The children may see this either as an addition problem or as a subtraction problem: □ + 3 = 8 or 8 − 3 = □. Repeat this for a similar problem, such as: *I think of a number, then add 4. The answer is 10. What was my number?*

Set another problem, such as: *Saleem and Moe have 9 marbles between them. If Saleem has 2 marbles, how many does Moe have?* Again, discuss with the children how they solved the problem. Write two number sentences on the board to show the problem: 9 − 2 = □ and 2 + □ = 9. Make sure the children understand that both of these number sentences are appropriate ways of showing the problem. Repeat this for another problem, such as: *Sam has 5 stickers and Paul has 6. How many do they have altogether?* Discuss what the children need to find out.
Group work: Ask the children to work in groups of four. They should each solve the following problems individually, write down a number sentence to show their solution, then compare how they solved the problem. The problems can be given orally, over a period of time:
● *There are an orange and an apple on the scales. They are balanced by 12 bricks. The apple can be balanced with five bricks. How many bricks will balance the orange?*
● *James went to school at 9 o'clock, and three hours later he had his lunch. When was lunchtime?*
● *Meena had 11p. Then she spent 8p. How much did she have left?*

Differentiation
Less able: Decide whether to simplify each problem by reducing the number range.
More able: Challenge the children to solve this problem: *Jack had 7 pens. Together, Jack and Mark had 15 pens. How many pens did Mark have?*

Plenary & assessment

Take each of the problems in turn and ask a group of four children to explain how they found the solution. It will be helpful to the other children if individuals who have used different methods explain these for all to hear. Encourage the children to write a number sentence on the board to represent the problem. If they find this difficult, ask the others to suggest what number sentence might be appropriate and why. Discuss the different methods used, asking questions such as:

- *What maths did you need to use? How did you decide that?*
- *Is there another way? Which way do you think is best? Why do you think that?*

Lesson

Starter

Repeat the Starter from Lesson 3. This time, ask the children to put up their hands to answer and to say the whole number sentence, including the answer.

Main teaching activities

Whole class: Explain that today's problems will concentrate on money. Set some problems, such as:

- *I have a 10p coin. I spend 8p. How much change will I get?*
- *A toffee costs 4p and a chew costs 5p. How much do they cost altogether?*
- *Crisps are 4p a pack. How much would two packs cost?*

For each problem, discuss how the children solved it. They may find it helpful to see the problem modelled using coins.

Now say: *I have something costing 5p and something costing 3p. Who can make up a number story about this for me?* Discuss the number stories that the children invent, and how they solve the problem set by each number story.

Group work: Provide each child with a set of price labels (from the 'Price labels' sheet) and some coins. Ask them to sort the labels into two piles: one with 1p to 5p and the other with 6p to 9p. They should take turns to choose a label from each pile and make up their own number story with the two labels, then write the number story and a number sentence to show the answer. The other child should check the number story and sentence each time.

Differentiation

Less able: Decide whether to work with this group, and to use only the labels 1p to 5p. The children can produce a group response, with an adult scribing for them.

More able: If the labels are shuffled and kept in one pile, the children can produce number stories and sentences with amounts up to 9p + 8p.

Plenary & assessment

Review the number stories that the children have invented. Talk about the mathematics they used to solve the problems, and how they recorded their number sentences. Ask questions such as:

- *What maths did you need to use? How did you decide that?*
- *Is there another way? Which way do you think is best? Why do you think that?*

Lesson ⑤

Starter

Repeat the Starter from Lesson 3, this time inviting individual children to read out the number sentence before it is answered by a show of fingers. They can read the answer space as 'box' or 'something'.

Main teaching activities

Whole class: Encourage the children to invent more number problems, this time involving quantities and measures. Ask how they worked out the solution to each one. Offer examples to help them think of problems, such as:

- *Jane had two ribbons, each one as long as five cubes. How long were both ribbons together?*
- *Peter balances an apple and an orange with ten cubes. Six cubes balance the orange. How many cubes balance the apple?*
- *A full jug of water holds three cups. How much will two jugs hold?*

Individual work: Write four number problems on the flip chart. For example:

- *Rashid left home at 8 o'clock. He arrived at the beach at 11 o'clock. How long did it take him to get to the beach?*
- *Rashid bought some sweets at the seaside. He bought a chew for 2p and a toffee for 5p. How much did he spend altogether?*
- *Rashid built a sandcastle. He put 4 red flags on it. Then he put 4 blue flags on it. How many flags were there in total?*
- *Rashid found 4 black pebbles. Then he found 3 white pebbles. How many pebbles did he find altogether?*

Ask the children to record their answers on paper.

Differentiation

Less able: These children may benefit from working with an adult, who can read the problems to them and guide them towards writing number sentences.
More able: They can make up their own word problems, with a seaside theme, for other children to try.

Plenary & assessment

Invite some children to explain how they solved the problems. Consider different methods used, and the mathematics involved. Ask questions such as:

- *How did you work that out? Is there another way?*
- *Which way of working out the problem do you like best? Why?*
- *What sort of maths did you use? Who used something different?*
- *Which way works best? Why do you think that?*

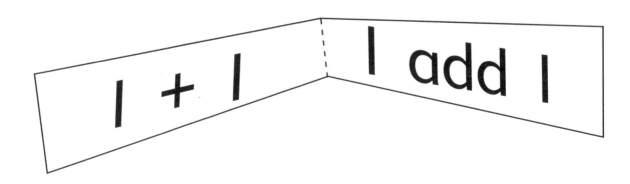

Data handling and weight

Children make decisions about how to sort objects for given properties. They make lists for given sets such as 'children with brown eyes'. They answer questions about data that they have collected. For weight the children make direct comparisons of two, then three, parcels, and check their estimates using a balance. They estimate, then choose appropriate uniform non-standard units to weigh items and justify their decisions.

LEARNING OBJECTIVES

		Topics	Starter	Main teaching activities
Lesson	**1**	Organising and using data	● **Order numbers to at least 10**, and position them on a number track.	● Solve a given problem by sorting, classifying and organising information in simple ways, such as: using objects or pictures; in a list or simple table. Discuss and explain results.
Lesson	**2**	Organising and using data	As for Lesson 1.	As for Lesson 1.
Lesson	**3**	Measures	● Begin to know addition facts for all pairs of numbers with a total up to at least 10, and the corresponding subtraction facts.	● Understand and use the vocabulary related to mass. ● **Compare two masses by direct comparison**; extend to more than two. ● Measure using uniform non-standard units (e.g. wooden cubes, plastic weights) or standard units. ● **Suggest suitable standard or uniform non-standard units and measuring equipment to estimate, then measure a mass**, recording estimates and measurements as 'about as heavy as 20 cubes'.
Lesson	**4**	Measures	As for Lesson 3.	As for Lesson 3.
Lesson	**5**	Measures	As for Lesson 3.	As for Lesson 3.

Lessons   overview

Preparation
Enlarge both sets of numeral cards onto thin card and cut them out to make a teaching set. Prepare a set of adhesive labels saying 'red', 'green', 'blue' and 'yellow'. Make a simple table for each group on sugar paper, with the headings '5 years old' and '6 years old'.

Learning objectives
Starter
● **Order numbers to at least 10**, and position them on a number track.
Main teaching activities
● Solve a given problem by sorting, classifying and organising information in simple ways, such as: using objects or pictures; in a list or simple table. Discuss and explain results.

Vocabulary
count, sort, vote, list, group, set, old, older, oldest

You will need:
CD pages
A teaching set of 'Numeral cards 0–9' and 'Numeral cards 10–20' (see General Resources).

Equipment
A washing line and pegs; classroom objects coloured red, blue, green and yellow; sorting hoops; adhesive labels; sugar paper; an interlocking cube for each child; a marker pen for each group.

Lesson ①

Starter

Put up the washing line. Tell the children that you have a set of 0 to 10 cards which need to be pegged on the line in order. Hold up the 0 and ask: *What number is this? Where do you think this card should go?* Invite a child to peg it to the line. Discuss whether the others agree with this position. Repeat for the 10 card. Taking the other cards in random order, ask children to peg each one to the line, repeating the questions above.

Now invite some children to take a given card from the line, saying, for example: *Take the 6 card… Take the card that is between 3 and 5…*

Main teaching activities

Whole class: Put two sorting hoops on the floor and label them 'red' and 'blue'. Invite some children to choose an object from your collection to go into one of the hoops. Ask: *Why did you put the toy car in that hoop?* Discuss with the children how the red and blue objects have been sorted. Now add two more hoops and label them 'green' and 'yellow'. Invite children to complete the sorting. Ask:

- *Why did you put that… in the yellow hoop?*
- *Why does that… belong there? Could it go in another hoop? Why?*

When the children are confident with this, explain that another way of sorting data is to make a list. Ask them to help you make a list of all the first names in the class that have four letters. Write the names on the board, with the heading 'Names with 4 letters'. Ask: *How many children have first names with four letters? How do you know that?* Discuss how lists of things are useful: they can help us to find information that we need. Ask the children to suggest other things that could be made into a list, such as the days of the week or who has a birthday this month.

Group work: Ask the children to work in groups of about six, making lists of:

- all the counting numbers between 3 and 15
- the names of all the children in their group
- the names of all the children in their group with brown eyes.

Give each group one sheet of sugar paper and a marker pen. The children can take turns to scribe for the group, writing large enough for the rest of the class to see what they have done later. Emphasise that the tasks should be done quickly and efficiently. Set a time limit of no more than 10 minutes for the whole activity, including the decisions about who will scribe and how the group will go about each task.

Differentiation

Less able: Decide whether to work with this group and act as scribe for them. Encourage the children to use the language of data handling (see 'Vocabulary' on previous page).
More able: When the children have completed the group task, challenge them to choose a topic and write another list of things.

Plenary & assessment

Invite each group to explain how they went about the task and to show their results. For each group, choose one list and ask questions about the data, such as:

- *What numbers are in the list? How many numbers is that? How did you find them?*
- *Who's in this group? Are there two children with the same name? How do you know that?*
- *So how many in this group have brown eyes? There are eight children in this group, so how many do not have brown eyes?*

Discuss how useful a list is for writing down things we know.

Lesson

Starter

Repeat the starter from Lesson 1, this time pegging the numeral cards on the line in the wrong order before the lesson begins. Encourage the children to discuss which number should go where, and why, before you ask individual children to move each numeral to its agreed new position.

Main teaching activities

Whole class: Give each child an interlocking cube. Put out a sheet of sugar paper with the headings '5 years old' and '6 years old'. Ask: *How old are you?* Invite the children to work in groups, placing their cubes into age piles and then placing these under the appropriate headings on the sugar paper.

Now ask questions such as:

- *How many in your group are five years old? How can you tell from this information?*
- *Which group has more five-year-olds than six-year-olds?*

Group work: Ask the children to collect information about how many pets each child in their group has and to record this on paper, making their own table. Ask them to decide what sort of table they will make. Say that you would like them to do this quickly and efficiently.

Differentiation

Less able: Provide a ready-prepared table outline for these children to use.

More able: If these children need a further task, ask them to collect information about how many clocks the members of their group have at home.

Plenary & assessment

Invite some children to explain how they collected and recorded their data. Discuss which ways of recording were best. The children will probably have written each child's name in one column and the number of pets each child has in the next column. Write the data from one group on the flip chart, and ask:

- *How many pets does… have? How do you know that?*
- *Who has the most pets? Who has the least?*
- *Who has no pets?*
- *Who has more/fewer pets than…? How did you work that out?*

4 2 9 5 1 8 3 0 7 6

Lessons   overview

Preparation
Make enlarged sets of teaching cards from 'Add facts to 5' and 'Take away facts to 5'. Make some parcels, including: two of the same size but different weights; two of the same weight but different sizes; a large 'light' parcel and a small 'heavy' parcel.

Learning objectives
Starter
- Begin to know addition facts for all pairs of numbers with a total up to at least 10, and the corresponding subtraction facts.

Main teaching activities
- Understand and use the vocabulary related to mass.
- **Compare two masses by direct comparison**; extend to more than two.
- Measure using uniform non-standard units (e.g. wooden cubes, plastic weights) or standard units.
- **Suggest suitable standard or uniform non-standard units and measuring equipment to estimate, then measure a mass**, recording estimates and measurements as 'about as heavy as 20 cubes'.

Vocabulary
measure, size, compare, guess, estimate, enough, not enough, too much, too little, too many, too few, nearly, roughly, close to, about the same as, just over, just under, weigh, weighs, balances, heavy/light, heavier/lighter, heaviest/lightest, balance, scales, weight

You will need:
CD pages
Teaching sets of 'Add facts to 5' and 'Take away facts to 5'; 'Measures chart 1' and 'Measures chart 2' for each pair (see General Resources).

Equipment
Individual whiteboards and pens; classroom items for weighing; non-standard units of mass such as cubes or scoops of sand; egg cups; bucket balances; a set of weighing scales; parcels for comparing; 100g weights; paper and pencils.

Lesson

Starter
Using the teaching set of 'Add facts to 5' cards, explain that you will hold up a card and you would like the children to write the answer on their whiteboard and hold it up when you say *Show me*. Ask: *How did you work it out? Is there another way?* Praise the children who are beginning to have rapid recall of these addition facts.

Main teaching activities
Whole class: Show the children the parcels. Pass two parcels around the class; ask the children to hold one in one hand and one in the other and decide which is heavier. Then ask: *Which parcel is heavier/lighter?*

Show the children a bucket balance and discuss how it is in balance when nothing is in the buckets. Now put one parcel in each bucket of the bucket balance, and discuss what the children observe. *How can you tell from this which parcel is heavier?* Repeat for other pairs of parcels. The children will begin to realise that visible size does not determine weight. Extend this to comparing three parcels, using superlatives: *Which is the heaviest/lightest parcel?*

Group work: Provide each group of four children with a set of objects to compare by weight and a bucket balance. Ask the children to take two items each time and compare how much they weigh by holding them, then check using the bucket balance. They should record their work in the form:

My estimate	My check
The _____ was lighter than the _____	The _____ was lighter than the_____

Then ask the children to choose three objects from their list. They should estimate which is the heaviest and which is the lightest and use a balance to check.

Differentiation
Less able: Work with this group and encourage the children to use the appropriate vocabulary.
More able: Challenge these children to put all of their objects in order of weight, starting with the lightest.

Plenary & assessment
Invite some children to compare three objects by picking them up. Ask:
- *Which is the heaviest/lightest? How can you check this?* Invite children to demonstrate with a bucket balance.
- *How can you tell by looking at a bucket balance which side is heavier/lighter?*

Lessons

Starter
For both lessons, repeat the Starter from Lesson 3; this time, use the 'Take away facts to 5' cards. Over two sessions, the children should begin to have rapid recall of some of these subtraction facts.

Main teaching activities
Whole class: Display some cubes, a balance and an object. Ask the children how many cubes they think will be needed to balance the object and write their estimates on the flip chart. Now invite a child to place the object in one pan of the balance and put cubes into the other pan one at a time, so the children can count how many are needed. Discuss whether the cubes balance the object 'exactly' or 'nearly'. In Lesson 5, repeat this for another object.
Group work: Choose from these activity suggestions for both lessons. Decide whether to set up a circus of activities for all the children to use, working in pairs.
- Estimate and then find the weight of one object using different non-standard units, such as cubes, marbles and rods. Record this on 'Measures sheet 1'.
- Estimate and then find the weight of different objects using one non-standard unit, such as cubes. Record this on 'Measures sheet 2'.
- Using a 100g weight, find items in the classroom that the children estimate weigh about that amount. Check how accurate their estimate is, using weighing scales. They can record this on 'Measures sheet 2'.
- Make a list of things that could be weighed with egg cups of sand, then choose some of these items and estimate and find how many egg cups of sand they weigh. They can record this on 'Measures sheet 2'.

Differentiation
Less able: Choose an activity that the children will enjoy, and limit the range of items for them to measure or use as units. Making estimates and comparing them with measures will help them to become more accurate. If possible, ask an adult to work with this group, encouraging the children to use the vocabulary of mass as they talk about what they are doing.
More able: Challenge the children to try the 100g weight activity. They should look for items of various sizes that they estimate weigh about 100g. Discuss how easy they found the estimate.

Plenary & assessment
Discuss the activities that each group has undertaken, asking questions such as:
- *Which units did you balance that with? Was that a good choice? Why?*
- *Which items did you balance with the … unit? Was that a good choice? Why?*
- *Were your estimate and measure about the same?*
- *What else could you balance with that unit? Why do you think that?*

Time, length, weight and handling data

Children order events, then learn to read o'clock times from an analogue clock. They learn the days of the week and their order. Then they solve practical problems for money, length and weight and record using simple charts. They are encouraged to explain the decisions that they made.

LEARNING OBJECTIVES

	Topics	Starter	Main teaching activities
Lesson 1	Measures	● Begin to know addition facts for all pairs of numbers with a total up to at least 10.	● Understand and use the vocabulary related to time. ● Order familiar events in time.
Lesson 2	Measures	● Begin to know addition facts for all pairs of numbers with a total up to at least 10, and the corresponding subtraction facts.	● Understand and use the vocabulary related to time. ● Read the time to the hour or half hour on analogue clocks.
Lesson 3	Measures	As for Lesson 2.	As for Lesson 2.
Lesson 4	Organising and using data Measures	● Know by heart addition doubles of all numbers to at least 5 (e.g. 4 + 4).	● Solve a given problem by sorting, classifying and organising information in simple ways, such as: using objects or pictures; in a list or simple table. Discuss and explain results. ● Understand and use the vocabulary related to length and mass. ● **Compare two lengths or masses by direct comparison**, extend to more than two. ● Measure using uniform non-standard units (e.g. straws, wooden cubes, plastic weights) or standard units. ● **Suggest suitable standard or uniform non-standard units and measuring equipment to estimate, then measure a length or mass**, recording estimates and measurements as 'about as heavy as 20 cubes'. ● Understand and use the vocabulary related to time. ● Order familiar events in time. ● Know the days of the week and the seasons of the year. ● Read the time to the hour or half hour on analogue clocks.
Lesson 5	Organising and using data Measures	As for Lesson 4.	As for Lesson 4.

Lessons   overview

Preparation
If necessary, make a teaching set of enlarged 'Add facts 6 to 10' and 'Take away facts 6 to 10' cards. Make a copy of 'David's birthday' on thin card. Copy 'Clock face' on to card, one for each child.

Learning objectives
Starter
● Begin to know addition facts for all pairs of numbers with a total up to at least 10, and the corresponding subtraction facts.
Main teaching activities
● Understand and use the vocabulary related to time.
● Order familiar events in time.
● Read the time to the hour or half hour on analogue clocks.

Vocabulary
time, morning, afternoon, evening, night, midnight, bedtime, dinnertime, playtime, today, yesterday, tomorrow, before, after, next, last, now, soon, early, late, hour, o'clock, half past, clock, watch, hands

You will need:
Photocopiable pages
'Jack and Jill' (see page 74) and 'Times of the day' (see page 75) for each child.

CD pages
'Add facts 6 to 10' (two sheets) and 'Take away facts 6 to 10' (two sheets) copied on to card; a copy of 'David's birthday'; 'Clock face' for each child (see General Resources).

Equipment
Scissors for each child; glue; paper fasteners; a teaching analogue clock.

Lesson

Starter

Tell the children that you will show them some addition fact cards for totals from 6 to 10. Ask them to use their fingers to show you the answers.

Main teaching activities

Whole class: Read the children the story 'David's birthday' on the resource sheet. Then ask them:

- *What happened first? Then what happened?*
- *Who can remember what happened next?*
- *What happened at the end of the story?*
- *Who would like to tell the story in their own words?*

Discuss how the events in the story took place in a particular order. Now ask the children questions about their own daily routine, such as: *What do you do when you get up in the morning? What do you do next?* and so on. Encourage them to use the vocabulary of ordering time.

Individual work: Remind the children of the nursery rhyme 'Jack and Jill'. Recite both verses together. Ask them to cut out the pictures on the 'Jack and Jill' activity sheet, then reassemble them in sequence to tell the story. When they are sure they have made the correct sequence, they should glue the pictures onto a sheet of paper.

Differentiation

Less able: Ask these children to cut out the pictures. Say both verses of the 'Jack and Jill' rhyme again, asking the children to point to the corresponding picture as you say each line or pair of lines. Repeat the rhyme, asking them to move the pictures into the correct time sequence.

More able: Challenge these children to choose another nursery rhyme and draw some pictures for it on a sheet of paper. They can swap with each other, cut out the pictures and put them into the correct time sequence.

Plenary & assessment

Review the activity with the children, inviting children to explain each time which picture comes next and why. Now ask questions about the lesson, such as:

- *What did we do first? And next?*
- *What did we do before/after…?*
- *What do you think we will do next?*

Lesson

Starter

Repeat the Starter from Lesson 1, this time using the 'Take away facts 6 to 10' cards.

Main teaching activities

Whole class: Set the hands on the teaching clock to 9 o'clock. Ask: *What time is this?* Repeat this for other o'clock times, until the children are confident with reading these. Now set the hands to 2.30. Ask the children to describe where the minute hand is, and explain that when it is 'straight down' or pointing to the 6, this means it is a 'half past' time. Encourage the children to say that the minute hand has moved halfway round the clock, and demonstrate this by moving the hands to show 3 o'clock and then 3.30. Set the clock to various o'clock and half past times for the children to read.

Group work: Give each child a card copy of 'Clock face'. They should take turns to say an o'clock or half past time; their partner should set the clock to show each time. Tell the children that they will have only about ten minutes for this activity.

Differentiation

Less able: Decide whether to limit the children to o'clock times.
More able: Decide whether to introduce 'quarter past' times as well.

Plenary & assessment

Ask the children to use their clock faces to show the times that you say. Ask for a variety of o'clock and half past times. Keep the pace sharp. Ask questions such as:

- *Where is the minute hand when it is o'clock/half past?*
- *Where does the hour hand point at 2 o'clock? And at half past 2?*
- *What do we call 12 o'clock? (midnight or mid-day)*

Lesson

Repeat the Starter from Lesson 2, encouraging more able children to begin to use rapid recall of some of these facts. During the whole-class teaching activity, review setting the clock to show o'clock and half past times. Provide copies of the 'Times of the day' activity sheet, which is not differentiated. Less able children may benefit from completing this activity as a group, discussing each picture and time shown. More able children could draw clocks and pictures of other daily activities on the back of the sheet. During the plenary session, review the activity and ask questions such as: *What do you do at 7 o'clock in the evening? What time is your bedtime? dinnertime? playtime?* Encourage the children to answer with a sentence, and to use the vocabulary of time appropriately.

Lessons   overview

Preparation
If necessary, make an enlarged teaching set of 'Double facts to 5 + 5' cards, and copy 'Clock face' on to card for each child.

Learning objectives
Starter
- Know by heart addition doubles of all numbers to at least 5 (e.g. 4 + 4).
Main teaching activities
- Understand and use the vocabulary related to length and mass.
- **Compare two lengths or masses by direct comparison**; extend to more than two.
- Measure using uniform non-standard units (e.g. straws, wooden cubes, plastic weights) or standard units.
- **Suggest suitable standard or uniform non-standard units and measuring equipment to estimate, then measure a length or mass**, recording estimates and measurements as 'about as heavy as 20 cubes'.
- Understand and use the vocabulary related to time.
- Order familiar events in time.
- Know the days of the week and the seasons of the year.
- Read the time to the hour or half hour on analogue clocks.

Vocabulary
count, sort, vote, list, group, set, measure, size, compare, guess, estimate, enough, not enough, too much, too little, too many, too few, nearly, roughly, close to, about the same as, just over, just under, weigh, weighs, balances, heavy/light, heavier/lighter, heaviest/lightest, balance, scales, weight, time, morning, afternoon, evening, today, yesterday, tomorrow, before, after, next, last, now, soon, early, late, hour, o'clock, half past, clock, watch, hands

You will need:
CD pages
'Double facts to 5 + 5' cards and 'Clock face' (see General Resources).

Equipment
Various objects and non-standard units for weighing; bucket balances; strips of paper; sugar paper; scissors; glue; non-standard units of length (such as rods or straws); flip chart or board; paper and pencils.

Lessons

Starter
Using the 'Double facts to 5 + 5' cards, ask the children to call out the total together each time you hold up a card and say: *Tell me.* Encourage all of the children to recall these facts from memory.

Main teaching activities
Whole class: Ask the children to say the days of the week. Chant these together. Write them on the flip chart. Ask questions such as: *What day is it today? What day will it be tomorrow? What day was it yesterday? Which days do we come to school? Which days are the weekend?*

In Lesson 5, include a discussion about the seasons, asking questions such as:
- *When do you go to the seaside? What season is that?*
- *When does it snow?*
- *What happens to the trees in spring/in autumn?*

Group work: Set groups to work on the following activities. These could be set up as a circus of activities for all the children to try.
- *Set the clock.* Work in groups of four. One child acts as leader and calls out o'clock and half past times. The others set their clocks. Swap the role of leader after each go, or after (say) four goes.
- *Balance these.* Decide which non-standard units of weight would be best to balance some items with. Record an estimate and then a measure, making a table in order to record the results.
- *Ten units long.* Use strips of paper and a variety of different non-standard units of length. Measure out a strip for ten units, then cut it out. Do this for each of the units. Record by gluing the strips onto sugar paper and writing the unit used under each one.
- *Draw your day.* Draw six pictures of your day. Start with getting up in the morning and finish with going to bed. Write the time to the nearest hour or half hour, or draw a small clock face and add the hands if you prefer.
- *The seasons.* Ask the children to work individually to write the names of the seasons and to draw an appropriate picture for each.

Differentiation
Less able: An adult can work with the group to complete the activities, where appropriate. The adult should ask questions that help the children to use the appropriate language in context, such as: *What time do you eat lunch? How many do you think you will need to balance/measure this? Which unit do you think will be best? Why is that?*
More able: Challenge the children to extend *Draw your day* to making a set of eight pictures.

Plenary & assessment
Review each of the activities that have been tried. Ask questions such as: *What did you try? How did you record your work? Who tried a different way?* For *Balance these* and *Ten units long*, which give the children an opportunity to use their data handling skills, ask the children to explain how they recorded their work and why they used that method. The children can show their results – especially where an efficient and effective method of recording has been used that others can learn from.

For *The seasons*, review the sequence of the seasons. Ask the children to say what is special about each of the seasons, such as the leaves falling from the trees in autumn.

Name	Date

Jack and Jill

You will need scissors, glue and a sheet of paper.

Cut out these pictures.

Put them in the right order to tell the story.

Glue the pictures in order onto the sheet of paper.

Name   Date

Times of the day

Join the clock to its picture.

EVERY DAY: Practise and develop oral and mental skills (e.g. counting, mental strategies, rapid recall of + and – facts)

- **Count reliably at least 20 objects.**
- Describe and extend number sequences: **count on and back in ones from any small number, and in tens from and back to zero.**
- **Read and write numerals from 0 to at least 20.**
- **Order numbers to at least 20**, and position them on a number track.
- Know by heart addition facts for all pairs of numbers with a total up to at least 5, and the corresponding subtraction facts.
- **Know by heart all pairs of numbers with a total of 10** (e.g. 3 + 7).
- Know by heart addition doubles of all numbers to at least 5 (e.g. 4 + 4).
- Read the time to the hour or half hour on analogue clocks.

Units	Days	Topics	Objectives
1	3	Counting, properties of numbers and number sequences	Describe and extend number sequences: **count in tens from and back to zero.** Describe and extend number sequences: count on in twos from zero, then one, and begin to recognise odd or even numbers to about 20 as 'every other number'.
2–4	15	Place value and ordering	**Read and write numerals from 0 to at least 20.** Begin to know what each digit in a two-digit number represents. Partition a 'teens' number and begin to partition larger two-digit numbers into a multiple of 10 and ones (TU). **Within the range 0 to 30, say the number that is 1 or 10 more or less than any given number.**
		Understanding addition and subtraction	**Understand the operation of addition and of subtraction (as 'take-away', 'difference', and 'how many more to make'), and use the related vocabulary.**
		Mental calculation strategies (+ and –)	Identify near doubles, using doubles already known (e.g. 6 + 5).
		Problems involving 'real life', money or measures	Recognise coins of different values. Find totals and change from up to 20p.
		Making decisions	Choose and use appropriate number operations and mental strategies to solve problems.
5–6	8	Measures	Understand and use the vocabulary related to length, mass and capacity. **Compare two lengths, masses or capacities by direct comparison**; extend to more than two. Measure using uniform non-standard units (e.g. straws, wooden cubes, plastic weights, yogurt pots), or standard units (e.g. metre sticks, litre jugs).
		Shape and space	**Use everyday language to describe features of familiar 3-D and 2-D shapes**, including the cube, cuboid, sphere, cylinder, cone, circle, triangle, square, rectangle, referring to properties such as the shapes of flat faces, or the number of faces or corners, or the number and types of sides. Make and describe models, patterns and pictures using construction kits, everyday materials, Plasticine… Use everyday language to describe position, direction and movement. Talk about things that turn. Use one or more shapes to make describe and continue repeating patterns…
		Making decisions	Choose and use appropriate number operations and mental strategies to solve problems.

EVERY DAY: Practise and develop oral and mental skills (e.g. counting , mental strategies, rapid recall of + and – facts)

- **Count reliably at least 20 objects.**
- Describe and extend number sequences: count on in twos from zero, then one, and begin to recognise odd or even numbers to about 20 as 'every other number'.
- Describe and extend number sequences: **count in tens from and back to zero.**
- **Read and write numerals from 0 to at least 20.**
- **Order numbers to at least 20**, and position them on a number track.
- **Know by heart all pairs of numbers with a total of 10** (e.g. 3 + 7).
- Know by heart addition facts for all pairs of numbers with a total up to at least 5, and the corresponding subtraction facts.
- Know by heart addition doubles of all numbers to at least 5 (e.g. 4 + 4).
- Read the time to the hour or half hour on analogue clocks.

Units	Days	Topics	Objectives
8	5	Counting, properties of numbers and number sequences	Count on in twos from zero, then one, and begin to recognise odd or even numbers to about 20 as 'every other number'. Count in steps of 5 from zero to 20 or more, then back again; begin to count on in steps of 3 from zero.
		Reasoning about numbers or shapes	Solve simple mathematical problems or puzzles; recognise and predict from simple patterns and relationships. Suggest extensions by asking 'What if?' or 'What could I try next?'
9–10	10	Place value and ordering	**Understand and use the vocabulary of comparing and ordering numbers**, including ordinal numbers to at least 20. Use the = sign to represent equality. Compare two familiar numbers, say which is more or less, and give a number which lies between them.
		Estimating	Understand the vocabulary of estimation. Give a sensible estimate of a number of objects that can be checked by counting (e.g. up to about 30 objects).
		Understanding addition and subtraction	**Understand the operation of addition, and of subtraction (as 'take-away', 'difference', and 'how many more to make'), and use the related vocabulary.**
		Mental calculation strategies (+ and –)	Use knowledge that addition can be done in any order to do mental calculations more efficiently. For example: begin to partition into '5 and a bit' when adding 6, 7, 8, or 9, then recombine (e.g. 6 + 8 = 5 + 1 + 5 + 3 = 10 + 4 = 14). Begin to bridge through 10, and later 20, when adding a single-digit number.
		Problems involving 'real life', money or measures	**Use mental strategies to solve simple problems** set in 'real life', money or measurement contexts, **using counting, addition, subtraction, doubling and halving, explaining methods and reasoning orally.** Find totals and change from up to 20p. Work out how to pay an exact sum using smaller coins.
		Making decisions	Choose and use appropriate number operations and mental strategies to solve problems.
11–12	10	Measures	Understand and use the vocabulary related to length, mass and capacity. **Suggest suitable standard or uniform non-standard units and measuring equipment to estimate, then measure, a length, mass or capacity**, recording estimates and measurement as 'about 3 beakers full' or 'about as heavy as 20 cubes'. Understand and use the vocabulary related to time. Know the days of the week and the seasons of the year.
		Organising and using data	Solve a given problem by sorting, classifying and organising information in simple ways, such as: using objects or pictures; in a list or simple table. Discuss and explain results.
Total	51		

Counting in tens and twos

Children count in ten from zero to 100 and back again, then count on or back from a given decade number. They count in twos, and begin to recognise odd and even numbers to about 20.

LEARNING OBJECTIVES

	Topics	Starter	Main teaching activities
Lesson **1**	Counting, properties of numbers and number sequences	● **Count reliably at least 20 objects.**	● Describe and extend number sequences: **count in tens from and back to zero.**
Lesson **2**	Counting, properties of numbers and number sequences	● **Read and write numerals from 0 to at least 20.**	● Describe and extend number sequences: count in twos from zero, then one, and begin to recognise odd or even numbers to about 20 as 'every other number'.
Lesson **3**	Counting, properties of numbers and number sequences	As for Lesson 2.	As for Lesson 2.

Lesson overview

Learning objectives
Starter
● **Count reliably at least 20 objects.**
Main teaching activites
● Describe and extend number sequences: **count in tens from and back to zero.**

Vocabulary
number, zero, ten, twenty… one hundred, count, count (up) to, count back (from, to), count in tens

You will need:
Photocopiable pages
'Tens and more tens' (page 81).

CD pages
'Decade cards 0–100' for each pair, 'Numeral cards 0–9' and 'Numeral cards 10–20' for each more able pair (see General Resources).

Equipment
For each pair: a container with about 40 cubes or counters; scissors; a paperclip.

Lesson

Starter
The children work in pairs. You say a number between 5 and 20, then they take turns to count out that number of cubes, then their partner checks the count. Ask: *How did you count them?* Strategies may include touch, count and move; touch and count; point and count. The children swap over and continue. Repeat until each child has counted out and checked five times.

Main teaching activities

Whole class: Explain to the children that they will be counting in tens. Ask them to count together in tens from zero to 100 and back. Count with them, keeping the pace sharp. Now ask the children to repeat the count individually around the class. As each child says a number, he or she should raise both hands and then lower them. This will produce a 'Mexican wave' and will help to maintain a lively pace. Repeat the count, starting from any decade number. Now say:

- *Count on in tens from 30… 40… 60… Count back in tens from 80… 50… 40…*
- *Count in tens until I say 'Stop'. I will keep a count on my fingers. How many tens did we count?*
- *Count on/back three tens from 30… 50… 60…*
- *Count round the circle in tens, starting with Paul at 30. Who will say 80?*
- *Listen to this counting pattern: 100, 90, 80. What are the next three numbers?*

Group work: Ask the children to play the game on the 'Tens and more tens' activity sheet in pairs. They should play the game for five turns each, then count their counters to see who has counted the most tens. If time permits, they can play the game again.

Differentiation

Less able: Decide whether to play the game as a group, with an adult checking the counting. Encourage the children to use their fingers to keep a count of how many tens they have counted.
More able: When the children have played the game, and if they are confident with counting in tens, provide them with a set of numeral cards from 0 to 20. They should take turns to draw a numeral card, with the other child counting on in tens from the number drawn to 100.

Plenary & assessment

Ask the children to count around the class, using the 'Mexican wave'. Start from 20… 30… 40… and count to 100. Then count back from 90… 80… 70… to zero. Ask the children to count on/back three tens from 30… 40… 50… Ask questions such as:

- *If I count back two tens from 90… 80… what number will I be at?*
- *Say the next three numbers in this pattern: 30, 40, 50…*
- *Say the next three numbers in this pattern: 80, 70, 60…*

Lessons   overview

Preparation
Enlarge a copy of 'Empty number track' to A3 size and pin to the flip chart.

Learning objectives
Starter
- **Read and write numerals from 0 to at least 20.**
Main teaching activities
- Describe and extend number sequences: count in twos from zero, then one, and begin to recognise odd or even numbers to about 20 as 'every other number'.

Vocabulary
zero, one, two, three… to twenty and beyond, count in twos…, odd, even, every other

You will need:
Photocopiable pages
'Odd and even' (see page 82) for each child.

CD pages
'Odd and even', less able, more able and blank versions (see Spring term, Unit 1); 'Numeral cards 0–9' and 'Numeral cards 10–20' for each pair, 'Numeral cards 21–30' for more able children, A3 copy of 'Empty number track' (see General Resources).

Equipment
Individual whiteboards and pens for each child; flip chart or board.

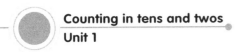

Lesson ②

Starter

Say some numbers for the children to write on their boards. When you say *Show me*, the children hold up their boards for you to check. Say: *Write 8… 9… 10… 12… 15… 19… 20. Write the number that has 1 ten and 3 units… Write the number that is between 13 and 15… Write the numbers between 14 and 17… How did you work that out?* (Some children may still need to start counting at 0 or 1.)

Main teaching activities

Whole class: Ask the children to count in twos from zero to 20. Count loudly with them, so that if the count falters you can keep it going. Repeat the count to 20, and count back to zero. Do this two or three times, keeping the pace sharp.

On the board, write two column headings: 'Odd numbers' and 'Even numbers'. Write 1 in the odd column and 2 in the even column, then ask the children to help you sort all the numbers from 1 to 20 into odd or even. When this is complete, together say all the odd numbers and then all the even numbers.

Group work: Give each pair a set of numeral cards 1–20. Ask them to shuffle the cards and place them in a stack. They take turns to turn over a card and say whether it is odd or even. They place the odd and even cards in separate lines, keeping the cards in counting order as they go.

Differentiation

Less able: Limit the range of numbers to 1–10 if the children need to build their confidence with these numbers. Decide whether to ask the children to place the cards into separate piles for odd and even; they can then place them in counting order once they have sorted all the cards.

More able: The activity can be extended to include 21–30.

Plenary & assessment

Say the nursery rhyme 'Two, four, six, eight, Mary at the garden gate' together. Ask: *Are these even or odd numbers? Tell me some more even numbers… some odd numbers.*

Say the rhyme 'One, two, buckle my shoe', asking the children to punch the air for each even number they say. Repeat for odd numbers.

Lesson ③

Repeat the Starter from Lesson 2, asking the children to draw the numerals in the air. For the whole-class activity, pin an A3 copy of the 'Empty number track' to the flip chart. Say: *Start at 2. Which is the next even number? And the next?* As the children say the numbers, write them on the track from 2 to 20. Repeat for the odd numbers from 1 to 19. Ask: *Which are the odd numbers? Which are the even numbers? What is the next odd/even number after…?*

Provide copies of 'Odd and even' and ask the children to complete it individually. Less able children can use the version with numbers to 10, and more able children, the version with numbers to 30. Review the sheet during the plenary session, using an A3 copy pinned to the flip chart: ask some children to write in the missing numbers. Say the number sequences together, identifying which sequences are even and which are odd. Ask the children to tell you some odd and even numbers.

Name	Date

Tens and more tens

Work with a partner.

You need a set of decade cards, counters and a paperclip.

Shuffle the cards and put them face down in a pile.

Take turns to spin the paper clip on the spinner and pick up two cards.

Count on or back between the two tens numbers.

Count how many tens were counted.

Take that number of counters.

After 5 turns each, the player with the most counters wins.

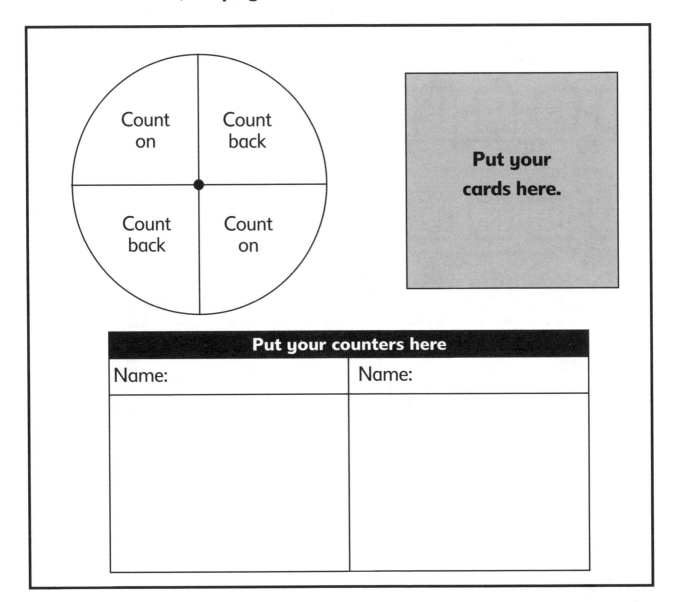

Name   Date

Odd and even

Colour in the odd numbers.

Colour in the even numbers.

Children read numerals and the words for numbers up to about 20. They use apparatus to identify the tens and the units of a number up to about 30. Using the hundred square they compare numbers up to about 30 for one more and one less, and then for 10 more and 10 less.

LEARNING OBJECTIVES

	Topics	Starter	Main teaching activities
Lesson 1	Place value and ordering	● Describe and extend number sequences: **count in tens from and back to zero.**	● **Read and write numerals from 0 to at least 20.**
Lesson 2	Place value and ordering	As for Lesson 1.	As for Lesson 1.
Lesson 3	Place value and ordering	● **Order numbers to at least 20,** and position them on a number track.	● Begin to know what each digit in a two-digit number represents. ● Partition a 'teens' number and begin to partition larger two-digit numbers into a multiple of 10 and ones (TU).
Lesson 4	Place value and ordering	As for Lesson 3.	● **Within the range 0 to 30, say the number that is 1 or 10 more or less than any given number.**
Lesson 5	Place value and ordering	As for Lesson 4.	As for Lesson 4.

Lessons   overview

Preparation
Make the teaching set of enlarged cards by enlarging each sheet to A3 size on card and cutting out. Make the pupil sets by copying each sheet onto A4 card and cutting out.

Learning objectives
Starter
● Describe and extend number sequences: **count in tens from and back to zero.**
Main teaching activities
● **Read and write numerals from 0 to at least 20.**

Vocabulary
zero, one, two, three... to twenty and beyond, greater, more, larger, bigger, less, fewer, smaller

You will need:
Photocopiable pages
'Numbers and number words' for each child (see page 88).

CD pages
'Numbers and number words', less able and more able versions (two sheets) (see Spring term, Unit 2); enlarged teaching sets of 'Number word cards 0–10', 'Number word cards 11–20', 'Number word cards 21–30', 'Numeral cards 0–9', 'Numeral cards 10–20' and 'Numeral cards 21–30', plus a set for each pair of children (see General Resources).

Equipment
A washing line, pegs.

Place value and ordering
Unit 2

Lesson

Starter

Ask the children to count together in tens from zero to 100 and back again. Join in, keeping the pace brisk. The children may find it helpful to punch the air in time with each number said. Now ask the children to count from, say, 20 to 80 and back again, still with a good pace. Repeat this for other counts, such as 10 to 40, 90 down to 30 and back again, and so on. Ask questions such as:

- *Keep a count on your fingers. Count from 40 to 100. How many tens did you say?*
- *If Jo begins the count on 30, who will say 70?*

Main teaching activities

Whole class: Shuffle a teaching set of 'Numeral cards 0–9'. Ask individual children to peg the cards onto the washing line one at a time in the correct order, leaving spaces for the cards still to come. When the cards are in order, explain that a number can be written in words as well as a numeral. Hold up the 'one' card, read it together, and invite a child to peg it over the '1' card. Repeat this for the other number word cards to ten, then include zero. Point to each card in turn, and read the number words together. Now remove the number word cards, shuffle them and hold each one up in turn; invite individual children to read the word, then peg the card in place.

Group work: Provide each pair of children with a set of 'Numeral cards 0–10' and 'Number word cards 0–10'. Ask them to shuffle both sets together, then play 'Snap'. Explain that before claiming the cards, the child who has said 'Snap' must read the number word.

Differentiation

Less able: Decide whether to limit the range of cards to 0–5, so that the children become confident with reading these number words.

More able: When the children are confident with 0–10, spend a few minutes with this group and introduce the number words for 11–20. The children can play 'Snap' with these numbers.

Plenary & assessment

Take the cards down from the washing line. Ask the children to read each number word card, and for one of them to peg the card onto the washing line in the correct place. Remind the children to leave room for the cards still to come. Ask:

- *What number word is this?*
- *Where does this card go? How did you work that out?*

Lesson ②

Starter

Repeat the Starter from Lesson 1, this time starting the count at 100 and counting back to zero, then up to 100. Encourage a quicker pace than before.

Main teaching activities

Whole class: Give each pair of children a set of 'Numeral cards 0–9' and 'Number word cards 0–10'. Ask them to sort these out on their tables. They may find it helpful to put the numerals in order first, then put the matching word card under each numeral card.

Explain that you will hold up a card. If it is a numeral, one of the pair should hold up the matching number word when you say: *Show me.* If it is a number word card, they should hold up the matching numeral. Invite some children to read their card aloud, so that the slower learners hear the number words spoken while seeing them. Extend the activity to cover the numbers 11–21, allowing the pairs to take turns.

Individual work: Give each child a copy of the 'Numbers and number words' activity sheet, which asks the children to match numerals and words.

Differentiation
Less able: Use the version of the sheet with numbers to 10.
More able: Use the version with numbers to 30 (two sheets). Spend a few minutes with this group introducing the number words for 21–30 beforehand.

Plenary & assessment
Hold up number word cards from 0–20, and ask the children to hold up the matching numeral card. Include some for more able children, if they have been introduced to the number words for 21–30, so that all the children begin to read these words. Ask questions such as: *What number is this word? What number is one before/after this?*

Lesson overview

Preparation
Make a teaching set of arrow cards by enlarging the sheet onto A3 card.

Learning objectives
Starter
- **Order numbers to at least 20**, and position them on a number track.

Main teaching activities
- Begin to know what each digit in a two-digit number represents.
- Partition a 'teens' number and begin to partition larger two-digit numbers into a multiple of 10 and ones (TU).

Vocabulary
units, ones, tens, exchange, digit, 'teens' number, the same number as, equal to

You will need:
Photocopiable pages
'Tens and units' (see page 89) for each child.

CD pages
'Tens and units', less able and more able versions (See Spring term, Unit 2); a teaching set of enlarged 'Number word cards 0–10', 'Number word cards 11–20' and 'Number word cards 21–30' and of 'Arrow cards', plus a set of arrow cards for each child (see General Resources).

Equipment
A washing line, pegs.

Lesson

Starter
Using the teaching set of 'Number word cards 0–10', ask children to read a card and peg it to the washing line in the correct place, leaving room for the cards that still have to be placed. Ask: *What number is this? Where does it go? What number comes one before/after this?* When the children are confident with these number words, extend to 11–20. Where appropriate, include 21–30 for the more able children.

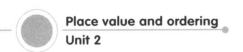

Main teaching activities

Whole class: Using the teaching set of arrow cards, hold up the 10 card and ask: *What number is this? How many tens does it have? How many units?* Show the children how to place a unit card onto a tens card by placing the 8. *What number is this? How many units are there? How many tens?* Repeat this for other 'teen' numbers. Now show the 20 card and repeat the process to produce numbers up to 29. Ask questions such as: *What does the 2 stand for? Which is the tens numeral? Which is the unit? What if I changed the tens number to 1 ten, what number would it be then?*

Individual work: Ask the children to complete the 'Tens and units' activity sheet.

Differentiation

Less able: Use the version of 'Tens and units' that covers only 'teen' numbers. This will help children who are still struggling with place value.

More able: Use the version of 'Tens and units' that covers numbers beyond 30. Where children are confident with numbers to 30, this will provide a further challenge.

Plenary & assessment

Give each child a set of arrow cards. Ask them to make the numbers that you say, then hold up the cards when you say: *Show me.* Say, for example:

- *Show me the number 15… 18… 21… 29… 30…*
- *Show me the number that has 1 ten and 4 units… 2 tens and 3 units… 2 tens and 6 units…*
- *How many tens/units does that number have?*

Lessons   overview

Preparation

Enlarge 'Animal cards' to A3 and copy onto card to make a teaching set (which could be coloured in). Enlarge 'Hundred square' to A3 and pin to the flip chart. Put a small dot below the sixth box on each track on 'Blank number tracks' before copying.

Learning objectives

Starter
- **Order numbers to at least 20**, and position them on a number track.

Main teaching activities
- **Within the range 0 to 30, say the number that is 1 or 10 more or less than any given number.**

Vocabulary

zero, one, two, three… to twenty and beyond, one more, one less, ten more, ten less

You will need:

Photocopiable pages
'10 more, 10 less' (see page 90) for each child.

CD pages
A teaching set of 'Animal picture cards' (two sheets) an A3 copy of 'Hundred square', 'Blank number tracks' and 'Numeral cards 10–20' for each pair and 'Numeral cards 21–30' for more able children (see General Resources).

Equipment
A washing line, pegs; flip chart or board.

Lesson

Starter

Show the children the animal cards. Ask a child to peg four of them onto the washing line. Say: *Which animal is first? Which is last? Which is between the second and the fourth?* Remove these cards, then ask a child to peg all ten cards to the line. Say: *John, swap over the fourth and tenth cards. What position is the elephant now? And the lion? Which animal is between the seventh and the ninth? Which animals are between the sixth and the last but one? Which animal is halfway between the fifth and the tenth?*

Main teaching activities

Whole class: Ask the children to look at the hundred square on the flip chart. Say: *Look at the number 15. What is one more/less than that? How do you know?* Discuss with the children how the number one more or less is next to a given number in the counting order. Repeat this for other numbers, up to about 30. Ask similar questions while hiding the hundred square, so that the children rely on their memory.

Group work: Give each pair of children a 'Blank number track'. Ask them to choose a numeral card at random from an 11–20 pack. They write this numeral in the sixth box on the track (marked with a spot). One child writes the numerals one more (below this number) and one less (above the number) on the track. The other child writes the numeral one more below the largest number and the numeral one less above the smallest number. They continue like this until the track is complete; then they start again with another random numeral card.

Differentiation

Less able: Decide whether to limit the number range to 10–15 in order to increase the children's confidence with these numbers.

More able: If the children are confident with numbers to 30, include the cards for 21–30 in their pack.

Plenary & assessment

Play the 'One more/less game' with the children, using enlarged 'Blank number tracks'. Invite a child to choose a starting number. Ask various children to write the one more/less than numbers until the track is full. Ask: *How do you know which is the one more/one less than number? How can you work it out?* Some children will 'know' the answer. Many will say the given number and count on or back one. Some may still need to say all of the counting numbers, which is an inefficient method. Encourage these children to count on or back from the given number.

Lesson

Starter

Repeat the Starter from Lesson 4 – but replace the washing line with ten children standing in a line at the front of the class, holding the pictures. Ask those sitting to swap places with a given ordinal position: *Swap places with the eighth person. Which position is between the lion and the elephant? Swap places with that person.*

Main teaching activities

Whole class: Repeat the activity from Lesson 4, this time for ten more and ten less. If the children are unsure, use the hundred square to count between the numbers so that they can see the pattern of 'decades'. Cover numbers from 10 to 90.

Individual work: Give each child a copy of '10 more, 10 less' to complete.

Differentiation

Less able: These children will find the hundred square helpful.

More able: Ask these children to write ten more/ten less numbers on the back of the sheet for *any* number from 10 to 90. For example: 19, 29, 39.

Plenary & assessment

Ask the children to say the number that is ten more or less than the number you say, without looking at the hundred square. Ask: *What is ten more/less than…? How did you work that out?* Some children will count. Others will see a pattern in the tens digits: ten more and it increases by one; ten less and it decreases by one.

Name	Date

Numbers and number words

Match the number words to the numbers.

Name	Date

Tens and units

Join each number to its tens and units.

1 ten and 4 units	23
1 ten and 9 units	18
2 tens and 3 units	11
2 tens and 0 units	29
2 tens and 9 units	13
1 ten and eight units	14
1 ten and 1 unit	16
1 ten and 6 units	25
1 ten and 3 units	20
2 tens and 5 units	19

Look at these arrow cards.

Write how many tens and how many units there are.

1 0	☐ ten and ☐ units
1 7	☐ ten and ☐ units
1 3	☐ ten and ☐ units
2 7	☐ tens and ☐ units
3 0	☐ tens and ☐ units
1 5	☐ ten and ☐ units

Name	Date

10 more, 10 less

On each sweet wrapper, write the 10 more number and the 10 less number.

For example:

Spring term
Unit 3

Addition and subtraction mental calculation strategies

Children identify near doubles and use these as a mental strategy for addition. They use the vocabulary of difference and counting on from the lower to the higher number to find differences.

LEARNING OBJECTIVES

	Topics	Starter	Main teaching activities
Lesson 1	Understanding addition and subtraction Mental calculation strategies (+ and –)	● Know by heart addition doubles of all numbers to at least 5 (e.g. 4 + 4).	● **Understand the operation of addition and use the related vocabulary.** ● Identify near doubles using doubles already known (e.g. 6 + 5).
Lesson 2	Understanding addition and subtraction Mental calculation strategies (+ and –)	As for Lesson 1.	As for Lesson 1.
Lesson 3	Understanding addition and subtraction Mental calculation strategies (+ and –)	● **Know by heart all pairs of numbers with a total of 10** (e.g. 3 + 7).	● **Understand the operation of subtraction (as 'difference') and use the related vocabulary.**
Lesson 4	Understanding addition and subtraction Mental calculation strategies (+ and –)	As for Lesson 3.	As for Lesson 3.
Lesson 5	Understanding addition and subtraction Mental calculation strategies (+ and –)	As for Lesson 3.	● **Understand the operation of subtraction (as 'take away' and 'difference') and use the related vocabulary.**

Lessons   overview

Preparation
Enlarge 'Double facts to 5 + 5' to A3 on thin card to make a teaching set of cards. Copy 'Double and double add 1' onto card and cut out the two spinners on each copy.

Learning objectives
Starter
● Know by heart addition doubles of all numbers to at least 5 (e.g. 4 + 4).
Main teaching activities
● **Understand the operation of addition and use the related vocabulary.**
● Identify near doubles using doubles already known (e.g. 6 + 5).

Vocabulary
add, more, plus, make, sum, total, altogether, score, double, near double, one more, two more

You will need:

Photocopiable pages
'Doubles and near doubles' (see page 96) for each child.

CD pages
'Doubles and near doubles', less able and more able versions (see Spring term, Unit 3); 'Number fan' for each child, an enlarged teaching set of 'Double facts to 5 + 5'; 'Double and double add 1' spinner for each pair (see General Resources).

Equipment
Interlocking cubes; a 1–6 dice; a pencil and paperclip for each child; flip chart or board.

Lesson ①

Starter

Explain that you will hold up a card with a double fact on it. Read the card to the children and ask them to hold up a blade of their number fan to show you the answer when you say: *Show me.* Keep the pace sharp, but allow time for those who do not yet have rapid recall to use a mental strategy such as counting on.

Main teaching activities

Whole class: Hold up a tower of four cubes and ask a child to count them. Agree that there are four. Now hold up a tower of five cubes and ask a child to count them. Ask: *What is 4 + 5? How did you work that out?* Discuss strategies; the children may have counted on in ones from 5. Explain that you will teach them a new strategy. Say: *What is 4 + 4? Yes, double 4 is 8. So 4 + 5 is double 4 and 1 more.* Ask the children to use this strategy to work out some near doubles: *What is 3 + 4? What is 5 + 4? What is 5 + 6?*

Some children may notice that it is also possible to double the larger number and subtract 1. Praise this, and explain that it is also a good strategy.

Group work: Provide each pair of children with a 'Double and double add 1' spinner, a paperclip, pencil and a 1–6 dice. Ask the children to take turns to spin the paperclip on the spinner and to throw the dice. They should write a sum using the outcomes. For example, for 'double add 1' and a dice score of 5, they should write 5 + 5 + 1 = 5 + 6 = 11.

Differentiation

Less able: Ask these children just to throw the dice and to write a 'double add 1' fact for the score. So if they throw 5, they should write 5 + 5 + 1 = 5 + 6 = 11.

More able: When the children have completed about eight sums, suggest that they write some 'double take away 1' number sentences. So for a dice score of 5, they would write 5 + 5 − 1 = 5 + 4 = 9.

Plenary & assessment

Review what the children have done. Invite some children to write one of their 'double add 1' sums on the board for the others to solve. Ask: *How did you work that out? How does knowing double facts help you?* Ask some more able children to demonstrate their 'double take away 1' number statements for the others to try. Repeat that this is also a good strategy to use.

Lesson ②

Starter

Repeat the Starter from Lesson 1. This time, write some addition words on the flip chart such as: *add, plus, make a sum, total.* Ask individual children to read out the number sentence on the card each time, using some of this vocabulary. All of the children can use their number fans to show the answer.

Main teaching activities

Whole class: Review the 'double add 1' and 'double subtract 1' strategies for adding near doubles. Ask questions such as:

- *What is 5 + 6? How did you work that out?*
- *What is 3 more than 4? How could you work it out?*

Individual work: Check that the children are confident with at least one of the two strategies, then ask them to complete the 'Doubles and near doubles' activity sheet.

Differentiation

Less able: Use the version of 'Doubles and near doubles' with numbers up to 5 + 6.
More able: Use the version with numbers up to 12 + 13.

Plenary & assessment

Ask the children more 'double add 1' questions. Choose individuals to answer, checking that they are using this strategy. Ask: *What is double 5? What is 5 + 6? How did you work that out? What is 4 + 5… 7 + 8… 9 +10…?*

Lessons   overview

Preparation
If necessary, copy 'Complements of 10' to A3 size on card to make a teaching set of cards.

Learning objectives
Starter
- **Know by heart all pairs of numbers with a total of 10 (e.g. 3 + 7).**

Main teaching activities
- **Understand the operation of subtraction (as 'take away' and 'difference') and use the related vocabulary.**

Vocabulary
how many more is … than …? subtract, take (away), minus, leave, how many are left/left over?, how many are gone?, one less, two less, ten less…, how many fewer is … than …?, how much less is…?, difference between

You will need:

Photocopiable pages
'Difference' (see page 97) for each child.

CD pages
'Difference', less able, more able and blank versions (see Spring term, Unit 3); a set of 'Numeral cards 0–9' for each pair, a teaching set of 'Complements of 10' cards and a 'Number fan' (see General Resources).

Equipment
Interlocking cubes; two 1–6 dice (with numerals) for each pair.

Lesson

Starter
Explain that you will hold up some cards with number facts, and that all of these number facts make a total of 10. Using the 'Complements of 10' cards, ask the children to hold up fingers to show the missing number. As they solve the problems, ask: *How did you work that out? Who knows this fact now?* Encourage rapid recall. Where children are working out the answer mentally, check which strategy they are using. It might be counting on, doubling or 'double plus/minus one'.

Main teaching activities
Whole class: Explain that in this lesson, the children will learn about subtraction as difference. Show them a tower of five interlocking cubes, and another of three. Place these towers side by side and ask: *How many more is 5 than 3?* When children give the answer, ask how they worked it out. Say: *5 is 2 more than 3. Count on from 3 until you reach 5: 3, 4, 5. We need to count on 2.*

Write the sum 5 – 2 = 3 on the board, and explain that this is how this type of number sentence is written. Children may find it helpful to keep a count with their fingers of how many they have counted on. Repeat this for other differences, such as: *How many more is 6 than 4? How many more is 6 than 2? How many more is 7 than 3?* Each time, say the counting on sentence together.

Explain that another way of saying *How many more…?* is to say *What is the difference between … and …?* Ask some 'difference' questions, such as: *What is the difference between 7 and 4? What is the difference between 6 and 1?* Again, say the counting on sentence together. For example: *The difference between 6 and 1 is 5. 1, 2, 3, 4, 5, 6. We need to count on 5.* Write 6 – 1 = 5 on the board.

Explain that finding the difference is a way of subtracting. Again, children may find it helpful to keep a count with their fingers of how many they have counted on.

Group work: Ask the children to work in pairs. They take turns to throw two 1–6 dice and find the difference between the scores, then write a subtraction sentence.

Differentiation
Less able: If these children find it difficult to count on from the lower number, suggest that they use interlocking cubes to model the difference. They can make a tower for each number, place the towers side by side and count on from the lower number to the higher.
More able: Encourage the children to calculate mentally without using their fingers. Suggest that they try to 'see' a number line in their heads when counting on.

Plenary & assessment
Review some of the children's number sentences as a class, and write them on the board. Ask: *How did you work this out?* Say the number sentences together, for example: *The difference between 6 and 2 is 4. We count on 4 from 2: 2, 3, 4, 5, 6.* Encourage the children to use their fingers to help them if necessary. Praise those who used a mental number line, and ask them to explain to the others how this helped them.

Lesson

Starter
Repeat the Starter from Lesson 3, this time asking the children to hold up their number fans to show the answer. Keep the pace sharp, but allow time for those who need to work out the answer.

Main teaching activities
Whole class: Review *How many more is … than …?* and *What is the difference between … and …?* questions. Introduce the concept of 'less than'. Ask: *How many less than 5 is 3? How can I work this out?* Explain that we can count on from the lower to the higher number in order to find the difference. Write 5 – 3 = 2 on the board. Explain that this is how 'less than' sentences are written. Repeat for some more examples.
Group work: Provide each pair of children with a 1–6 dice and a set of 0–9 numeral cards. Ask them to take turns to throw the dice and take a card from the top of the shuffled pack. They write a subtraction number sentence for each difference.

Differentiation
Less able: Decide whether to limit these children to the numeral cards 0–6 and to encourage them to count on in ones, keeping a count with their fingers.
More able: These children could use two shuffled sets of 0–9 cards instead of dice.

Plenary & assessment
Review the number sentences that the children have written, asking individuals to say a 'more than', 'less than' or 'difference' number sentence (as requested by you) for each subtraction sum. If necessary demonstrate this, so that all the children are clear about what vocabulary to use.

Lesson ⑤

Starter

Use the 'Complements of 10' cards as in Lesson 3, but this time read each sentence without showing the card. Vary your vocabulary, saying *more than*, *difference* or *less than*. For example, □ + 4 = 10 could be read as *What is the difference between 10 and 4? How many more is 10 than 4?* or *How many less is 4 than 10?*

Main teaching activities

Whole class: Review the 'more than', 'less than' and 'difference' vocabulary, using examples with a difference of up to 10 (such as 10 – 5 and 6 – 0). Write each example on the board as a number sentence, and say it together (using 'take away' or 'difference') when the children have supplied the answer.

Individual work: Ask the children to complete the 'Difference' activity sheet.

Differentiation

Less able: Use the version of 'Difference' with questions involving differences to 6.
More able: Use the version with questions involving differences to 12.

Plenary & assessment

Review some of the questions, choosing from each of the activity sheets used. Encourage the children to explain their answers. Ask: *What strategy did you use? Who counted in ones, using their fingers to help them? Who can use a mental number track and count along that?* Note which children use which strategy, so that all of them can be encouraged over time to use mental methods of calculation and rapid recall.

Name   Date

Doubles and near doubles

Write in the missing numbers.

5 + 5 = ☐

4 + 3 = ☐

2 + 1 = ☐

6 + 5 = ☐

6 + 6 = ☐

6 + 7 = ☐

8 + 8 = ☐

9 + 9 = ☐

10 + 9 = ☐

7 + 8 = ☐

4 + ☐ = 9

3 + ☐ = 5

☐ + 5 = 11

☐ + 4 = 8

6 + ☐ = 11

Name	Date

Difference

Join the questions to the answers.

How many more is 6 than 3?

How many less is 8 than 10?

How many more is 9 than 2?

How many less is 4 than 8?

What is the difference between 7 and 5?

What is the difference between 9 and 3?

What is the difference between 10 and 1?

What is the difference between 10 and 0?

How many less is 1 than 6?

How many more is 8 than 7?

9

4

6

2

10

5

3

2

7

1

Solving problems involving 'real life', money and measures

Children sort and name coins, then find equivalent values using coins. They take turns to be the customer or shopkeeper and practise giving change for amounts to about 10p. They solve problems involving giving change and explain how they worked out the answer and the mathematics they chose to use.

LEARNING OBJECTIVES

	Topics	Starter	Main teaching activities
Lesson 1	Problems involving money	● Describe and extend number sentences: **Count in tens from and back to zero.**	● Recognise coins of different values. ● Find totals from up to 20p.
Lesson 2	Problems involving money	As for Lesson 1.	● Recognise coins of different values. ● Find totals and change from up to 20p.
Lesson 3	Problems involving money	As for Lesson 1.	As for Lesson 2.
Lesson 4	Problems involving 'real life', money or measures Making decisions	● **Count reliably at least 20 objects.**	● Recognise coins of different values. ● Find totals and change from up to 20p. ● Choose and use appropriate number operations and mental strategies to solve problems.
Lesson 5	Problems involving 'real life', money or measures Making decisions	As for Lesson 4.	As for Lesson 4.

Lessons   overview

Preparation
Set up a class newsagent's shop, and label the items for sale using the 1p–20p price labels. Provide a 'till': a box with some 1p, 2p, 5p, 10p and 20p coins in it. Enlarge 'The fairground game' to A3 size and pin it to the flip chart.

Learning objectives
Starter
● Describe and extend number sequences: **count in tens from and back to zero.**
Main teaching activities
● Recognise coins of different values.
● Find totals and change from up to 20p.

Vocabulary
money, coin, penny, pence, pound, price, cost, buy, sell, spend, spent, pay, change, dear, costs more, cheap, costs less, cheaper, costs the same as, how much…?, how many…?, total

You will need:
Photocopiable pages
'The fairground game' (see page 103) for each pair.

CD pages
'The fairground game', less able and more able versions and an A3 teaching version (see Spring term, Unit 4); 'Price labels 1p–10p', 'Price labels 11p–20p' (see General Resources).

Equipment
A pot of coins (all values from 1p–£2) and a 1–6 dice for each pair; items for a class newsagent's shop, such as newspapers, comics and sweet boxes; a metal or wooden box; a pad of paper; flip chart or board; paper and pencils.

Lesson ①

Starter

Ask the children to count together in tens, from zero to 100 and back again. Do this several times, keeping the pace sharp. The children may find it helpful to hold up fingers for each decade number. Repeat, counting around the class. To keep up the pace, ask the children to put their hands in the air as they say the number. This will produce a 'Mexican wave'. Repeat this several times.

Main teaching activities

Whole class: Ask the children to sort out the coins in the containers. Say: *Hold up a penny. Now show me 2p. Find a 5p and hold it up. Now a 10p. Which coin is worth 20p? Hold that up. And 50p? And £1?*

Ask the children to put a 20p coin in front of them. Say: *How many pennies is the same as a 20p coin? How many 2p… 5p… 10p coins are the same as a 20p coin? What other ways can we make 20p using other coins?*

Remind the children that each coin is worth the same as so many pennies: only the 1p coin is worth 1 penny.

Group work: Ask the children to fold a piece of A4 paper into four sections. They should then draw in each quarter a different selection of coins totalling 20p.

Differentiation

Less able: Work with this group. Encourage them to put out coins to make 20p, and to count up. For example: *1p and 1p makes 2p; 2p and 2p and 1p makes 5p…*

More able: Challenge the children to go on to find different ways of making 30p.

Plenary & assessment

Invite some children each to show a different way of making 10p. Record them on the flip chart, and encourage the children to check that each new suggestion is different from the others. The same coins in a different order should *not* count as a new way. Ask: *How many different ways did you find? Which way to make 20p would use the least/most coins? If you could have 20p in any coins, what coins would you choose? Why?*

Lesson ②

Starter

Repeat the Starter from Lesson 1. This time, also ask the children to start and stop counting in tens on different numbers. They can use their fingers to help them keep count. For example:
● *Start on 20. Stop on 80. How many tens did you count?*
● *If Iqbal starts on 30, what number will Sara say? How did you work that out?*

Main teaching activities

Whole class: Choose some items from the 'shop' priced between 1p and 10p. Choose a child to be the customer. In role as the shopkeeper, say: *This costs 3p. If the customer gives me 5p to pay for it, how much change will I need to give?* As you count out pennies into the customer's hand, say: *Let's count up together. 3p: 4p, 5p. So I need to give 2p change.* On the flip chart, write 5p – 3p = 2p. *What if the customer gave me a 10p coin: what change would I give then?* As you put the 1p coins into the customer's hand, say: *Count up again. 3p: 4p, 5p, 6p, 7p, 8p, 9p, 10p. So the change is 7p.* On the flip chart, write 10p –3p = 7p. Children may find it helpful to keep a tally on their fingers as they count up. Repeat for the other items the 'customer' has chosen.

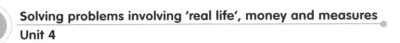
Now say: *Does change always come in pennies? Can we give other coins too?* Demonstrate the change from 5p for a 1p purchase. Ask the children to count up with you in steps of 2p: *1p and 2p is 3p, and 2p more is 5p. So I can use 2p coins to give 4p in change.* Repeat this for other amounts, such as the change from 10p for spending 4p: *4p and 1p is 5p, and 5p more is 10p. The change is 6p: 1p and 5p coins.*

Group work: Ask one group to work in the shop. They take turns to be shopkeeper and customer, choosing items and paying for them using a 10p coin. The shopkeeper counts out the change. Encourage the children to use coins other than 1p to give change.

The other children work in pairs, using a set of price labels 1p–10p and a pot of 1p, 2p, 5p and 10p coins. They take turns to be shopkeeper and customer. The customer chooses a price label and offers the shopkeeper a 10p coin; the shopkeeper counts out the change into the customer's hand. Encourage the children to use coins other than 1p to give change. They can write a subtraction sentence for each transaction.

Differentiation

Less able: If the children are unsure about equivalent coin values, limit the range of prices to 1p–5p and change from 5p until they understand how to count up in 2p coins as well as 1p coins.
More able: If the children are confident about giving change from 10p, extend the price label range to 12p.

Plenary & assessment

Invite pairs of children to act as shopkeeper and customer, giving change for prices to 10p. Encourage the other children to suggest alternative ways of giving the change. Ask: *Is there another way to give this change? Which way uses the least number of coins?*

Lesson

Starter

Repeat the Starter from Lesson 2. This time, include counting back from any decade number.

Main teaching activities

Whole class: Repeat from Lesson 2, this time including some prices for 11p to 20p and offering 20p in order to extend more able children. Again, encourage the children to count up using larger coins, so that fewer coins are used.
Group work: Ask the children to work in pairs on 'The fairground game'. Most of the class can use the version that involves finding prices and change within 10p.

Differentiation

Less able: Use the version of 'The fairground game' with amounts to 5p.
More able: Use the version with amounts to 20p.

Plenary & assessment

Play the game as a class, using an A3 version of the game (the version with amounts to 10p). Ask questions such as: *How did you work out the change? Which way of giving the change would use the least number of coins?*

Lessons   overview

Preparation
Make a screen to hide the tambourine behind, for example with a Big Book or an easel.

Learning objectives
Starter
- **Count reliably at least 20 objects.**

Main teaching activities
- Recognise coins of different values.
- Find totals and change from up to 20p.
- Choose and use appropriate number operations and mental strategies to solve problems.

Vocabulary
money, coin, penny, pence, pound, price, cost, buy, sell, spend, spent, pay, change, dear, costs more, cheap, costs less, cheaper, costs the same as, how much…?, how many…?, total, greatest, biggest, largest, fewest, smallest

You will need:
CD pages
'Price labels 1p–10p' and 'Price labels 11p–20p' (see General Resources).

Equipment
A tambourine; class shop resources (see Lessons 1–3).

Lesson

Starter
Explain that you will tap a tambourine that is hidden behind a screen. Ask the children to listen and count how many taps there are. As some of them may find this difficult, suggest that they shut their eyes to help them concentrate. Begin with two taps, then three, and continue up to ten.

Main teaching activities
Whole class: Explain that during these two lessons, the children will be solving problems involving money. Say: *John bought some toffees that cost 6p. He gave the shopkeeper a 10p coin. What change did he get? Which coins do you think the shopkeeper would have used?* Discuss the problem. Ask the children how they worked it out. Some children may have rapid recall; others will have counted up to 10p from 6p. Encourage the children to think about the coins that could be used for the change. *What is the smallest number of coins that could be used?* Discuss the answer (two 2p coins). Together, count up from 6p to 10p: *6p and 2p is 8p, and 2p more is 10p. So the change is two 2p coins.* Repeat this for other problems.

For example:
- *James buys a biscuit for 7p. What change will he get from 10p?*
- *Marie buys two 2p chews. How much does she spend? How much change will she have from 10p?*
- *Amy buys an apple for 3p and a banana for 4p. How much does she spend? How much change will she have from 10p?*

Group work: The following is a suggested list of activities for the children to work on over this and the next lesson.

1. A group of four children work in the class shop, taking turns to be a customer and the shopkeeper. The customer chooses two items each time and pays 10p; the shopkeeper adds up the prices and calculates the change.
2. Children work in pairs. They take turns to choose two price labels from 1p to 5p and add the prices. The other child gives change from 10p using the least number of coins. They can record the transaction: for example '5p + 2p = 7p. Our change is 3p. 2p + 1p.'
3. Children work in pairs to find different ways of making 10p, 12p, 15p and 18p. They can record by writing sums, such as 5p + 5p = 10p.
4. Children work in pairs to make up a number story for each of these: 2p + 5p = 7p; 10p – 6p = 4p; 10p – 10p = 0.

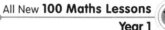

Differentiation

Less able: In activities 1 and 2, work with the children; encourage them to count on aloud as they give the change. Decide whether to limit activity 3 to making 7p, 8p, 9p and 10p. Simplify the numbers in activity 4, perhaps keeping the totals to no more than 6p. This activity can be undertaken orally with an adult.

More able: In activity 1, extend the price limit to 20p. In activity 2, the children can use labels to 10p and give change from 20p. In activity 3, ask the children to find the least number of coins that will make each value. In activity 4, include number sentences such as 4p + 2p + 3p = 9p.

Plenary & assessment

Review the group activities. Ask the children to explain how they worked out each problem:
- *How did you work this out? Is there another way?*
- *Which mathematics did you choose? Did this work well?*
- *Who did this problem in a different way?*
- *Which way do you think is better? Why is that?*

Check that the children are using rapid recall of number facts, and relating these to money, and are using counting on strategies, such as counting up from the total spent to find the change.

Lesson

Repeat the Starter from Lesson 4, this time starting with six taps. During the whole-class teaching activity, give the children a problem such as: *Sam paid 12p for some toffees. He gave three coins. Which three coins do you think he used?* As the children suggest solutions, ask them to explain how they worked it out and what maths they used. Set group activities from those listed for Lesson 4. Review these during the plenary session, again checking what maths was used and why the children made this choice.

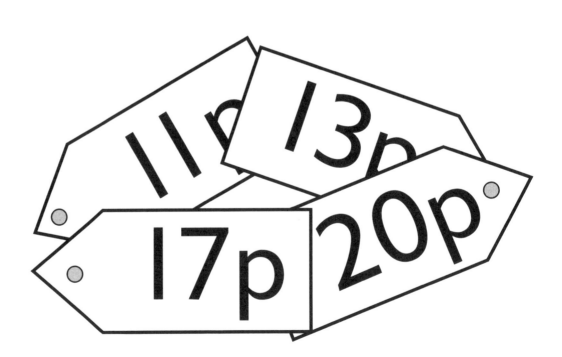

Name

Date

The fairground game

You will need a partner to play this game.

You need scissors and a pot of coins.

Cut out these cards and shuffle them.

Take turns to take a card.

Answer the question on the card.

Pick up the answer in coins.

When all the cards have been picked up, count your coins.

The player with the most money wins the game.

 How much are two 5p rides on the dodgems?	 I buy some candy floss for 6p. How much change do I get from 10p?
 I buy a toffee apple for 3p and a lolly for 2p. What is the total cost?	 I buy two tickets for the helter-skelter at 4p each. How much do I spend?
The water splash costs 7p. How much change will I have from 10p?	I have two goes on the hoopla. They cost 4p each. How much do I spend?
 One turn on the coconut shy costs 7p. How much change will I get from 10p?	The ghost train costs 9p. How much change will I get from 10p?
 Two of us go in the house of mirrors. It costs 4p each person. How much change will I get from 10p?	 The Ferris wheel costs 7p. How much change will I get from 10p?

SCHOLASTIC
photocopiable

Spring term
Unit 5
Shape and space, and reasoning about numbers and shapes

Children name 3-D shapes and their faces. They explore the properties of shapes. They make repeating patterns with shapes. They explore position, direction and movement through a PE lesson. They play a simple number game and try to develop a winning strategy for playing the game. They explore simple shape puzzles.

LEARNING OBJECTIVES

		Topics	Starter	Main teaching activities
Lesson	1	Shape and space	● Read the time to the hour or half hour on analogue clocks.	● **Use everyday language to describe features of familiar 3-D and 2-D shapes,** including the cube, cuboid, sphere, cylinder, cone, circle, triangle, square, rectangle, referring to properties such as the shapes of flat faces, or the number of faces or corners, or the number and types of sides. Make and describe models, patterns and pictures using construction kits, everyday materials, Plasticine…
Lesson	2	Shape and space	As for Lesson 1.	As for Lesson 1. ● Use one or more shapes to make, describe and continue repeating patterns…
Lesson	3	Shape and space	● Read the time to the hour or half hour on analogue clocks.	● Use everyday language to describe position, direction and movement. ● Talk about things that turn.
Lesson	4	Making decisions	● Know by heart addition facts for all pairs of numbers with a total up to at least 5, and the corresponding subtraction facts.	● Choose and use appropriate number operations and mental strategies to solve problems.
Lesson	5	Making decisions	As for Lesson 4.	As for Lesson 4.

Lessons   overview

Learning objectives
Starter
- Read the time to the hour or half hour on analogue clocks.

Main teaching activities
- **Use everyday language to describe features of familiar 3-D and 2-D shapes**, including the cube, cuboid, sphere, cylinder, cone, circle, triangle, square, rectangle, referring to properties such as the shapes of flat faces, or the number of faces or corners, or the number and types of sides.
- Make and describe models, patterns and pictures using construction kits, everyday materials, Plasticine…
- Use one or more shapes to make, describe and continue repeating patterns…

Vocabulary
shape, flat, curved, straight, round, hollow, solid, corner, point, pointed, face, side, edge, end, sort, make, build, draw, cube, cuboid, pyramid, sphere, cone, cylinder, circle, triangle, square, rectangle, star

You will need:
Equipment
A teaching clock; construction kits; commercial packaging materials; Plasticine; a teaching set of 3-D shapes (cubes, cuboids, cylinders, pyramids, cones, spheres) and 2-D shape tiles (squares, rectangles, circles, triangles); coloured sticky paper; sugar paper; glue; scissors.

Lesson ①

Starter

Explain that you will show the children a time on the teaching clock, and you would like them to read it aloud when you say: *Go.* Show them: 6 o'clock; half past 3; 9 o'clock; 12 o'clock; half past 7…

Main teaching activities

Whole class: Hold up a cube and say: *What shape is this? What shape is this face? What shape are all of the faces of a cube?* Agree that each face is a square. Hold up a square tile. Repeat this for a cuboid, using the rectangle tile (and if appropriate, the square as well). Discuss how the cuboid has six faces, with opposite faces matching and all faces either rectangular or square. Hold up the cylinder. The children should observe that the ends are circular. Elicit or explain the idea that the curved surface could be spread out to make a rectangle. Roll up a rectangular sheet of paper into a cylinder, and show the children that the hole at each end is circular. Discuss how the cone has a circle as one face.

Discuss which 3-D shapes are good for making models. Ask: *Which shapes have flat/curved faces? Which shapes would be good at the bottom of a tower? Why? Which shapes would not be good at the bottom of a tower? Why?* Look together at a sphere, and agree that other shapes cannot be balanced on it safely. Agree that the same is true of a cone.

Group work: The children work in pairs, making a model of a castle with a construction kit and/or commercial packaging materials (held together with Plasticine). They should be ready to explain why they have used 3-D shapes in particular places, referring to the properties of these shapes.

Differentiation

Less able: If possible, ask an adult to work with the children and encourage them to discuss what they are doing, using the vocabulary of shape.

More able: Ask the children to draw what they have made, showing how the parts fit together.

Plenary & assessment

Choose some children to demonstrate what they have made and describe the shapes they have used. Ask questions such as: *What shapes can you see? Which have curved/flat faces? What shapes can you think of that have both curved and flat faces?*

Lesson ②

Starter

Repeat the Starter for Lesson 1, asking questions such as:
- *What time does the clock show? What time will it be in half an hour… one hour… two hours?*
- *The clock shows 2 o'clock. If I turn the hands to half past 4, how much later would that be?*

Main teaching activities

Whole class: Use 2-D shape tiles. Display a square, rectangle, square and rectangle. Ask: *Which shape should come next? Why?* Now display a square, circle, triangle, square, circle and triangle. Discuss this repeating pattern.

Group work: Provide shape tiles, scissors and sticky coloured paper. The children work in pairs to make a pattern with the shape tiles. They then cut out the shapes, using the shape tiles as templates, and stick their pattern onto sugar paper. Encourage them to make three different repeating patterns.

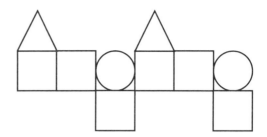

Differentiation
Less able: Limit the range of shape tiles to two types initially, so that the children can be successful in making AB or AAB type patterns.
More able: Challenge the children to make more complex patterns, as shown in the example here:

Plenary & assessment
Review some of the patterns that the children made, choosing examples from each ability range. Ask questions such as: *What shapes are there in this pattern? Who can 'say' the pattern? What comes before/after the…?*

Make a repeating pattern with some shapes to show the children. Now ask them to shut their eyes. Remove two pieces from the pattern and close the gaps. Say: *Open your eyes. What is wrong with my pattern?* Repeat this for other patterns, checking that the children can 'read' each pattern and identify faults.

Lesson overview

Preparation
Photocopy 'Clock face' onto card for each child. Ask children to cut out and make up the clock face, which they may like to decorate and personalise.

Learning objectives
Starter
- Read the time to the hour or half hour on analogue clocks.
Main teaching activities
- Use everyday language to describe position, direction and movement.
- Talk about things that turn.

Vocabulary
position, over, under, underneath, above, below, top, bottom, side, on, in, outside, inside, around, in front, behind, front, back, before, after, beside, next to, opposite, apart, between, middle, edge, centre, corner, direction, journey, left, right, up, down, forwards, backwards, sideways, across, next to, close, far, along, through, to, from, towards, away from, movement, slide, roll, turn, stretch, bend

You will need:
CD pages
'Clock face' for each child (see General Resources).

Equipment
Paper fasteners; large PE apparatus; small PE apparatus such as hoops, quoits, balls.

Lesson

Starter
Each child should have a 'Clock face' sheet made from the CD page. Explain that you would like them to set their clocks to the times that you say, and hold them up when you say: *Show me.* Say, for example:
- *Half past 1… 3… 7… 10 o'clock… 2 o'clock… 5 o'clock.*
- *Set your clock to 3 o'clock. Now set it four hours on.*
- *Use your clock to help you to work this out. If Jane gets up at 7 o'clock and has her lunch at 12 o'clock, how much time has passed?*

Main teaching activities

Whole class: This will be a PE lesson in the hall. Explain that this lesson is about using the vocabulary of position, direction and movement. Ask the children to put out some hoops around the edge of the hall, then run around the hall. When you say *Stop*, they move to stand inside a hoop. Now ask them to hold the hoop above their heads when you say *Stop*. Repeat for other position words, such as *stand outside/inside the hoop; four of you stand around it…*

Ask the children to put the hoops away and put out the large apparatus. Now ask them to move in pairs carefully around the hall, finding which pieces of apparatus they can go over or under. Then invite some pairs to demonstrate what they have found out, using the appropriate vocabulary. Repeat for words such as *top, bottom, side, on, in, in front of, behind…*

Group work: The children work in groups of four to six. Assign each group to a piece of apparatus. Ask them to develop a sequence of movements.

Differentiation

Less able: Decide whether to limit the children to a more limited range of positions and movements, so that they become familiar with these words. The activity can be repeated to introduce different vocabulary at a later date.

More able: Challenge the children to include words such as *turn* and *centre*.

Plenary & assessment

Ask each group in turn to demonstrate its sequence. Ask the other children to describe what they see, using the vocabulary of position, direction and movement. Check that they can use the vocabulary appropriately. When the floor is clear, ask the children to stand up and then to move quietly around the hall. Say: *Move forwards. Stop. Stretch up as far as you can.* Then say: *Find a partner. One of you lead, the other one is the shadow. The shadow copies the moves of the other person.* Now say: *Stand on your own. Move forwards; backwards; sideways; turn left/right…*

Lessons   overview

Preparation
Enlarge the 'Snail trail' sheet to A3 size and pin it to the flip chart. Also enlarge 'Town and country jigsaw' to A3.

Learning objectives
Starter
- Know by heart addition facts for all pairs of numbers with a total up to at least 5, and the corresponding subtraction facts.

Main teaching activities
- Choose and use appropriate number operations and mental strategies to solve problems.

Vocabulary
pattern, puzzle, answer, right, wrong, what could we try next?, how did you work it out?, count out, share out, left, left over, number sentence, sign, operation

You will need:

Photocopiable pages
'Snail trail' for each pair (see page 109) and 'Town and country jigsaw' (see page 110) for each child.

CD pages
A teaching set of 'Add facts to 5' and 'Take away facts 6 to 10'; 'Number fan' for each child (see General Resources).

Equipment
Individual whiteboards and pens; two cubes or counters for each pair; scissors and paper for each child; glue; temporary adhesive; flip chart or board.

Lesson

Starter

Ask the children to hold up their number fans when you say *Show me*, and display the answers to the number sentences that you show them. Hold up the cards, keeping the pace sharp so as to encourage rapid recall.

Main teaching activities

Whole class: Explain that you would like the children to solve some problems. Show them the A3 copy of 'Snail trail'. Explain to the children that they should use cubes or counters to represent the snails, and take turns to move their counter one or two places. Tell them that what you are interested in is how they find a way of winning. They should decide how to record their work, so they can explain what they have done.

Group work: The children play the game in pairs. Check that they do not spend too long playing it as a game: encourage them to move on to finding a strategy for winning.

Differentiation

Less able: The children can play the game in a larger group, with an adult. They can work in pairs to model a strategy, using two colours of cubes to record moves of one square and two squares.

More able: Ask the children to keep a systematic record of what they have done.

Plenary & assessment

Ask various children to explain their solutions. Encourage them to explain accurately. They will find it helpful to say how many squares the snail has moved, and how many are left. Discuss a strategy for winning. Move your finger along the track and ask: *What square must the snail be on to be sure of winning?* (8) *Why?* Discuss (and if necessary, demonstrate) this with the children.

Now ask: *What squares are best to visit?* (2, 4, 6, 8.) *What kind of numbers are these?* (Even.) *What if I visit 1, 3 and 5? What kind of numbers are these?* (Odd.) Discuss how, by using even numbers, the snail can reach the square in just five moves. Say the even numbers together. Ask two children to play the game, making a two-square move each time. This will show that the first snail to reach 10 wins.

Lesson

Starter

Repeat the Starter from Lesson 4. This time ask the children to write their answers on their whiteboards and, when you say *Show me*, they hold up their boards. Again, keep the pace sharp to encourage rapid recall.

Main teaching activities

Whole class: Show the children the A3 version of the 'Town and country jigsaw'. Discuss what the children can see, so that the pictures are familiar to them. Ask them to cut up the pictures as indicated on the sheet, then arrange the pieces to make the pictures again.

Individual work: Remove the A3 version of the activity sheet, then ask the children to start working. They can glue their reassembled pictures onto paper.

Differentiation

Less able: Let the children see the A3 version of the activity sheet as they work.

More able: Challenge the children to make ten cuts in the pictures and reassemble the pieces.

Plenary & assessment

Ask the children how they solved the puzzle. Cut up the A3 version of the sheet and ask some children to help you reassemble the pictures. If a temporary adhesive is used, the pictures can be moved around the board. Ask questions such as: *What shape is …? How did that help you?*

Name

Date

Snail trail

Work with a partner.

Cut out the snails.

Take turns to move the snails along the track.

The snails are very slow.

They can only move one or two squares at a time.

How can you help your snail to win?

Name	Date

Town and country jigsaw

Cut along the dotted line.

Now make six straight cuts through the two pictures.

Mix up the pieces.

Put the two pictures back together again.

Children make direct comparisons of the capacity of two vessels, then extend this to more than two. They use uniform non-standard units to estimate then measure capacity. They are introduced to the litre as a unit of measure for capacity.

LEARNING OBJECTIVES

	Topics	Starter	Main teaching activities
Lesson 1	Measures	● **Order numbers to at least 20**, and position them on a number track.	● Understand and use the vocabulary related to capacity. ● **Compare two capacities by direct comparison**; extend to more than two.
Lesson 2	Measures	As for Lesson 1.	As for Lesson 1. ● Measure using uniform non-standard units (e.g. yogurt pots), or standard units (e.g. litre jugs).
Lesson 3	Measures	As for Lesson 1.	As for Lesson 2.

Lessons   overview

Preparation
Label six containers with different capacities A–F. Remove the labels from the one-litre containers. Mix up all the containers and label them with numbers.

Learning objectives
Starter
● **Order numbers to at least 20**, and position them on a number track.
Main teaching activities
● Understand and use the vocabulary related to capacity.
● **Compare two capacities by direct comparison**; extend to more than two.
● Measure using uniform non-standard units (e.g. yogurt pots), or standard units (e.g. litre jugs).

Vocabulary
full, half full, empty, holds, container, measure, size, compare, guess, estimate, enough, not enough, too much, too little, too many, too few, nearly, roughly, close to, about the same as, just over, just under, most, least

You will need:
Photocopiable pages
'Filling', (see page 114) one for each group.

CD pages
Teaching set of and 'Numeral cards 0–9' and 'Numeral cards 10–20'; 'Measures chart 1', 'Measures chart 2' (see General Resources).

Equipment
A washing line; pegs; containers such as cups, egg cups, yogurt pots, margarine tubs; scoops or spoons; filling material such as sand, water, cubes; a set of one-litre containers with various shapes.

Lesson

Starter

Explain that you have some shuffled numeral cards from 0–20 and you would like these pegged to the line, in order. Hold up each numeral; ask the children to read it together, then invite a child to peg it to the line in a suitable position. Carry on until all the numerals are on the line, in order. Now say, for example: *Jamil, take the number that is between 9 and 11. Sara, take the number that is two more than 17. Clare, take the next odd number after 13.* Continue in this way, using facts that the children should know, until all the cards have been removed.

Main teaching activities

Whole class: Show the children two containers, and ask: *Which container do you think holds more? Why do you think that? How could you check?* Explain that their estimate could be checked by filling. Ask a child to fill one container with sand, then pour the sand into another container. Ask:

- *Did all the sand from this container fit into that one? What does this tell you?*
- *Which container was full? Which container was nearly full?*
- *Which container held more? How can you tell? Which one held less?*

Repeat with two more containers. When the children are confident with this, extend to three containers. Encourage the children to use the superlatives *most* and *least*.

Group work: Provide each group of four children with a set of containers to compare for capacity, and some filling material, such as sand or water. Ask them to compare two containers each time by looking at them, then check by filling and pouring. They can record their work on the 'Filling' activity sheet; this also asks them to compare three containers, using appropriate vocabulary.

Differentiation

Less able: Work with these children, encouraging them to use the appropriate vocabulary.
More able: Challenge these children to put all their containers in order of capacity, starting with the one that holds the least.

Plenary & assessment

Use the containers labelled A–F. Invite the children to compare three of these by looking at them. Ask: *Which holds the least/most? How can you check this?* Invite children to demonstrate this by pouring sand from the one they think holds the most to the next, then the one that holds the least. Ask: *Why do you think this container holds more than that one? Did you make a good guess/estimate? Which container holds the most/least? How do you know?*

Lesson

Starter

Repeat the Starter from Lesson 1. This time, invite children to stand at the front holding numeral cards and lining up in order. Then ask some children who are still seated to change places: *Tom, change places with the person holding the number that is ten more than 10. Sakina, change places with the person holding the number that is the next even number after 4…* Carry on until everyone has had a turn standing at the front.

Main teaching activities

Whole class: Show the children two containers and say: *Which one do you think holds more? Today we are going to find out how much more one container holds than another container.* Invite a child to fill one container with scoops of sand. Record on the board how many scoops were needed. Ask another child to fill the other container. Ask: *Which container holds more/less? How much more/less? How do you know that?* Discuss how we can compare how much different containers hold by filling them with the same non-standard units.

Group work: Choose from these activities. They could be set up as a circus of activities for all the children to use over time, working in pairs.

1. Estimate and then measure the capacity of one container using different non-standard units. Record this on 'Measures sheet 1'.
2. Estimate and then measure the capacity of several containers using one non-standard unit, such as scoops of sand. Record this on 'Measures sheet 2'.
3. Use a one-litre jug to choose containers which they estimate hold roughly that amount. Check by filling. Record this on 'Measures sheet 2'.
4. Make a list of things that could be measured for capacity with egg cups of sand. Choose some of these things to estimate and measure in this way. Record this on 'Measures sheet 2'.

Differentiation

Less able: Choose the activity that the children will enjoy most, and limit the range of items for them to measure or use as units. If possible, ask an adult to work with this group, encouraging the children to use the vocabulary of capacity in sentences. Making and checking estimates will help them to estimate more accurately.

More able: Challenge the children to try activity 3, estimating one litre. They should search for containers with a variety of shapes. Discuss how easy they found the activity, particularly with more unusually shaped containers.

Plenary & assessment

Discuss the activities each group has undertaken, asking key questions such as:

- *Which units did you use to measure that? Was that a good choice? Why?*
- *Which items did you measure with …? Was that a good choice? Why?*
- *Were your estimate and your measure about the same?*
- *What else could you measure with that unit? Why do you think that?*
- *What else could you use to measure that container? Why do you think that?*

Lesson 3

Repeat the Starter from Lesson 2, asking different children to stand at the front with the numeral cards. In the whole-class teaching activity, explain that the litre is the standard unit of measure for capacity. Show the children a one-litre jug, pointing out how the 'litre' level is marked with a line. Ask the children which liquids are sold in litres. Continue the group activities from Lesson 2. During the plenary session, use questions from the plenary in Lesson 2 to discuss the activities undertaken today.

| Name | Date |

Filling

You will need some containers, sand and a scoop.

Choose two containers.

Estimate which one holds more.

Check by filling.

Write your results in the table below.

Compare more containers.

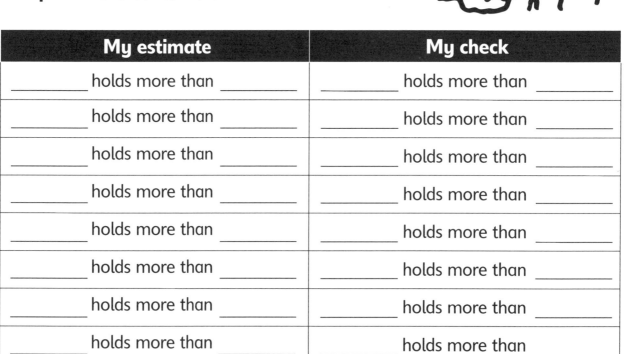

My estimate	My check
_____ holds more than _____	_____ holds more than _____
_____ holds more than _____	_____ holds more than _____
_____ holds more than _____	_____ holds more than _____
_____ holds more than _____	_____ holds more than _____
_____ holds more than _____	_____ holds more than _____
_____ holds more than _____	_____ holds more than _____
_____ holds more than _____	_____ holds more than _____
_____ holds more than _____	_____ holds more than _____

Now choose three containers.

Estimate which holds most and which holds least.

Check by filling.

Write a sentence about what you found out.

_____

_____

_____

Counting in twos, threes and fives, and reasoning about numbers or shapes

The children count in twos from zero or one, to about 20 and back again. They sort numbers to 20 into odd and even numbers. They count in fives, then threes, from zero to 20 and back again. They begin to recall the sequence of multiples of five from zero to about 20. They solve number problems.

LEARNING OBJECTIVES

	Topics	Starter	Main teaching activities
Lesson 1	Counting, properties of numbers and number sequences	● **Count reliably at least 20 objects.**	● Count on in twos from zero, then one, and begin to recognise odd or even numbers to about 20 as 'every other number'.
Lesson 2	Counting, properties of numbers and number sequences	As for Lesson 1.	● Count in steps of 5 from zero to 20 or more, then back again.
Lesson 3	Counting, properties of numbers and number sequences	As for Lesson 1.	● Count in steps of 5 from zero to 20 or more, then back again; begin to count in steps of 3 from zero.
Lesson 4	Reasoning about numbers or shapes	● Describe and extend number sequences: count on in twos from zero, then one, and begin to recognise odd or even numbers to about 20 as 'every other number'.	● Solve simple mathematical problems or puzzles; recognise and predict from simple patterns and relationships. Suggest extensions by asking 'What if?' or 'What could I try next?'
Lesson 5	Reasoning about numbers or shapes	As for Lesson 4.	As for Lesson 4.

Lessons   overview

Preparation
Enlarge 'Blank number tracks' and 'Missing numbers' (the 'more able' version) to A3 size and pin them to the flip chart.

Learning objectives
Starter
● **Count reliably at least 20 objects.**
Main teaching activities
● Count on in twos from zero, then one, and begin to recognise odd or even numbers to about 20 as 'every other number'.
● Count in steps of 5 from zero to 20 or more, then back again; begin to count in steps of 3 from zero.

Vocabulary
number, zero, one, two, three… to twenty and beyond, how many…?, count, count (up) to, count back (from, to), count in twos, odd, even, every other, how many times?, pattern, pair

You will need:

Photocopiable pages
'Missing numbers' (see page 120), one for each child.

CD pages
'Missing numbers', more able, less able and blank versions (see Spring term, Unit 8); two sets of 'Numeral cards 0–9' and 'Numeral cards 10–20' for each pair, and 'Numeral cards 21–30' for each more able pair, 'Work mat' for each child and A3 copies of 'Blank number tracks' (see General Resources).

Equipment
20 cubes in a pot for each child; a counting stick; some 20cm rulers marked in cm only; flip chart or board; paper and pencils.

Lesson

Starter

Ask the children to count out cubes onto their work mat. Say:

- *Count out ten cubes. Put them in a straight line. Now check the number by touching, counting and moving the cubes. How many are there? Put the cubes back.*
- *Now count out 12… 15… 20 cubes. Check the number by touching, counting and moving the cubes. How many are there?*

Main teaching activities

Whole class: Ask the children to count around the class in twos, from zero to about 20 and back. Repeat this, starting from one. Ask: *Which are the odd numbers? Which are the even numbers? Tell me an odd/even number less/more than 7… 8… 12…* Now ask the children to count individually around the class in twos, from zero to 20 and back, then from one to 19 and back. Keep the pace sharp.

Show the children the counting stick, and explain that one end shows zero. Count together in twos, and point to each segment as you count. Explain that you will point to a segment, and you would like the children to say which number it represents. Wipe the stick and pretend to empty the 'numbers' onto the floor. Now repeat the process with odd numbers (starting from one).

Group work: Ask the children to work in pairs with a set of numeral cards 0–20. They take turns to take a card and say whether it shows an odd or an even number. They can record this on a sheet of paper with the headings 'Odd numbers' and 'Even numbers'.

Differentiation

Less able: Provide a number track, such as a ruler marked in cm only up to 20cm. The children can count along this to check whether their number is odd or even.

More able: When the children are confident with the group activity, decide whether to give them a set of numeral cards 21–30 as well.

Plenary & assessment

Write the headings 'Odd numbers' and 'Even numbers' on the flip chart. Explain that you will say a number. Ask the children to say together 'odd' or 'even' for each number. Invite a child to write the odd numbers, and another child to write the even numbers, on the flip chart. Ask questions such as: *Is this number odd or even? How can you tell?* Discuss how the odd or even numbers in a counting sequence are 'every other number'.

Lesson ②

Starter

Repeat the Starter from Lesson 1. This time, the children work in pairs and take turns to count out the amounts you say. The other child checks by touching and counting, but not moving, the cubes.

Main teaching activities

Whole class: Tell the children that today, they will start to count in fives. Say the counting pattern for fives loudly, from zero to 20, inviting the children to join in. Repeat this, counting forwards and back. Keep up a good pace, even if this means that the children are not saying all of the numbers.

Now say that you want to list these numbers. Write 'Counting in fives' on the board. Ask the children which numbers they would say when counting in fives from zero. Write up 0, 5, 10, 15, 20. Ask: *What do you notice about this pattern?* The children should notice that the units number is either 5 or zero. *How does this help you to say the pattern of fives? What would the next number be after 20?*

Group work: The children play a 'Snap' game in pairs. Provide each pair with two sets of 0–20 numeral cards. They take turns to put down a card, and take matching cards if they can say 'Snap' first. However, if the matching card is a multiple of five (5, 10, 50, 20), they say 'Fives snap' and take a counter too. The child with the most counters at the end of the game wins. They can play several times to find the overall winner.

Differentiation

Less able: The children can play in a group with an adult, using four sets of 0–20 numeral cards. The adult checks that the children recognise the multiples of five. If the children are not sure, they can count each number (using their fingers) in order to recognise the multiples.

More able: Decide whether to add two sets of 21–30 numeral cards for each pair.

Plenary & assessment

Invite the children to count with you. This time, instead of saying the multiples of five, they should nod: *One, two, three, four, [nod], six, …* Repeat this several times, counting up to 20 and back again. Ask: *Which numbers come in the pattern of fives? Say some numbers that do* not *come in the pattern of fives.*

Lesson ③

Starter

Repeat the Starter for Lesson 2. This time, the child who checks the count should point to the cubes but not touch them.

Main teaching activities

Whole class: Count together in fives, from 0 to 20 and back again. Ask: *Which numbers come in the pattern of fives? What can you tell me about these numbers?* The children should recall that these numbers have either a 5 or a 0 in the units. Using the A3 'Blank number tracks' sheet, invite children to say which numbers you should write for the pattern of fives (0, 5, 10, 15, 20).

Now ask the children to help you count in threes. Ask them to say 'zero', then count in their heads and tell you the next number. Write this on a blank number track. Build up the sequence: 0, 3, 6, 9, 12, 15, 18, 21. Ask the children to recite these numbers with you; keep the pace sharp.

Individual work: Ask the children to complete the 'Missing numbers' activity sheet individually.

Differentiation
Less able: The children can use the version of 'Missing numbers' with counting numbers to 15.
More able: The children can use the version with counting numbers to 30.

Plenary & assessment
Using an A3 copy of the 'more able' version of 'Missing numbers', invite the children to take turns to suggest missing numbers. This will ensure that all of the children hear number patterns to 30, and will encourage more able children to demonstrate what they know. Ask:
- *What number comes next in the pattern? How did you work that out?*
- *Count on from 20 in fives. What is the next fives number?*

Lessons   overview

Preparation
Enlarge 'Hops and jumps' to A3 size and pin it to the flip chart.

Learning objectives
Starter
- Describe and extend number sequences: count on in twos from zero, then one, and begin to recognise odd or even numbers to about 20 as 'every other number'.

Main teaching activities
- Solve simple mathematical problems or puzzles; recognise and predict from simple patterns and relationships. Suggest extensions by asking *What if?* or *What could I try next?*

Vocabulary
pattern, puzzle, answer, right, wrong, what could we try next?, how did you work it out?, count out, share out, left, left over, number sentence, sign, operation

You will need:
Photocopiable pages
'Hops and jumps' for each pair (see page 121) and an A3 copy of 'Hops and jumps'.

Equipment
A counting stick; a pot of about 20 counters, in two colours, for each pair; coloured pens; flip chart or board.

Lesson

Starter
Point to one end of the counting stick and say: *This is zero.* Count along in twos, asking the children to count with you. Now point to different places on the stick and ask: *What number is this?* Repeat this, starting at one.

Main teaching activities
Whole class: Tell the children that they will be solving a problem. Show them the A3 version of 'Hops and jumps' and say: *Tom and Sara are playing 'hops and jumps'. Tom hops along the track in twos from the Start line. Sara jumps along the track in fives from the Start line. Can you find out which numbers they both land on?* Give each pair a copy of the sheet and a pot of counters. Ask them to talk in their pairs about how they will solve the problem and decide how they will record their work.
Group work: The children work in pairs to solve the problem and record their work. Allow them about 15–20 minutes.

Differentiation
Less able: Decide whether to simplify the problem so that the children go from the Start line to 10.
More able: Challenge the children to consider Josh, who leaps in threes, and extend the number track to 30. They need to find the numbers all three children land on.

Plenary & assessment

Using the A3 copy of 'Hops and jumps', invite some children to say which numbers Tom and Sara land on. Mark the hops in twos in one colour and the jumps in threes in another. Ask: *Which numbers does Tom visit? Which numbers does Sara visit? Which numbers do both children visit? Who visited just even numbers? Who visited odd and even numbers?*

Ask the more able children to explain how they extended the problem, and to say which numbers were visited. Discuss these facts: the only number visited by all three children is 30; Tom and Sara both visited 10 and 20; Sara and Josh both visited 15.

Lesson

Starter

Repeat the Starter for Lesson 4, this time asking the children to identify the odd and even numbers.

Main teaching activities

Whole class: Explain that the children have a problem to solve. Write the number '10' on the flip chart and say: *Tell me a number sentence that has ten as the answer. How many different number sentences can you find? Talk to your neighbour for about a minute, and think of as many as you can.*

Write the children's suggestions on the flip chart. Point out that there is a pattern if the number sentences are written in order: 0 + 10 = 10; 1 + 9 = 10; 2 + 8 = 10…

Group work: Ask the children to work in pairs, finding as many number sentences as they can with 12 as the answer. Suggest that they start with addition number sentences where the total is 12, and write these in order. Then they can find subtraction number sentences that begin with '12 subtract…'

Differentiation

Less able: If the children struggle with 12, suggest that they use eight as the answer.
More able: Challenge the children to use 15 as the answer.

Plenary & assessment

Invite some children to write an addition sentence where the total is 12 on the flip chart. When the children can find no more addition sentences, invite a child to rewrite them on the flip chart in a logical order, so that the pattern of the numbers can be seen. For example:

$$12 + 0 = 12$$
$$11 + 1 = 12$$
$$10 + 2 = 12…$$

Repeat this for subtraction, finishing with the number sentences in a logical order.

Ask the children to look at the two sets of number sentences and tell you what they can see. Encourage them to notice that, for example, 8 + 4 = 12 and 12 − 4 = 8 contain the same numbers. Ask: *What can you tell me about the addition and subtraction number sentences? What patterns can you see in the numbers?*

If the more able children used 15 as their answer, review this so that all of the class can see and hear these number sentences.

Name	Date

Missing numbers

Look at the number patterns.

Write in the missing numbers.

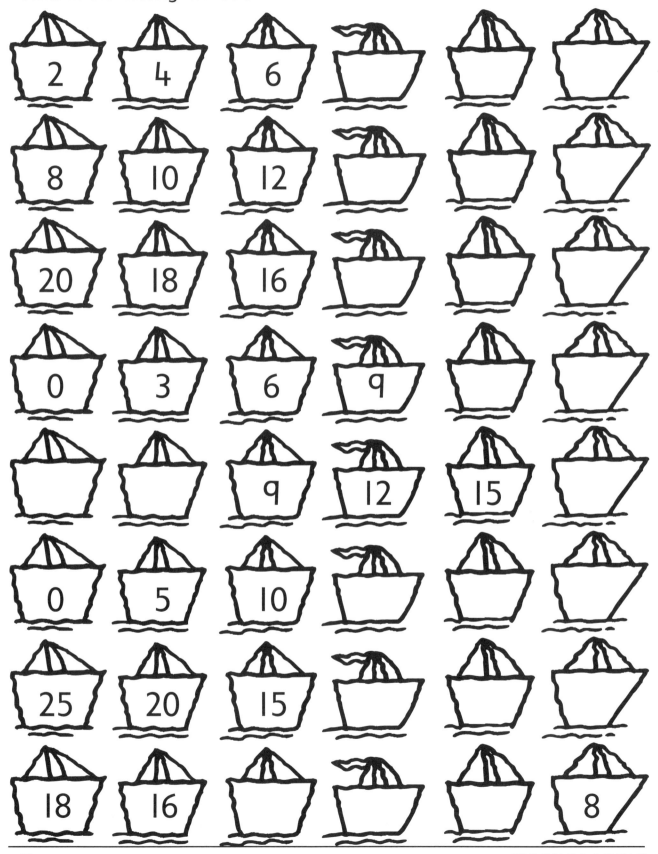

All New **100 Maths Lessons**
Year 1

SCHOLASTIC

photocopiable

Name	Date

Hops and jumps

Tom and Sara play a game on a 1–20 number track.

They both stand on the Start square.

Tom hops in 2s.

Sara jumps in 5s.

Which numbers does Tom land on?

Which numbers does Sara land on?

Which numbers do they both land on?

Mental calculations for addition and subtraction

Children learn and practise the addition strategies of partitioning into '5 and a bit' and bridging through 10. They practise take-away and difference questions, and explain the mental strategies that they used.

LEARNING OBJECTIVES

	Topics	Starter	Main teaching activities
Lesson 1	Understanding addition and subtraction Mental calculation strategies (+ and −)	● **Know by heart all pairs of numbers with a total of 10** (e.g. 3 + 7).	● **Understand the operation of addition, and use the related vocabulary.** ● Use knowledge that addition can be done in any order to do mental calculations more efficiently. For example: begin to partition into '5 and a bit' when adding 6, 7, 8 or 9, then recombine (e.g. 6 + 8 = 5 + 1 + 5 + 3 = 10 + 4 = 14).
Lesson 2	Understanding addition and subtraction Mental calculation strategies (+ and −)	As for Lesson 1.	As for Lesson 1.
Lesson 3	Understanding addition and subtraction Mental calculation strategies (+ and −)	● Know by heart addition facts for all pairs of numbers with a total up to at least 5, and the corresponding subtraction facts.	● **Understand the operation of addition, and use the related vocabulary.** ● Begin to bridge through 10 when adding a single-digit number.
Lesson 4	Understanding addition and subtraction Mental calculation strategies (+ and −)	As for Lesson 3.	As for Lesson 3.
Lesson 5	Understanding addition and subtraction	● Describe and extend number sequences: count on in twos from zero, then one, and begin to recognise odd or even numbers to about 20 as 'every other number'.	● **Understand the operation of addition, and of subtraction (as 'take-away', 'difference', and 'how many more to make'), and use the related vocabulary.**

Lessons   overview

Preparation
Make a tower of five and a tower of eight from the cubes.

Learning objectives
Starter
● **Know by heart all pairs of numbers with a total of 10** (e.g. 3 + 7).
Main teaching activities
● **Understand the operation of addition, and use the related vocabulary.**
● Use knowledge that addition can be done in any order to do mental calculations more efficiently. For example: begin to partition into '5 and a bit' when adding 6, 7, 8 or 9, then recombine (e.g. 6 + 8 = 5 + 1 + 5 + 3 = 10 + 4 = 14).

Vocabulary
add, more, plus, make, sum, total, altogether, equals, sign, is the same as

You will need:
Photocopiable pages
'Find the totals' (see page 127) for each pair.
CD pages
'Find the totals', less able, more able and blank versions (see Spring term, Unit 9); a teaching set of 'Complements of 10' cards, a '6, 7, 8 and 9 spinner' for each pair and a 'Number fan' for each child (see General Resources).

Equipment
About 20 interlocking cubes; paperclips; pencils; an individual whiteboard and pen for each child; flip chart or board.

Lesson ①

Starter

Explain that you will show the children a number sentence on a card. Ask an individual to read each 'Complements of 10' card aloud, then ask the children to hold up fingers to show the missing number.

Main teaching activities

Whole class: Explain that today, the children will learn a new strategy to help them add. On the flip chart, write the addition sentence 5 + 8 = . Show the children a tower of five cubes, and another of eight. Explain that the eight tower can be broken into a five and a 'bit'. Invite a child to do this, making towers of five and three. Invite the children to check by counting the cubes in each tower. Now say: *5 add 8 is the same as 5 add 5 add 3.* Write on the board: 5 + 8 = 5 + 5 + 3. Ask: *What is 5 add 5? Yes, 10. And 10 add 3 is? 13. So 5 add 8 is 13.* Write on the board:

    5 + 8 = 5 + 5 + 3
    10 + 3 = 13
    So 5 + 8 = 13.

If the children do not recognise that, for example, 10 + 3 is 13, ask them to count on in ones from 10.
Repeat this for another example of adding 6, 7, 8 or 9 to 5.

Group work: Ask the children to work in pairs. They take turns to spin a paperclip around a pencil on the '6, 7, 8 and 9 spinner', then add the number to 5. Encourage them to work quickly, and to carry out the partition and then the addition mentally. This is a practice activity; they do not need to record their work.

Differentiation

Less able: The children will benefit from working in a group, with an adult, to carry out the activity. The adult should check that the children can partition and then add; if necessary, they can add by counting on in ones from 10.

More able: Challenge the children to use their knowledge of tens and units numbers to find totals such as 10 + 3 rapidly.

Plenary & assessment

Ask the children to complete a sum mentally, such as 5 + 7. Discuss how they can partition 7 into 5 and 2. Check that they understand that, for example, 10 + 2 is 12 because 12 is 1 ten and 2 units. Ask: *What is 5 + 6? How did you work that out? What is 10 + 3? How did you work that out?*

Lesson

Starter

Repeat the Starter from Lesson 1. This time, invite the children to respond orally when you say: *Tell me.*

Main teaching activity

Whole class: Remind the children of the new strategy they have learnt: add 6, 7, 8 or 9 by partitioning into 5 and a 'bit' and recombining. Check the children understand that there is no need to count on in ones from 10. For example, 5 + 9 is 10 + 4, which is 14.

Individual work: Provide the 'Find the totals' sheet for the children to complete.

Differentiation

Less able: Use the version of the sheet with totals to 13.

More able: Use the version with totals to 20.

Plenary & assessment

Discuss the strategies the children used. Ask questions such as: *Which strategy did you use? How did you work that out? Who used counting on in ones… partitioning into 5 and a bit and recombining… double facts… double add 1 facts…? Which strategy do you think was best? Why is that?*

Lessons   overview

Preparation

Photocopy the 'Number line 0–20' sheet onto card and cut out the number lines.

Learning objectives

Starter
- Know by heart addition facts for all pairs of numbers with a total up to at least 5, and the corresponding subtraction facts.

Main teaching activities
- **Understand the operation of addition, and use the related vocabulary.**
- Begin to bridge through 10 when adding a single-digit number.

Vocabulary

add, more, plus, make, sum, total, altogether, equals, sign, is the same as

You will need:

Photocopiable pages
'Bridging 10' (see page 128) for each child.

CD pages
A teaching set of 'Add facts to 5' and 'Take away facts to 5' cards, a 'Number fan' and a set of 'Numeral cards 0–9' for each child, 'Numeral cards 10–20' for each more able child, individual 'Number line 0–20' for less able children (see General Resources).

Equipment

Individual whiteboards and pens; flip chart or board.

Lesson

Starter

Explain that you will hold up a card with an addition or subtraction number sentence on it. Ask the children to show you the answer with their number fan when you say: *Show me.* Use the 'Add facts to 5' and 'Take away facts to 5' cards. Keep the pace lively, as most of the children should have rapid recall of the majority of these facts.

Main teaching activities

Whole class: Explain that today, the children will learn another strategy to use for adding. On the flip chart, write: 6 + 7 = . Explain that it is possible to simplify this by 'making a ten'. Ask: *What do I need to add to 6 to make 10? Yes, 4.* Write: 6 + 4 + 3 = . Say: *The 7 can be made into a 4 and a 3. So now, 6 + 4 is 10, add 3 is 13.* Ask the children to repeat this sentence with you. Remind them that adding any digit to 10 just changes the units digit of the 10 from 0 to the digit being added.

Write 7 + 8 = on the flip chart. Ask the children how they can work this out. They may suggest 7 + 3 + 5 or (starting with the larger digit) 8 + 2 + 5. Ask for a volunteer to explain how to complete the sum. For example: *7 + 3 is 10, and 5 more is 15.*

Group work: Ask the children to work in pairs. They will need two sets of numeral cards 6–9. They shuffle the cards together and take turns to take the top two cards. Using the digits on the cards, they write an addition sentence and use the new strategy to find the answer. At this stage, they may find it helpful to write out an intermediate stage in the process, e.g.: 6 + 9 = 6 + 4 + 5 = 10 + 5 = 15.

Differentiation

Less able: The children may find it helpful to use a 0–20 number line.
More able: Decide whether to include a set of numeral cards for 16, 17, 18 and 19, asking the children to bridge 20 in the same way.

Plenary & assessment

Invite some children to write one of their sums on the board. Ask: *How did you work that out? Which strategy did you use? Say the whole number sentence for us. Write it on the board.* Check that the children understand that they can start with either number when adding two numbers, and that they are using knowledge of the complements of 10.

Lesson 4

Starter

Repeat the Starter from Lesson 3. This time, ask the children to write the answer on their whiteboard and hold it up when you say: *Show me.*

Main teaching activities

Whole class: Review the 'bridging through 10' strategy from Lesson 3. Encourage individual children to explain how they found the answers, and to write extended number sentences to show the bridging on the flip chart.
Individual work: Provide each child with a copy of 'Bridging 10', which contains sums with totals to 17.

Differentiation

Less able: Provide the children with 0–20 number lines if they need help with counting on, but check that they are using the bridging strategy and not just counting on in ones.
More able: Challenge the children to write some 'bridging through 20' sums on the back of the sheet and solve them.

Plenary & assessment

Review some of the examples on the activity sheet. Ask questions such as:
- Which did you find easy to do? Why was that?
- Which were more difficult? Why?

Lesson ⑤ overview

Learning objectives

Starter
- Describe and extend number sequences: count on in twos from zero, then one, and begin to recognise odd or even numbers to about 20 as 'every other number'.

Main teaching activities
- **Understand the operation of addition, and of subtraction (as 'take-away', 'difference', and 'how many more to make'), and use the related vocabulary.**

Vocabulary

add, more, plus, make, sum, total, altogether, subtract, take (away), minus, leave, how many are left/left over?, how many are gone?, how many fewer is … than …?, how much less is …?, difference between

You will need:

Photocopiable pages
'Subtraction' (see page 129) for each child.

CD pages
'Subtraction', less able and more able versions (see Spring term, Unit 9).

Equipment
A counting stick; pencils.

Lesson ⑤

Starter

Show the children the counting stick. Label one end zero, then count along the stick in twos to 20. Point to different sections. Ask: *What number is this? And this?* Now label one end '1' and count along the stick in twos. *Are these odd or even numbers?* Point again to different sections and ask the children to say what number goes there. Count forwards and backwards along the stick, first in odd numbers and then in even numbers.

Main teaching activities

Whole class: Explain that today, the children will be revising what they know about subtraction. Ask subtraction questions that use a range of vocabulary, such as: *What is 9 subtract 4? How many more is 8 than 2? How many fewer is 3 than 6? What is the difference between 6 and 9? How did you work that out?*

Check that the children remember the strategy of counting on. So for 9 − 4, they could count: *4: 5, 6, 7, 8, 9. That is 5 more. So 9 − 4 is 5.*

Group work: Provide copies of the 'Subtraction' activity sheet. The children work individually to answer the questions.

Differentiation

Less able: Decide whether to provide the version of 'Subtraction' with numbers to 8.
More able: Decide whether to provide the version with numbers to 13.

Plenary & assessment

Review some of the examples from the activity sheet. Ask individual children to explain how they worked out their answer, and which strategy they used. Ask questions such as:
- *What is 9 subtract 2? How did you work that out?*
- *Do some of you remember the answers to these? If you do, then remembering is a good strategy to use.*

Name

Date

Find the totals

Join the answers to the sums.

4+3

5+7

5+8

13

14

5+9

6+6

5

12

11

14

9+5

5+6

2+3

7

12

8+7

4+4

10

8+5

5+5

15

13

8

Name   Date

Bridging 10

Write the answers to these addition sentences.

6 + 7 =

9 + 6 =

4 + 8 =

8 + 7 =

7 + 5 =

3 + 9 =

6 + 8 =

9 + 7 =

8 + 9 =

7 + 8 =

9 + ☐ = 13

☐ + 8 = 15

6 + ☐ = 13

☐ + 4 = 12

☐ + 9 = 17

6 + ☐ = 14

8 + ☐ = 17

4 + ☐ = 13

☐ + 6 = 15

7 + ☐ = 16

Name	Date

Subtraction

Read these subtraction questions.

Write the answers.

What is 8 subtract 4?

How many more is 9 than 3?

How many fewer is 4 than 10?

What is the difference between 4 and 7?

Clare has 10 pencils.

She has 5 more than Dilshad.

How many pencils does Dilshad have?

Pip has 6 fewer sweets than Jack.

Jack has 9 sweets.

How many sweets does Pip have?

Place value, ordering, estimating and solving problems

The children order numbers to at least 20 and recognise ordinal numbers. They identify the missing numbers which form a sequence. They estimate how many for quantities up to about 30. They solve money problems and money word problems.

LEARNING OBJECTIVES

	Topics	Starter	Main teaching activities
Lesson 1	Place value and ordering	● **Count reliably at least 20 objects.**	● **Understand and use the vocabulary of comparing and ordering numbers**, including ordinal numbers to at least 20. ● Use the = sign to represent equality. ● Compare two familiar numbers, say which is more or less, and give a number which lies between them.
Lesson 2	Place value and ordering	As for Lesson 1.	As for Lesson 1.
Lesson 3	Estimating	As for Lesson 1.	● Understand and use the vocabulary of estimation. ● Give a sensible estimate of a number of objects that can be checked by counting (e.g. up to about 30 objects).
Lesson 4	Problems involving 'real life', money or measures Making decisions	● **Read and write numerals from 0 to at least 20.**	● **Use mental strategies to solve simple problems** set in 'real life', money or measurement contexts, **using counting, addition, subtraction, doubling and halving, explaining methods and reasoning orally.** ● Find totals and change from up to 20p. ● Work out how to pay an exact sum using smaller coins. ● Choose and use appropriate number operations and mental strategies to solve problems.
Lesson 5	Problems involving money	As for Lesson 4.	As for Lesson 4.

Lessons   overview

Preparation
Enlarge 'Blank number lines' and 'Number monsters' (core version) to A3 size and pin them to the flip chart.

Learning objectives
Starter
● **Count reliably at least 20 objects.**
Main teaching activities
● **Understand and use the vocabulary of comparing and ordering numbers**, including ordinal numbers to at least 20.
● Use the = sign to represent equality.
● Compare two familiar numbers, say which is more or less, and give a number which lies between them.

Vocabulary
compare, order, size, first, second, third… tenth, eleventh… twentieth, last, last but one, before, after, next, between, halfway between

You will need:
Photocopiable pages
'Number monsters' (see page 135) for each child plus an A3 copy.

CD pages
'Number monsters', less able, more able and blank versions (see Spring term, Unit 10); 'Work mat' for each child; a teaching set of 'Numeral cards 0–9' and 'Numeral cards 10–20' and a set for each group of four; 'Numeral cards 21–30' for each more able group, an A3 copy of 'Blank number lines' (see General Resources).

Equipment
About 20 cubes for each child; a washing line, pegs; flip chart or board.

Lesson ①

Starter

Ask the children to count out given numbers of cubes onto their work mat. They should check their partner's counting by touching, but not moving, the cubes as they count them. Include quantities from 10 to 20. Say: *Count out … cubes. Now check your partner's cubes. Touch the cubes as you count them. Put the cubes back.*

Main teaching activities

Whole class: Explain that you would like the children to help you peg the numeral cards on the washing line. Say that you have all of the numerals from 0 to 20. Invite individual children to take a card and peg it where they think it should go, taking into account which numerals are still to come. When all the cards are on the line, ask questions such as: *Which number comes between 14 and 16? Tell me three numbers that are between 10 and 16. Which numbers are more than 15 and less than 18?*

Now invite individual children to remove a numeral card, leaving the numbers 0, 1, 2, 6, 7, 12, 19 and 20 in place. Ask: *Which numbers need to go between 2 and 6? Which numbers are missing between 7 and 12? How do you know? Which numbers go between 12 and 19?*

Group work: Provide each group of four children with a set of 0–20 numeral cards. They shuffle the cards, then deal them out between them. They hide their own cards. The dealer starts by placing any card on the table (for example, 10). The next child has to place a card that fits on either side (9 or 11). If they cannot do this, they say 'pass' and the next child has a turn. The object of the game is to be the first player to get rid of all their cards. The children should play this game four times, so that everyone has a turn at being the dealer.

Differentiation

Less able: Decide whether to limit the number range to 10 or 15.
More able: Decide whether to extend the number range to 30.

Plenary & assessment

Write part of a number line on the board: 8, 10, 11, 15, 18. Ask: *Which numbers come before 8? What is missing between 8 and 10? Which numbers are between 11 and 15? And between 15 and 18? What comes after 18?* Ask the children to explain how they worked out the answers. Some children may have used a mental number line; others may have counted.

Lesson ②

Starter

Repeat the Starter from Lesson 1; this time, ask the children to check each other's count by pointing, but not touching.

Main teaching activities

· **Whole class:** Use an A3 copy of the 'Blank number lines' sheet. Write in parts of a number line. For example: 9 10 _ _ _ 14 15 _ _ _ 19 _. Ask questions such as:
- *What numbers come between 10 and 14? And 15 and 19?*
- *Tell me a number that is less than 18/more than 14.*

Individual work: Provide copies of 'Number monsters' and ask the children to complete this individually.

Differentiation
Less able: Use the version of the activity sheet with numbers to 12.
More able: Use the version with numbers to 30.

Plenary & assessment
Using an A3 copy of 'Number monsters' (the core version with numbers to 20), invite children to write in the missing numbers. Ask: *How do you know those numbers go there?* Encourage the use of mental counting, rather than using fingers, where appropriate.

Lesson overview

Learning objectives
Starter
- **Count reliably at least 20 objects.**

Main teaching activity
- Understand and use the vocabulary of estimation.
- Give a sensible estimate of a number of objects that can be checked by counting (e.g. up to about 30 objects).

Vocabulary
guess, how many, estimate, nearly, roughly, close to, about the same as, just over, just under, too many, too few, enough, not enough

You will need:

Equipment
A set of about eight transparent containers that contain, for example, 20 cubes, 15 counters, 10 dice, 26 marbles, 18 pieces of pasta, 14 conkers, 30 beads and 23 buttons; a picture (from a Big Book or poster) of items that can be counted; about 30 counters for each pair of children.

Lesson

Starter
Ask the children to look carefully at the picture from the Big Book or poster. Ask questions such as: *How many … can you see? Are there more/fewer … than …? How many more/fewer?*

Main teaching activities
Whole class: Explain that you have some containers with between 10 and 30 things in each one. You will show the children one container at a time and ask them to estimate how many things there are inside. Hold up one container and ask: *How many … do you think there are?* Write some of the estimates on the flip chart, then ask two children to open the container. One child can count the items, the other can check. Repeat for another container. Ask: *Did you make a good estimate? Were there too many/too few for your estimate?* Discuss how checking helps us to make better estimates.
Group work: Ask the children to work in pairs. They take turns to take a handful of counters which they estimate to be between 20 and 30 counters. They record their estimate, then check by counting and writing the count. Ask the children to devise their own means of recording this. Encourage them to become more accurate in their estimates as they work.

Differentiation
Less able: Suggest that the children aim for numbers between 10 and 20.
More able: Suggest that the children try counting the items in twos.

Plenary & assessment

Discuss how much more accurate the children's estimates became through practice. Invite them to look at another transparent container and estimate how many items are inside it. Ask two children to count the items and check the count. Ask: *Was your estimate close? Who estimated just under/just over the count?*

Lessons   overview

Learning objectives

Starter
- **Read and write numerals from 0 to at least 20.**

Main teaching activity
- **Use mental strategies to solve simple problems** set in 'real life', money or measurement contexts, **using counting, addition, subtraction, doubling and halving, explaining methods and reasoning orally.**
- Find totals and change from up to 20p.
- Work out how to pay an exact sum using smaller coins.
- Choose and use appropriate number operations and mental strategies to solve problems.

Vocabulary

money, coin, penny, pence, price, cost, buy, sell, spend, spent, pay, change, dear, costs more, cheap, costs less, cheaper, costs the same as, how much…?, how many…?, total.

You will need:

Photocopiable pages
'Money problems' (see page 136) for each pair.

CD pages
'Money problems', less able and more able versions (see Spring term, Unit 10); a teaching set of 'Number word cards 0–10' and 'Number word cards 11–20' and sets of 'Price labels 1p–20p' (see General Resources).

Equipment
Individual whiteboards and pens; a pot of several 1p, 2p, 5p, 10p and 20p coins for each pair.

Lesson

Starter

Use the number word cards 0–20. Explain that you will hold up a card with a number word on it. Ask the children to read the word and write the number on their whiteboard, using digits, then hold it up when you say: *Show me.*

Main teaching activities

Whole class: Explain that today's lesson is about solving money problems. Ask: *What coins can I use to pay for an ice cream that costs 15p?* Invite some children to suggest how they would do this, and write their suggestions on the board. Ask questions such as: *Which way uses the least number of coins? Which way uses the largest number of coins?* Repeat this for other amounts, such as 14p, 12p and 18p.

Group work: Ask the children to work in pairs, using a pot of coins. They take turns to choose a price label from 11p to 20p and try to make this price using the least possible number of coins. They record the price and the coins used, writing an addition sentence (for example, 10p + 5p = 15p).

Differentiation

Less able: Decide whether to use price labels from 1p to 10p.
More able: Challenge the children to write three different ways of making the price.

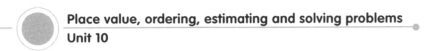

Plenary & assessment
Invite individual children to suggest how to make the prices, using the least number of coins possible. Ask them to record an addition sentence on the board. Ask questions such as: *How do you know that this way uses the least number of coins?*

Now ask some money problem questions, such as:
- *Josh bought a 6p toffee. He gave the shopkeeper 10p. What was his change?*
- *Which coins do you think the shopkeeper gave him?*
- *Marie bought a lolly for 7p. She gave the shopkeeper 10p. What change did she get?*

Lesson

Starter
Ask the children to write given numbers in numeral form on their whiteboards, then show them to you. For example: *Write the numbers that are between 9 and 12. Write a number that is more than 7 and less than 11. Write a number that is odd/even and is more than 14.*

Main teaching activities
Whole class: Explain that you will be asking some money word problems. Ask the children to listen and answer. Say: *Mark had 15p. He spent 6p. How much did he have left? How can we work this out?* Children may suggest counting on in ones from 6p, or using coins to count up to 15p. Demonstrate using coins and say: *6p and 2p is 8p, and 2p more is 10p. 10p and 5p is 15p. The coins we used are 2p and 2p and 5p. How much is that? Yes, 9p change.*

Repeat this for other amounts spent and initial amounts, such as 8p and 15p or 12p and 20p.
Group work: The children work in pairs with the 'Money problems' activity sheet and a pot of coins. They read each problem together; then one child acts as shopkeeper and the other as customer. Using the coins, they model the spending and the change, then write the change on the sheet.

Differentiation
Less able: Use the version of 'Money problems' involving change from 10p.
More able: Use the version involving change from 30p.

Plenary & assessment
Invite various children to explain how they solved the first problem on the activity sheet. Invite them to model the problem with coins, and ask other children to check their answers. Ask:
- *What is the least number of coins you could use? What are these coins? How did you work that out?*
- *Which other ways could we give this amount of change? Which way would you prefer? Why?*

Name	Date

Number monsters

Look at the numbers on the monsters' tails.

Write in the missing numbers.

Name	Date

Money problems

Work with a partner.
Use some coins to help you.

Read each problem together.
Take turns to be the shopkeeper and the customer.
Write how much change is given from 20p.

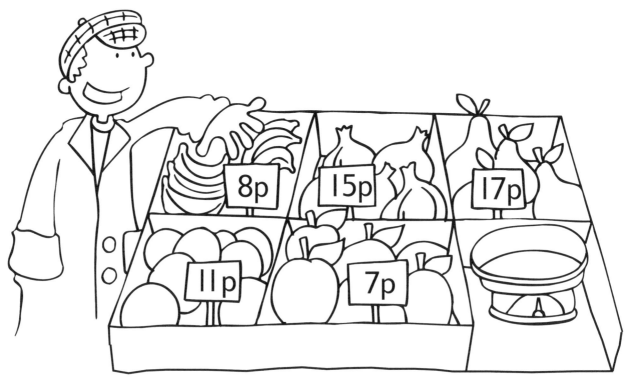

1. Mrs Smith buys a banana for 8p.
   What is her change from 20p?

   ☐ p

2. Mr Desai buys an orange for 11p.
   What is his change from 20p?

   ☐ p

3. Sam buys an onion for 15p.
   What is her change from 20p?

   ☐ p

4. Treena buys an apple for 7p.
   What is her change from 20p?

   ☐ p

5. Harry buys a pear for 17p.
   What is his change from 20p?

   ☐ p

Organising and using data and time

Children collect data, write lists and make simple picture graphs from the data. They interrogate the data and answer questions about it. They order the days of the week and the seasons of the year. They estimate how long one, two and three minutes are through practical activities.

LEARNING OBJECTIVES

		Topics	Starter	Main teaching activities
Lesson	1	Organising and using data	● **Order numbers to at least 20**, and position them on a number track.	● Solve a given problem by sorting, classifying and organising information in simple ways, such as: using objects or pictures; in a list or simple table.
Lesson	2	Organising and using data	As for Lesson 1.	As for Lesson 1.
Lesson	3	Organising and using data	As for Lesson 1.	As for Lesson 1.
Lesson	4	Measures	● Describe and extend number sequences: **count in tens from and back to zero.**	● Understand and use the vocabulary related to time. ● Know the days of the week and the seasons of the year.
Lesson	5	Measures	As for Lesson 4.	As for Lesson 4.

Lessons   overview

Preparation
Make an A3-sized copy of 'Pet show' and pin it to the flip chart.

Learning objectives
Starter
● **Order numbers to at least 20**, and position them on a number track.
Main teaching activities
● Solve a given problem by sorting, classifying and organising information in simple ways, such as: using objects or pictures; in a list or simple table.

Vocabulary
count, sort, vote, list, group, set, table

You will need:
Photocopiable pages
'Pet show' (see page 142) for each child, plus an A3 copy.

CD pages
A 'Number fan' for each child (see General Resources).

Equipment
Individual whiteboards and pens; a cube for each child; large sheets of sugar paper; small identical squares of blank paper; glue; flip chart or board.

Lesson ①

Starter

On the board, write three numbers out of order, such as 6, 1, 3. Ask the children to write these numbers in order on their individual whiteboards and hold them up when you say: *Show me*. Repeat this, using three or four numbers up to 10 each time.

Main teaching activities

Whole class: Explain that today the children will be using their data handling skills to solve problems. Write a list of ice-cream flavours, such as vanilla, strawberry, toffee, chocolate and banana, across the flip chart as column headings. Ask: *How can we find out who likes which flavour best?* Give the children a short time to discuss, in groups of three or four, how they would collect the data. Their suggestions may include:

- Make a list of everyone in the class and write what they like best against their name.
- Make a list of which ice-cream flavours everyone likes on each table, then put the lists together.

  Discuss these two options, pointing out that both are good ideas, but that the first one would probably take longer. Provide a further suggestion: *Suppose I give everyone in the class a cube. Take turns to put your cube by your favourite ice-cream flavour. Would that work?* Invite each child to put their cube quickly on the board ledge in the column of their favourite ice cream. Ask: *Which is the flavour that most people like? How can you tell? Which is the flavour that the least number of people like? How can you tell?*

  Discuss how graphs like this can also be made using pictures stuck onto paper. Explain that the children will be doing this during the group activity. Talk about why it is necessary to use the same size of paper for each picture, and to stick the pictures onto the graph evenly – so that you can easily tell which set of pictures has more or fewer pictures in without counting them.

Group work: Ask the children to work in groups of about eight, making a graph with pictures. Choose one question from those listed below. The children draw on a square of paper to represent their favourite item, then combine their pictures to make a group chart. They can write their own column labels.

- *What pets do you have?*
- *Which is your favourite crisp flavour?*
- *Which is your favourite cartoon programme on television?*
- *How many teeth have you lost?*

Differentiation
Less able: Decide whether to work with the children to help them make the graph.
More able: Challenge the children to make graphs for two of the ideas above.

Plenary & assessment
Choose one of the graphs made and ask questions about it. For example, for a graph about pets, you could ask: *How many dogs/cats/rabbits are there? Which is the most popular animal? Which animal is the least popular? Which are there more/fewer of: dogs or cats? How can you tell? How many more/fewer … than … are there?*

Lesson

Starter
Repeat the Starter from Lesson 1. This time, ask the children to extend the number range from 11 to 20.

Main teaching activities
Whole class: Recap on the idea of picture graphs. Ask the children what each picture in a picture graph stands for. Remind them to stick their pictures onto the graph in neat, tidy lines, so that it is easy to compare how many there are in each column without counting.
Group activity: Choose another group activity idea from Lesson 1 for the children to try. Differentiate the work as before.

Plenary & assessment
Ask similar questions to those used in Lesson 1. Also ask: *How easy is it to tell which column has most/ least pictures without counting? Why is it important to stick the pictures on carefully in straight lines?*

Lesson

Starter
Repeat the Starter from Lesson 1. This time, include four or five numbers from the range of 0–20 each time. The children can respond by putting up their hands, so that you can choose a volunteer to answer.

Main teaching activities
Whole class: Using the A3 copy of 'Pet show', explain that this activity sheet shows a graph about the animals in a pet show. Ask questions such as: *How many dogs were in the show? How many cats? How many more/fewer … than … were there?*
Individual work: Give each child a copy of 'Pet show' to complete independently.

Differentiation
Less able: The children may benefit from completing this activity as a group, with an adult to help with the reading.
More able: Challenge the children to make a graph showing their group's favourite zoo animals.

Plenary & assessment
Review the activity sheet together, working through the questions. Ask further questions such as: *How many more rabbits than mice were there? Which animal was there the biggest number of?* Ask more able children: *How many animals were there altogether? How did you work that out?*

Lessons   overview

Learning objectives
Starter
- Describe and extend number sequences: **count in tens from and back to zero**.

Main teaching activities
- Understand and use the vocabulary related to time.
- Know the days of the week and the seasons of the year.

Vocabulary
time, *days of the week:* Monday, Tuesday…, *seasons:* spring, summer, autumn, winter, day, week, month, year, weekend, quick, quicker, quickest, quickly, fast, faster, fastest, slow, slower, slowest, slowly, takes longer, takes less time

You will need:

Equipment
A one-minute sand timer for each group of four children; a box of cubes for each group; a sheet of dotted paper for each child; paper and pencils.

Lesson

Starter
Ask the children to count with you, in tens, from zero to 100 and back again. Keep the pace sharp. Now ask the children to count around the class; but if anyone falters, supply the counting word so that the pace is maintained. Repeat this several times.

Main teaching activities
Whole class: Say the days of the week together. Ask: *Which days do you come to school? Which days are the weekend? What day is it today? What day was it yesterday? What day will it be tomorrow?*

Show the children a one-minute timer. Explain that the time the sand takes to run through is about a minute. Say: *While the sand is running through the timer, how many times do you think you can write your first name? Write your estimate. Now let's find out! When I turn the sand timer over, start writing.* Call *Stop* when the sand has run through. Ask for some estimates and how many times the name was written. Remind the children that this was done in one minute. Ask: *Were you faster or slower than you estimated?*

Group work: Provide each group of about four children with a sand timer. Encourage the children to think of actions that they can count in one minute. For example, build a tower with cubes, draw squares, touch my toes. They should record their results in the form:

I can	My estimate	My count
build a tower with cubes		

Differentiation
Less able: Work with this group, emphasising each time that the sand timer is measuring one minute.
More able: Challenge the children to suggest other actions that they can do several times in one minute. They can check their estimates by timing.

Plenary & assessment
Ask various children about the actions they tried. Ask: *How many did you estimate? How much was your count? Did you make a good estimate?*

Invite the children to shut their eyes when you say *Shut,* and to keep them shut for what they estimate to be a minute while you time a minute with a sand timer. Ask: *How did you do? Was that easy? Was it difficult? Why?*

Lesson ⑤

Starter

Repeat the Starter from Lesson 4. This time, the children can make a Mexican wave as they say the count individually. When it is an individual's turn to say the next number, he or she raises and then lowers both hands. If the pace of the count is sharp, this will produce a wave effect. Then repeat, starting the count at any ten up to 100; count back to zero; then count up to the starting number.

Main teaching activities

Whole class: Review the days of the week and seasons of the year. Ask the children to name the seasons in order, and to suggest a feature of each season (such as: *We go to the seaside in the summer*).

Ask the children to prepare for a PE lesson. In the hall, ask the children to do various things for one minute, two minutes and three minutes. For example:

- *How many giant steps can you take in two minutes?*
- *How many times can you touch your toes in one minute?*
- *Line up in a row. Take it steady. How many of you can run up to this mat, then do a somersault, in three minutes?*

Differentiation

Encourage all the children to take part in the activities.
Less able: Decide whether to limit the counting time to one minute.
More able: Decide whether to extend the counting time to four minutes.

Plenary & assessment

Ask questions such as: *How close was your estimate to your count? Who thinks they can estimate a minute well? Let's try!* Ask the children to shut their eyes when you say *Shut* and keep them shut for what they estimate to be a minute, while you time them using the one-minute sand timer.

Name	Date

Pet show

This chart shows how many pets were at the pet show.

Write the answers to the questions below.

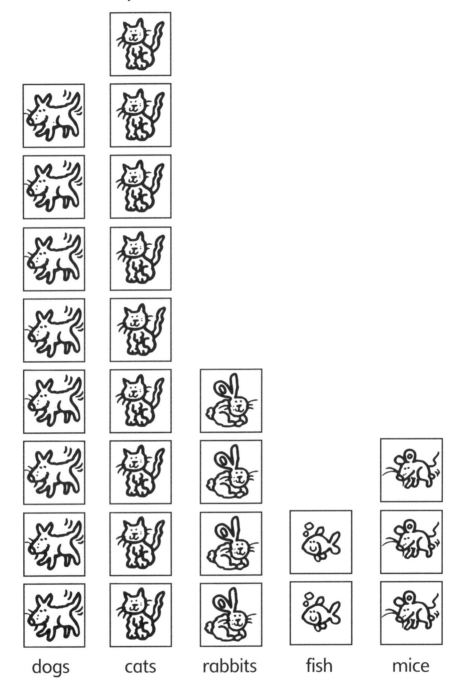

| dogs | cats | rabbits | fish | mice |

1. How many cats were there?

2. How many more dogs than rabbits were there?

3. How many fewer fish than mice were there?

Length, weight and capacity

Children work with length, weight and capacity to make estimates and check using uniform non-standard units. They decide which non-standard units they would choose for a particular measurement.

LEARNING OBJECTIVES

		Topics	Starter	Main teaching activities
Lesson	1	Measures	● Know by heart addition doubles of all numbers to at least 5 (e.g. 4 + 4).	● Understand and use the vocabulary related to length, mass and capacity. ● **Suggest suitable standard or uniform non-standard units and measuring equipment to estimate, then measure, a length, mass or capacity**, recording estimates and measurements as 'about 3 beakers full' or 'about as heavy as 20 cubes'.
Lesson	2	Measures	As for Lesson 1.	As for Lesson 1.
Lesson	3	Measures	As for Lesson 1.	As for Lesson 1.
Lesson	4	Measures	Read the time to the hour or half hour on analogue clocks.	As for Lesson 1.
Lesson	5	Measures	As for Lesson 4.	As for Lesson 1.

Lessons overview

Preparation
Make up some parcels of different sizes and weights. Make an A3-sized copy of 'Match the units' and pin it to the flip chart.

Learning objectives
Starter
● Know by heart addition doubles of all numbers to at least 5 (e.g. 4 + 4).
● Read the time to the hour or half hour on analogue clocks.
Main teaching activities
● Understand and use the vocabulary related to length, mass and capacity.
● **Suggest suitable standard or uniform non-standard units and measuring equipment to estimate, then measure, a length, mass or capacity**, recording estimates and measurements as 'about 3 beakers full' or 'about as heavy as 20 cubes'.

Vocabulary
measure, size, compare, guess, estimate, enough, not enough, too much, too little, too many, too few, nearly, roughly, close to, about the same as, just over, just under, length, width, metre, ruler, metre stick, balance, scales, weight, full, half full, empty, holds, container

You will need:
Photocopiable pages
'How long?' (see page 148) and 'Match the units' (see page 149) for each child and an A3 copy of 'Match the units'.

CD pages
A set of teaching cards of 'Double facts to 5 + 5', 'Measures vocabulary' copied onto card for each pair of children, 'Number fan', 'Arrow cards' and a 'Clock face' for each child (see General Resources).

Equipment
An individual whiteboard and pen for each child; a pair of scissors for each pair of children; parcels and reading books of different sizes and weights; cubes; balances; containers for filling and pouring; scoops and spoons; sand or water; a teaching clock; string; about 10 straws; flip chart or board.

Lesson ①

Starter

Explain to the children that you will be holding up cards with double facts on. Ask them to hold up their fingers to show you the answer when you say: *Show me.* Use the 'Double facts to 5 + 5' cards. Keep the pace sharp.

Main teaching activities

Whole class: Explain to the class that this week, they will be working with length, mass and capacity. Today they will be making estimates and measures using non-standard units. Hold up a book in one hand and a cube in the other. Ask: *How many cubes do you think I will need to fit across this book?* On the board, write some of the estimates. Now invite a child to make a tower of cubes that will fit across the book. Ask: *How many cubes did we need?* Talk about any space left, using the words *nearly* and *not enough*. Put one more cube onto the tower and show the children the fit. Talk about how this is *too many, just over…* On the flip chart, write a sentence about what has just been done. For example: *Just over/under 15 cubes fitted across the book.*

Group work: Provide each pair of children with a copy of the 'Measures vocabulary' sheet on card, about 15 cubes, and two different-sized reading books. Ask them to cut out the vocabulary cards. Read through the words with all of the children. Ask them to estimate, and then measure, the length and width of the books using the cubes. They should write down their estimate and measure, then use the vocabulary cards to help them write a sentence about how accurate their measure was.

Differentiation

Less able: Ask an adult to work with the children as a group. The children can carry out the estimation and measuring in pairs. Then they can discuss the accuracy of the measure with the adult, who should encourage the children to use the vocabulary cards to help them record a sentence about it.

More able: Challenge the children to choose a much taller and wider book to estimate, measure and write a sentence about.

Plenary & assessment

Invite some pairs of children to report back on what they found. Discuss how close their estimate was. Discuss how closely they measured with the cubes. Ask questions such as: *Did the cubes fit across the book? Was the fit just under, just over or about the same as the width of the book?*

too much | just over | roughly

about the same as | measure | about the same as

just under

width

Lesson

Starter

Repeat the Starter from Lesson 1. This time, ask the children to use arrow cards to show the answer when you say: *Show me.*

Main teaching activities

Whole class: Explain to the children that today they will be making estimates and measures of mass. Pass one of the parcels that you have made around the class for the children to weigh in their hands and pass on quickly. Then ask: *How many cubes do you think will balance the parcel?* Write some suggestions on the flip chart. Invite a child to balance the parcel with some cubes. Ask the children to describe how it was balanced. For example, they might say:

- 'We used ten cubes to balance the parcel.'
- 'Ten cubes nearly balanced the parcel. Eleven cubes was too much.'
- 'The parcel needed nearly/close to ten cubes to balance it.'
- 'It weighed just over ten cubes.'
- 'It weighed just under 11 cubes.'

Write some of these sentences on the flip chart. Read out the appropriate vocabulary from the 'Measures vocabulary' sheet for the children to hear.

Group work: Ask the children to work in groups of about four. Each group should choose four different reading books to estimate and then balance with cubes. They should make a group record of their estimate and balance. They can use the measures vocabulary cards to help them write some sentences about their estimates and measures.

Differentiation

Less able: Ask an adult to work with the children. The children can carry out the estimation and measuring in groups of four. Then they can discuss the accuracy of the measure with the adult, who can use the vocabulary cards to help them record a sentence about it.

More able: Challenge the children to choose a book which they estimate to be heavier than the other book they have used. Then they should weigh it and write a sentence about how its weight compares with that of the first book.

Plenary & assessment

Invite some pairs of children to report back on what they have found. Discuss how close their estimates were, and how accurately they were able to measure with the cubes. Ask questions such as: *How many cubes did you need to balance the parcel? So the parcel weighed just over how many cubes? And it weighed just under how many cubes?*

Lesson ③

Starter

Repeat the Starter from Lesson 1. This time, ask the children to write their responses on their individual whiteboards and hold them up when you say: *Show me*.

Main teaching activities

Whole class: Explain that today the children will be estimating and measuring capacity (how much something holds). Show the children a container (such as a jug) and ask them to estimate how many cups of water it will hold. Write some of their estimates on the board. Ask a child to check by filling the container and counting the number of cupfuls used. Ask: *Did the container hold all of the last cup of water? Is it full to the top? How many cups of water did it hold?* Encourage the children to talk about 'just over four cups', 'nearly five cups' and so on.

Group work: Ask the children to work in groups of four. Each group chooses four different containers. They estimate the capacity of each, then measure by filling with scoops or spoonfuls of water. They make a group record of their estimates and measures. They can use the measures vocabulary cards to help them write some sentences about their estimates and measures.

Differentiation

Less able: Ask an adult to work with the children. The children can carry out the estimation and measuring in groups of four. Then they can discuss the accuracy of the measure with the adult, who can use the vocabulary cards to help them record a sentence about it.

More able: Challenge the children to find a container that holds more than any of those they have used so far in this lesson.

Plenary & assessment

Invite some pairs of children to report back on what they have found. Discuss how close their estimates were, and how accurately they could measure with the scoops or spoonfuls of water. Ask questions such as: *How many scoops of water did you need to fill the container? So the jug contained just over how many scoops of water? And it contained just under how many scoops of water?*

Lesson ④

Starter

Show the children the teaching clock. Explain that you will set it to various o'clock and half past times. Ask questions such as: *What time does the clock show? What time will it be in half an hour/in one hour? What time was it half an hour/an hour/an hour and a half/two hours ago?*

Main teaching activities

Whole class: Draw a straight line on the board. Ask the children to look carefully at this line and estimate how long it is in straws. Ask them how they could measure this line. Children may suggest putting straws against the line until they have gone along its length, then counting the straws.

Explain that another way to do this would be to use a line of straws on the table. Ask a child to make this. Now show the children how to measure the line on the board with a piece of string, then measure the string against the straws. Emphasise that you are matching the end of the string to the end of the line of straws. Compare the measured length with the children's estimates.

Draw a curved line on the board. Ask the children to estimate how long this is. Then invite two children to take some string and match the string along the line. They can cut off the extra string if this helps. Now ask them to match the length of string against the line of straws. Can they say how long the line on the board was? Compare the measure with the children's estimates.

Group work: Ask the children to work in pairs. Each pair will need a long piece of string, scissors, cubes and a copy of the 'How long?' activity sheet. They should estimate and measure the length of each line on the sheet, using string and matching it to a line of cubes, and record their estimates and measures on the sheet.

Differentiation

Less able: Ask an adult to work with this group. The children may need help with matching the string along the line, then matching the length cut off to cubes.

More able: Challenge the children to draw lines for each other and to use this method of measuring, estimating first.

Plenary & assessment

Discuss how well the children managed this method of measuring. Invite them to talk about what was easy about it, and what they found more difficult. Ask: *Was your measure about the same as ... cubes? Was your estimate just over what you measured? Was it just under?*

Lesson 5

Starter

Repeat the Starter from Lesson 4. This time, ask the children to show you the times that you say on their individual clock faces.

Main teaching activities

Whole class: Ask the children to suggest things in the classroom that could be measured for length (or width, or height) using rulers, garden canes, matchsticks, metre sticks. Now repeat this for weighing (or balancing) with cubes, marbles, cups of sand. Repeat this for finding capacity with egg cups, scoops, litre jugs of water.

Individual work: Ask the children to complete the 'Match the units' activity sheet, which asks them to choose the most appropriate units to measure the length, weight and capacity of various objects.

Differentiation

Less able: Ask an adult to work with these children, encouraging them to explain their decisions.

More able: Encourage the children to suggest something at home that could be measured using each of the units on the sheet.

Plenary & assessment

Review the activity sheet, using an A3 copy. Ask questions such as: *Why did you choose that unit? Who chose something else? Which unit would be better for measuring that? Why?*

Name	Date

How long?

You will need scissors, some string and some cubes.

Put some string along the first line drawn below.

Cut off the string.

Now measure the string with the cubes.

Write how many cubes you used in the box next to the line.

Measure the other lines in the same way.

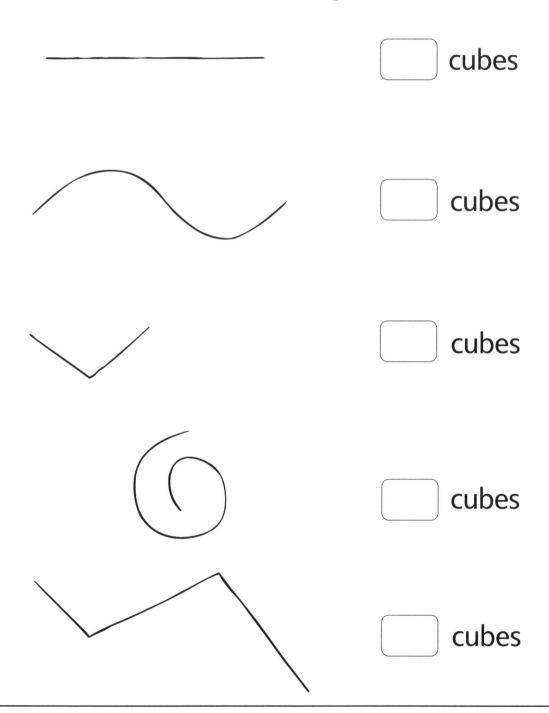

cubes

cubes

cubes

cubes

cubes

Name   Date

Match the units

Which units would you use to measure these things?

Draw a line to match each thing to the right unit.

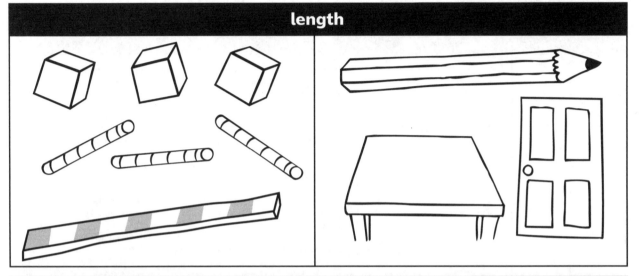

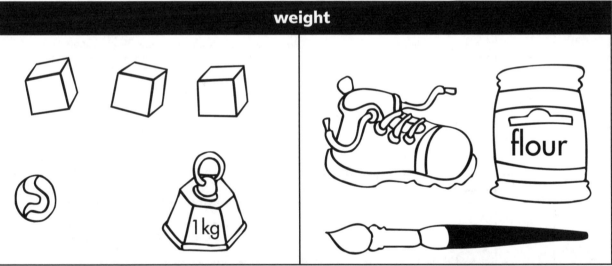

EVERY DAY: Practise and develop oral and mental skills (e.g. counting, mental strategies, rapid recall of + and – facts)

- Know the number names and recite them in order to at least 20.
- **Count reliably at least 20 objects**.
- Describe and extend number sequences: **count on in ones from any number**.
- Describe and extend number sequences: count in steps of 5 from zero to 20 or more, then back again.
- Order numbers to at least 20, and position them on a number track.
- Know by heart addition facts for all pairs of numbers with a total up to at least 5, and the corresponding subtraction facts.
- Know by heart addition doubles of all numbers to at least 5 (e.g. 4+4).
- **Know by heart all pairs of numbers with a total of 10** (e.g. 3 + 7).

Units	Days	Topics	Objectives
1	3	Counting, properties of numbers and number sequences	Describe and extend number sequences: count in steps of 5 from zero to 20 or more, then back again; begin to recognise odd and even numbers to 20 as 'every other number'.
2–4	15	Place value and ordering	**Within the range 0 to 30, say the number that is 1 or 10 more or less than any given number.** Compare two familiar numbers, say which is more or less, and give a number which lies between them.
		Understanding addition and subtraction	**Understand the operation of addition and subtraction (as 'takeaway', 'difference',** and 'how many mroe to make '), **and use the related vocabulary**. Begin to use the +, – and = signs to record mental calculations in a number sentence, and to recognise the use of symbols to stand for an unknown number.
		Mental calculation strategies (+ and –)	Use known number facts and place value to add or subtract a pair of numbers mentally within the range 0 to at least 10, then to 0 to at least 20.
		Problems involving 'real life', money or measures	**Use mental strategies to solve simple problems** set in 'real life', money or measurement contexts, **using counting, addition, subtraction, doubling and halving, explaining methods and reasoning orally**. Recognise coins of different values. Find totals and change from up to 20p. Work out how to pay an exact sum using smaller coins.
		Making decisions	Choose and use appropriate number operations and mental strategies to solve problems.
5–6	8	Measures	Understand and use the vocabulary related to length, mass and capacity. **Compare two lengths, masses or capacities by direct comparison**; extend to more than two. Measure using uniform non-standard units (e.g. straws, wooden cubes, plastic weights, yogurt pots), or standard units (e.g. metre sticks, litre jugs).
		Shape and space	Fold shapes in half, then make them into symmetrical patterns. Begin to relate solid shapes to pictures of them. Use everyday language to describe position, direction and movement. Talk about things that turn. Make whole turns and half turns. Use one or more shapes to make, describe and continue repeating patterns…
		Reasoning about numbers or shapes	Investigate a general statement about familiar numbers or shapes by finding examples that satisfy it.

EVERY DAY: Practise and develop oral and mental skills (e.g. counting, mental strategies, rapid recall of + and – facts)

- **Count reliably at least 20 objects.**
- **Understand the operation of subtraction (as 'difference') and use the related vocabulary.**
- Describe and extend number sequences: begin to count on in steps of 3 from zero.
- **Read and write numerals from 0 to at least 20.**
- **Order numbers to at least 20**, and position them on a number track.
- **Know by heart all pairs of numbers with a total of 10** (e.g. 3 + 7).
- Know by heart addition doubles of all numbers to at least 5 (e.g. 4 + 4).
- Begin to know addition facts for all pairs of numbers with a total up to at least 10, and the corresponding subtraction facts.

Units	Days	Topics	Objectives
8	5	Counting, properties of numbers and number sequences	Describe and extend number sequences: begin to count on in steps of 3 from zero.
		Reasoning about numbers or shapes	Investigate a general statement about familiar numbers or shapes by finding examples that satisfy it. Explain methods and reasoning orally
9–11	15	Place value and ordering	**Order numbers to at least 20**, and position them on a number track.
		Understanding addition and subtraction	Begin to recognise that more than two numbers can be added together.
		Mental calculation strategies (+ and –)	Add 9 to single-digit numbers by adding 10 then subtracting 1. Begin to bridge through 10, and later 20, when adding a single-digit number. Use known number facts and place value to add or subtract a pair of numbers mentally within the range of 0 to at least 10, then 0 to at least 20.
		Problems involving 'real life', money or measures	**Use mental strategies to solve simple problems** set in 'real life', money or measurement contexts, **using counting, addition, subtraction, doubling and halving, explaining methods and reasoning orally.**
		Making decisions	Choose and use appropriate number operations and mental strategies to solve problems.
12–13	10	Measures	**Suggest suitable standard or uniform non-standard units and measuring equipment to estimate, then measure, a length, mass or capacity**, recording estimates and measurements as 'about 3 beakers full' or 'about as heavy as 20 cubes'. Read the time to the hour or half hour on analogue clocks.
		Organising and using data	Solve a given problem by sorting, classifying and organising information in simple ways, such as: using objects or pictures; in a list or simple table. Discuss and explain results.
Total	56		

Counting in twos and fives

Children begin by counting in twos from zero to 20 and back again, then from 1. They recognise odd and even numbers to about 20. They count in fives from zero to 20 and back again, and complete sequences of counting in fives.

LEARNING OBJECTIVES

	Topics	Starter	Main teaching activities
Lesson 1	Counting, properties of numbers and number sequences	● **Count reliably at least 20 objects.**	● Describe and extend number sequences: count on in twos from zero, then one; begin to recognise odd or even numbers to about 20 as 'every other number'.
Lesson 2	Counting, properties of numbers and number sequences	As for Lesson 1.	As for Lesson 1.
Lesson 3	Counting, properties of numbers and number sequences	As for Lesson 1.	● Describe and extend number sequences: count in steps of 5 from zero to 20 or more, then back again.

Lessons   overview

Preparation
Enlarge 'Counting picture' to A3 size and pin it to the flip chart.

Learning objectives
Starter
● **Count reliably at least 20 objects.**
Main teaching activities
● Describe and extend number sequences: count on in twos from zero, then one; begin to recognise odd or even numbers to about 20 as 'every other number'.

Vocabulary
number, zero, one, two, three… to twenty and beyond, count, count (up) to, count back (from, to), count in twos, odd, even, how many more to make …?, how many more is … than …?

You will need:
Photocopiable pages
'Odd and even numbers' (see page 155) for each child.

CD pages
'Odd and even numbers', less able and more able versions (see Summer term, Unit 1); 'Counting picture' enlarged to A3 and a copy for each child; 'Numeral cards 0–9' and 'Numeral cards 10–20' for each pair; 'Numeral cards 21–30' for each more able pair (see General Resources).

Equipment
Flip chart or board; pencils.

Lesson

Starter

Give each child a copy of the 'Counting picture'. Ask the children to count pictures by pointing to and touching them. Say: *How many birds can you count? How many squirrels are there? Are there more birds or more squirrels? How many more? How many flowers can you count? How many stepping stones are there? How many more/fewer … are there than …?* Remind the children that as they count, they must remember which items they have already counted and which are still to be counted.

Main teaching activities

Whole class: Ask the children to count together in twos from zero to at least 20, then back again. Keep the pace sharp. Repeat the count. Then ask them to count quite quickly around the class, with each child raising both hands as they say their number, then bringing them down again. This will produce a Mexican wave effect. Repeat all of this, this time counting from 1.

Ask: *Which are the even numbers? Which are the odd numbers?* Choose two children to write even and odd numbers on the flip chart; divide the class into halves to say even and odd numbers. Now ask the children to count slowly from zero (even) or 1 (odd), with one child writing each number pattern on the flip chart. Continue to 20 (even) or 21 (odd). Discuss how odd/even numbers are 'every other number' starting with 1/zero. Remind the children that if a number has 0, 2, 4, 6, or 8 in its units it is even, and if it has 1, 3, 5, 7 or 9 in its units it is odd.

Group work: Ask the children to work in pairs with the numeral cards 0–20. They shuffle the cards, then take turns to take a card from the pile, read it aloud and place it in an 'odd' or 'even' pile. When they have sorted all the cards, ask them to place each set of cards in order.

Differentiation

Less able: The number range can be limited to 10 initially.
More able: The number range can be extended to 30.

Plenary & assessment

Remove the numbers from the flip chart. Write the headings 'Odd' and 'Even'. Explain that you will say a number and the children should say odd or even together, quietly; then you will write the number in the correct column. Begin with the numbers 0–10, but not in order; extend the range to 20 and then, if appropriate, to 30. Ask: *How can you tell that a number is even/odd? Tell me some odd numbers between 2 and 8… some even numbers between 9 and 15…*

Lesson

Starter

Repeat the Starter from Lesson 1, but use the enlarged 'Counting picture'. Ask the children to look carefully at it. They can count by pointing, but not by touching.

Main teaching activities

Whole class: Ask the children to tell you some odd and even numbers. Repeat the odd and even numbers counting activity from Lesson 1.
Individual work: Let the children complete the activity sheet 'Odd and even numbers' individually.

Differentiation

Less able: Provide the version of 'Odd and even numbers' with numbers to 20.
More able: Provide the version with numbers to 31.

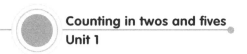

Plenary & assessment

Write the headings 'Odd' and 'Even' on the flip chart. Working around the class, ask each child to say an odd or even number. Ask: *How do you know that is an odd/even number? What will the next odd/even number be?*

Lesson overview

Preparation

Make an A3 copy of 'Counting in 5s' and pin it to the flip chart.

Learning objectives

Starter
- **Count reliably at least 20 objects.**

Main teaching activities
- Describe and extend number sequences: count in steps of 5 from zero to 20 or more, then back again.

Vocabulary

number, zero, one, two, three… twenty and beyond, count, count (up) to, count back (from, to), how many more to make …?, how many more is … than … ?

You will need:

Photocopiable pages
'Counting in 5s' (see page 156) for each child and an A3 copy.

Equipment
A picture from a 'Big Book' with lots of things for counting; flip chart or board; pencils.

Lesson

Starter

Repeat the Starter from Lesson 2, this time using a picture from a Big Book. Remind the children to point and count, and to remember which items they have counted and which are still to be counted.

Main teaching activities

Whole class: Ask the children to count from 0 to 20 in fives, then back again. Repeat this several times, keeping the pace sharp. Now ask the children to count around the class in fives, making a Mexican wave as in Lesson 1.

Individual work: Ask the children to complete the activity sheet 'Counting in 5s' individually.

Differentiation

Less able: The children may find it helpful to count along a number line.
More able: Challenge the children to complete the sheet quickly, then work with a partner to write the numbers that continue the last counting pattern from 30 to 50.

Plenary & assessment

Review the activity sheet, using an A3 enlargement with individual children taking turns to write in the answers. Ask: *How can you tell whether a number is in the count of fives?* (It has either 5 or 0 in its units.) *Which numbers in the count of fives are odd? Which numbers are even? How do you know that?*

Name	Date

Odd and even numbers

Look at these odd and even number patterns.

Write in the missing numbers.

Name	Date

Counting in 5s

Look at these counting in 5s patterns.

Write in the missing numbers.

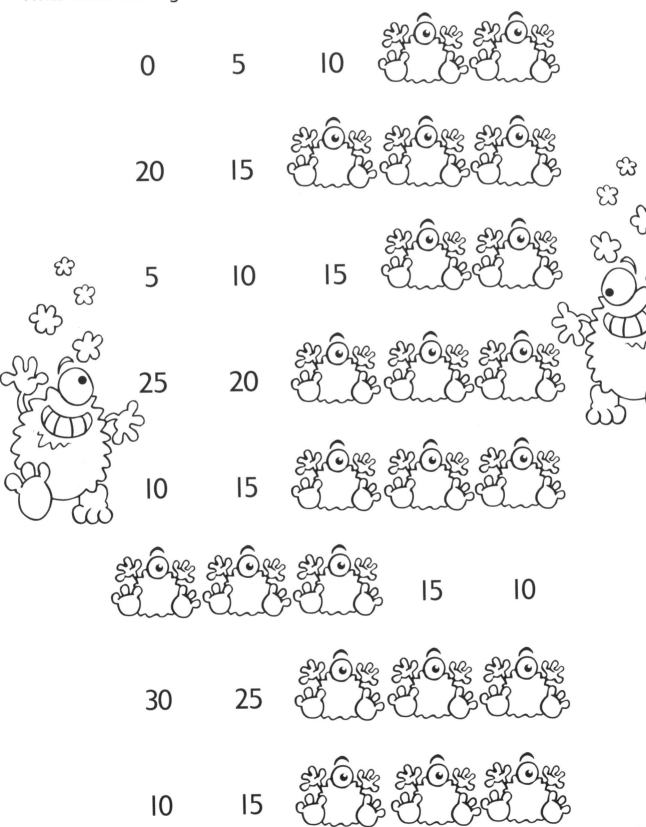

0　　5　　10

20　　15

5　　10　　15

25　　20

10　　15

15　　10

30　　25

10　　15

Summer term

Unit 2

Place value and ordering

Children count from zero to 30 and back again. They identify numbers that are 1 or 10 more or less than a given number. They complete missing numbers in sequences of numbers chosen from up to 20, then extended to 30. They answer word problems about sequences of numbers.

LEARNING OBJECTIVES

	Topics	Starter	Main teaching activities
Lesson 1	Place value and ordering	● Describe and extend number sequences: count in steps of 5 from zero to 20 or more, then back again.	● **Within the range 0 to 30, say the number that is 1 or 10 more or less than any given number.**
Lesson 2	Place value and ordering	As for Lesson 1.	As for Lesson 1.
Lesson 3	Place value and ordering	● **Know by heart all pairs of numbers with a total of 10** (e.g. 3 + 7).	● Compare two familiar numbers, say which is more or less, and give a number which lies between them.
Lesson 4	Place value and ordering	As for Lesson 3.	As for Lesson 3.
Lesson 5	Place value and ordering	As for Lesson 3.	As for Lesson 3.

Lessons overview

Learning objectives

Starter
● Describe and extend number sequences: count in steps of 5 from zero to 20 or more, then back again.

Main teaching activities
● **Within the range 0 to 30, say the number that is 1 or 10 more or less than any given number.**

Vocabulary
one more, ten more, one less, ten less, compare, order, how many more to make …?, how many more is … than …?, how much more is …?

You will need:

Photocopiable pages
'More and less' (see page 162) for each child.

CD pages
'More and less', less able and more able versions (see Summer term, Unit 2); 'Numeral cards 0–9', 'Numeral cards 10–20' and 'Numeral cards 21–30' for each child (see General Resources).

Lesson

Starter

Ask the children to count with you from zero to 20 or more, in fives, and back to zero. Keep the pace of the count sharp. Repeat this, counting around the class. Ask, for example: *If Jane says 10, what will Neeta say? If I count back three fives from 20, what number will I say?*

Main teaching activities

Whole class: Ask the children to count with you from zero to 30 and back again. Repeat this, keeping the pace sharp. Now ask:

- *What is one more than 6?*
- *What is one less than 8?*
- *How did you work that out?*

Repeat this for various numbers up to 10, then to 20, then to 30. Encourage the children to respond to the questions quickly.

Group work: Ask the children to work in pairs with numeral cards to 30. Explain that you would like them to take turns to take the top card from the shuffled pack and to say and write the one more and one less number. They can record this on paper.

is 1 less than		is 1 more than
14	15	16
20	21	22

Differentiation

Less able: Decide whether to limit the number range to 15 or 20, then gradually extend the range over time.

More able: If the children are confident with one more and one less, ask them to repeat the activity for two more and two less.

Plenary & assessment

Ask some children from the less able group to challenge the class with some of their numbers: they say the middle number for others to say the numbers one more and one less. Repeat this for the average group. Ask some more able children to challenge the class with some two more and two less numbers. Ask:

- *What is one more than and one less than 25? How did you know that?*
- *Tell me another set of three numbers like these. How did you work that out?*

Lesson

Starter

Repeat the Starter from Lesson 1. This time extend the count to (and back from) 30 for all, and to (and back from) 40 for the more able children.

Main teaching activities
Whole class: Repeat the activity from Lesson 1, this time for ten more and ten less, using the number range to 30.
Individual work: Ask the children to complete the activity sheet 'More and less', which involves finding numbers ten more and ten less as well as one more and one less.

Differentiation
Less able: Give the children the version of 'More and less' that shows numbers to 15.
More able: Give the children the version that shows numbers to 39.

Plenary & assessment
Ask children from each ability group to challenge the class with some of their number problems, as in Lesson 1. All the groups should say both one more/less and ten more/less problems. Ask:
Is there a quick way to work out ten more and ten less than a number?

Lessons   overview

Preparation
Enlarge 'Blank number tracks' to A3 size and pin to the board. Make a teaching set of enlarged 'Complements of 10' cards.

Learning objectives
Starter
● **Know by heart all pairs of numbers with a total of 10** (e.g. 3 + 7).
Main teaching activities
● Compare two familiar numbers, say which is more or less, and give a number which lies between them.

Vocabulary
compare, order, size, first

You will need:
Photocopiable pages
'Comparing and ordering' (see page 163) for each child.

CD pages
'Comparing and ordering', less able and more able versions (see Summer term, Unit 2); a teaching set of enlarged 'Complements of 10' cards, an A3 copy of 'Blank number lines', 'Numeral cards 0–9', 'Numeral cards 10–20' and 'Numeral cards 21–30' for each pair of children, a 'Number fan' for each child (see General Resources).

Equipment
An individual whiteboard and pen for each child; flip chart or board; paper and pencils.

Lesson ③

Starter

Explain to the children that you will show them some number sentences that all have to do with the number ten. Use a teaching set of 'Complements of 10' cards. Ask the children to hold up their hands when they have worked out each answer. Encourage them to use rapid recall of these number facts. Less able children may need to use their fingers to help them count on to ten and see how many they have counted.

Main teaching activities

Whole class: Write 15 and 20 on the flip chart, leaving a space between them. Say: *Tell me a number that is between 15 and 20. What other numbers go between 15 and 20?* Repeat this for other pairs of numbers, using numbers from 0 to about 20, then extend to 30. Ask, for each pair of numbers: *How did you work out which numbers could fit?*

Group work: Ask the children to work in pairs with numeral cards 0–20. The children shuffle the cards, then take turns to take the top two cards. If these are consecutive numbers, they put them back and shuffle again. If not, they write down the pair of numbers and a number that goes between them. If the larger number has been picked up first, they put the smaller number first before choosing a number to fit between the two numbers. They record their number sets on paper.

Differentiation

Less able: Decide whether to limit the number range to 10 or 15, then increase the range over time.
More able: The children can work with numeral cards 0–30. Ask them to write two intermediate numbers for each pair of numbers chosen, where this is possible. (For example, only one number can go between 23 and 25.)

Plenary & assessment

Invite children from each ability group to say pairs of numbers, challenging the other children to suggest numbers that fit in between. Start with some less able children, then extend the number range to suit the average and then the more able children. Ask:
- *What numbers could fit between … and …? How do you know this? How did you work it out?*
- *Tell me all the numbers that will fit between 13 and 16… between 18 and 23…*

Lesson ④

Starter

Repeat the Starter from Lesson 3, this time asking the children to hold up the answer using their number fans when you say: *Show me.*

Main teaching activities

Whole class: Pin up the A3 copy of the 'Blank number lines' resource sheet. Write on the first number line the numbers 12, 13, 14, _, _, _, _,19, 20. Ask the children to suggest what the missing numbers are. Repeat this for other number sequences within the range 0–30.
Group work: Ask the children to work in pairs, using numeral cards 0–30. They can choose any two cards and write the lower number, the higher number and the numbers in between. Suggest to them that they choose pairs of numbers that are not too far apart.

Differentiation

Less able: Limit the number range to 20.
More able: Challenge the children to use pairs of numbers that are further apart, such as 13 and 27.

Plenary & assessment

Invite some children from each ability group to give examples of pairs of numbers and challenge the other children to say what numbers are between them. Write the examples on the flip chart. Ask: *How do you know these numbers fit between … and …?*

Lesson 5

Starter

Repeat the Starter from Lesson 3, this time asking the children to write the answer on their whiteboards and hold them up when you say: *Show me.* Encourage the children to use rapid recall, rather than working out each number fact. Keep the pace sharp.

Main teaching activities

Whole class: Explain to the children that you will ask them some questions. To answer these, they will need to compare and order numbers. Say, for example:

- *The time is between 3 and 8 o'clock. What time could it be?*
- *There are between 10 and 18 pencils in the pot. How many could there be?*
- *The children ate between 14 and 21 sweets. How many could they have eaten?*

Ask more questions like these, each time encouraging the children to give the complete range of possible answers. Check that they are comfortable with the idea of a range of possible answers that they could choose, rather than just one.

Individual work: Give the children the 'Comparing and ordering' activity sheet to complete individually. This presents some word problems that involve comparing and ordering numbers within the range 0–30.

Differentiation

Less able: Provide the version of 'Comparing and ordering' that uses the number range 0–20.
More able: Provide the version that uses the number range 10–40.

Plenary & assessment

Review some of the word problems from each version of the activity sheet, again encouraging the children to provide the complete range of possible answers. Write the answers given on the flip chart, so that the children can use them as a visual clue to find any numbers that are still missing. Ask:

- *What other numbers would fit?*
- *Have we found all of them? How do you know that?*
- *Make up your own problem like these ones. Tell it to me. What are the answers?*

Name	Date

More and less

Write the number that is
1 less on the left suitcase.

Write the number that is
1 more on the right suitcase.

Write the number that is
10 less on the left suitcase.

Write the number that is
10 more on the right suitcase.

Name   Date

Comparing and ordering

Read these problems.

Write the answers.

1. Which number is **less**, 16 or 19?

2. Which number is **more**, 16 or 20?

3. Write a number between 23 and 27.

4. Write a number in each box so that the three numbers are in order.

1		8
3		9
10		15
26		29

3 ? 9

Children use the +, – and = signs for recording mental calculations. They recognise that symbols such as ☐ or △ stand for an unknown number which they must find through an addition or subtraction calculation. They use facts they already know and their knowledge of place value to carry out addition or subtraction mentally, such as using addition facts to 10 to answer 15 + 2.

LEARNING OBJECTIVES

	Topics	Starter	Main teaching activities
Lesson 1	Understanding addition and subtraction Mental calculation strategies (+ and –)	● Know by heart addition doubles of all numbers to at least 5 (e.g. 4 + 4).	● **Understand the operation of addition, and use the related vocabulary.** ● Begin to use the + and = signs to record mental calculations in a number sentence, and to recognise the use of symbols to stand for an unknown number. ● Use known number facts and place value to add a pair of numbers mentally within the range 0 to at least 10.
Lesson 2	Understanding addition and subtraction Mental calculation strategies (+ and –)	As for Lesson 1.	As for Lesson 1, except: ● Use known number facts and place value to add a pair of numbers mentally within the range 0 to at least 20.
Lesson 3	Understanding addition and subtraction Mental calculation strategies (+ and –)	● Begin to know addition facts for **all pairs of numbers with a total up to at least 10**, and the corresponding subtraction facts.	● **Understand the operation of subtraction (as 'take away', 'difference' and 'how many more to make'), and use the related vocabulary.** ● Begin to use the – and = signs to record mental calculations in a number sentence, and to recognise the use of symbols to stand for an unknown number. ● Use known number facts and place value to subtract a pair of numbers mentally within the range 0 to at least 10.
Lesson 4	Understanding addition and subtraction Mental calculation strategies (+ and –)	As for Lesson 3.	As for Lesson 3, except: ● Use known number facts and place value to subtract a pair of numbers mentally within the range 0 to at least 20.
Lesson 5	Understanding addition and subtraction Mental calculation strategies (+ and –)	As for Lessons 1 and 3.	As for Lesson 4.

Lessons   overview

Preparation
Cut out the sets of cards. Enlarge a copy of 'Addition' to A3 size.

Learning objectives
Starter
- Know by heart addition doubles of all numbers to at least 5 (e.g. 4 + 4).

Main teaching activites
- **Understand the operation of addition, and use the related vocabulary.**
- Begin to use the + and = signs to record mental calculations in a number sentence, and to recognise the use of symbols to stand for an unknown number.
- Use known number facts and place value to add a pair of numbers mentally within the range 0 to at least 10.

Vocabulary
add, more, plus, make, sum, total, altogether, equals, sign, is the same as

You will need:
Photocopiable pages
'Addition' (see page 169) for each child and an A3 copy.

CD pages
A teaching set of enlarged 'Double facts to 5 + 5' cards, a 'Number fan' for each child, a set of 'Addition to 10 trio cards' for each pair (see General Resources).

Equipment
An individual whiteboard and pen for each child; flip chart or board.

Lesson

Starter

Provide each child with a number fan. Explain that you will hold up a card with a double fact written on it. Ask the children to use recall, or a mental method such as counting on in ones, to find the answer. They hold up the answer on their number fans when you say: *Show me.* Hold up 'Double facts to 5 + 5' cards. Ask questions as the children respond, such as: *How did you work that out? Who used a mental number line to count along?*

Main teaching activities
Whole class: Explain that the focus for today's work is addition to at least 10. Write 2 + 4 = on the flip chart and ask: *What is 2 add 4? How did you work that out?* By this stage, most of the children should have rapid recall of this number fact. Now write 2 + △ = 6 and ask: *What do I add to 2 to make 6? How did you work that out?* Some children may point out the link between the two number sentences: if you know 2 + 4 = 6, then the missing number must be 4. Now write □ + 4 = 6 and ask: *What is the missing number? Yes, 2. How do you know that?* The children should make the link between the three number sentences. Repeat this for other number sentences, such as: 3 + 4 = 7; 5 + 6 = 11; 2 + 6 = 8. Remind the children that if there is a missing number in an addition sentence, then one way to find it is to use facts that they already know.

Group work: The children work in pairs with a set of 'Addition to 10 trio cards'. They shuffle the cards and take turns to take the top card. They read out the problem, saying '*What?*' for the unknown number. Their partner says and writes down the complete addition number sentence.

Differentiation
Less able: Work with this group. Read out each problem and ask the children to write the numbers. Ask them to say an addition number sentence that links these numbers, and to say how they worked it out. With children who find this difficult, discuss where the largest numbers will fit.
More able: Challenge the children to complete the cards quickly, and to use rapid recall. Ask them to find some more addition number trios and to write these down as addition number sentences.

Plenary & assessment
Review some of the addition trio problems with the children. Encourage them to respond quickly. Invite some of the more able children to present their own number trios to the other children.

Invite children from each ability group to write the complete number sentences on the board. Ask questions such as: *What strategies could you use to work this out? Where does the largest number fit in the addition sentence? Why is that?*

Lesson

Starter
Repeat the Starter from Lesson 1. This time, ask the children to record their answers on their whiteboards and to hold these up when you say: *Show me.*

Main teaching activities
Whole class: Explain that in today's lesson the children will be using what they know about addition to 10 to help them to work out addition to 20. Say: *What is 10 add 4? How do you know that? If I add 10 to a units number, the units stay the same. So 10 + 4 is 14.* Ask the children some more '10 add …' questions, such as 10 + 7 and 10 + 3. Write the number sentence on the board each time. Point out how the 10 and the single-digit number combine to make the answer. Now ask: *What is 15 + 2? How could you work this out?* Discuss how it is the same as 10 + 5 + 2. Repeat this for other additions (with totals below 20).
Group work: Ask the children to complete the 'Addition' activity sheet individually. This presents addition problems within 10, then within 20 (but not crossing the tens boundary).

Differentiation
Less able: The 'Addition' sheet can be cut in half and just the top half (with addition to 10) given to the children. Encourage the children to use rapid recall when they can.
More able: Challenge the children to use rapid recall. If they finish early, ask them to write some more sentences where a TU number is added to a U number. Their totals should be within 20.

Plenary & assessment
Review the answers to the problems on the 'Addition' sheet, using an A3 enlargement of it. Ask individual children from each ability group to give an answer, and to explain how they worked it out. Encourage the use of rapid recall. Ask: *What is 5 + 3? So what is 15 + 3? How do you know that?* Repeat this for other TU + U questions (with answers that do not cross the 10 or 20 boundary).

Lessons   overview

Learning objectives
Starter
- Begin to know addition facts for **all pairs of numbers with a total up to at least 10**, and the corresponding subtraction facts.

Main teaching activites
- **Understand the operation of subtraction (as 'take away', 'difference'** and 'how many more to make'), **and use the related vocabulary.**
- Begin to use the – and = signs to record mental calculations in a number sentence, and to recognise the use of symbols to stand for an unknown number.
- Use known number facts and place value to add or subtract a pair of numbers mentally within the range 0 to at least 20.

Vocabulary
subtract, take (away), minus, leave, how many fewer is … than …?, how much less is …?, difference between, equals, sign, is the same as

You will need:
Photocopiable pages
'Subtraction' (see page 170) and 'Add and subtract' (see page 171) for each child.

CD pages
A teaching set of 'Add facts to 5', 'Add facts 6 to 10', 'Take away facts to 5' and 'Take away facts 6 to 10' cards, a 'Number fan' for each child, a set of 'Addition to 10 trio cards' for each pair (see General Resources).

Equipment
Flip chart or board.

Lesson ③

Starter

Provide each child with a number fan. Hold up the 'Add facts to 5' and 'Add facts 6 to 10' cards and ask the children to hold up the appropriate fan blade for the answer when you say: *Show me.*

Main teaching activities

Whole class: Explain that today's lesson is about subtraction of numbers to 10. Write on the flip chart 8 – 5 = and ask: *What is 8 subtract 5? Yes, 3. How did you work that out?* Praise particularly those children who used rapid recall methods to work this out. Repeat for other subtractions, all within the range up to 10. Now write on the board: 7 – □ = 2. Ask the children to work out the missing number. Some children may say:

● 'I counted on in ones from 2 to 7 and that made 5.'
● 'I know that 7 subtract 5 is 2.'

Praise those who knew or found the answer. Encourage the others to use a counting on method to find the missing answer. Now write □ – 5 = 2 and ask: *How can you work this out?* Some children will make the link with the previous subtraction sentence. Others may say that they added 5 and 2. Repeat this for other pairs of subtraction sentences with missing numbers.

Group work: Ask the children to work in pairs, using the 'Addition to 10 trio cards'. They shuffle the cards, then take turns to take a card and read the problem. Their partner says and writes the answer and a subtraction sentence for the same trio. For example, for 1 + 8 = □, the child could write '9' and then '9 – 8 = 1'.

Differentiation

Less able: Work with this group. Read out each problem and invite the children to say the answer, and then to think of a subtraction sentence that uses these numbers. If the children find this difficult, ask them where they think the largest number should go in the sentence and why. Encourage the use of rapid recall.

More able: Challenge the children to complete the number sentences quickly. Ask them to make up some subtraction trios for themselves, keeping the largest number to no more than 10.

Plenary & assessment

Review some of the children's subtraction sentences with the class. Encourage them to respond quickly. Invite some of the more able children to present their subtraction trios to the other children. Invite children from each ability group to write the completed number sentences on the flip chart. Ask questions such as:

● *What strategies could you use to work this out?*
● *Where does the largest number fit in the subtraction sentence? Why is that?*

Lesson ④

Starter

Repeat the Starter for Lesson 3, this time using the 'Take away facts to 5' and 'Take away facts 6 to 10' cards.

Main teaching activities

Whole class: Explain that today the children will be subtracting from 'teens' numbers. Ask the children to work out, for example, 7 – 5 and then 17 – 5; ask them to explain their answers. Repeat this for other pairs of subtraction sentences, including 10 – … and 20 – …

Individual work: Provide each child with a copy of the 'Subtraction' activity sheet to complete individually.

Differentiation

Less able: The activity sheet can be folded and only the top half (with a focus on subtraction within 10) given to the children.

More able: The children should be encouraged to complete these examples using rapid recall of subtraction facts.

Plenary & assessment

Review some of the examples from the activity sheet. Ask questions such as: *What is 9 – 4? What is 19 – 4? How do you know this?*

 Lesson **⑤**

Starter

Using a selection of addition and subtraction facts cards from 'Add facts to 5', 'Add facts 6 to 10' and 'Take away facts to 5', repeat the Starter from Lesson 3.

Main teaching activities

Whole class: Write the numbers 4, 5 and 9 on the flip chart. Ask the children to suggest two addition sentences and two subtraction sentences that use these three numbers. They should suggest: 4 + 5 = 9; 5 + 4 = 9; 9 – 4 = 5; 9 – 5 = 4. Now repeat this with the numbers 19, 14 and 5: 14 + 5 = 19; 5 + 14 = 19; 19 – 5 = 14; 19 –14 = 5. Discuss how, if one fact of the three is known, the others can be worked out.

Individual work: Provide each child with a copy of the 'Add and subtract' activity sheet to complete individually.

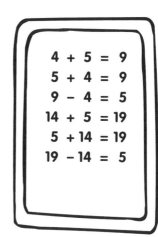

$$4 + 5 = 9$$
$$5 + 4 = 9$$
$$9 - 4 = 5$$
$$14 + 5 = 19$$
$$5 + 14 = 19$$
$$19 - 14 = 5$$

Differentiation

Less able: The activity sheet can be folded and only the top half (with a focus on addition and subtraction within 10) given to the children.

More able: Encourage the children to complete the sheet by using rapid recall of addition and subtraction facts.

Plenary & assessment

Review some of the examples from the activity sheet. Ask the children to provide four different number facts for a trio of numbers such as: 15, 12 and 3. Ask:

- *What are the addition facts?*
- *What are the subtraction facts?*
- *How can you work out a subtraction fact from an addition fact?*

Remind the children that using known facts is another strategy that might help them with addition and subtraction problems.

Name	Date

Addition

Write the answers to these addition sentences.

3 + 5 = ☐

4 + 6 = ☐

3 + 6 = ☐

2 + 7 = ☐

1 + 3 = ☐

2 + 4 = ☐

5 + 3 = ☐

4 + 4 = ☐

6 + 2 = ☐

5 + 5 = ☐

12 + 5 = ☐

18 + 1 = ☐

11 + 6 = ☐

13 + 4 = ☐

16 + 1 = ☐

13 + 6 = ☐

15 + 4 = ☐

14 + 4 = ☐

12 + 7 = ☐

15 + 3 = ☐

| Name | Date |

Subtraction

Write the answers to these subtraction problems.

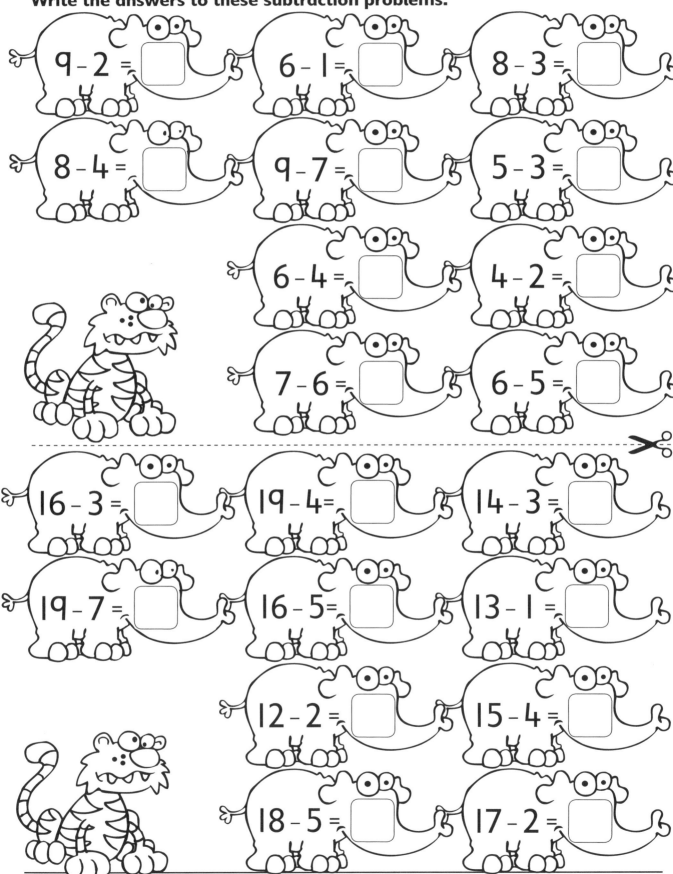

9 − 2 =

6 − 1 =

8 − 3 =

8 − 4 =

9 − 7 =

5 − 3 =

6 − 4 =

4 − 2 =

7 − 6 =

6 − 5 =

16 − 3 =

19 − 4 =

14 − 3 =

19 − 7 =

16 − 5 =

13 − 1 =

12 − 2 =

15 − 4 =

18 − 5 =

17 − 2 =

Name

Date

Add and subtract

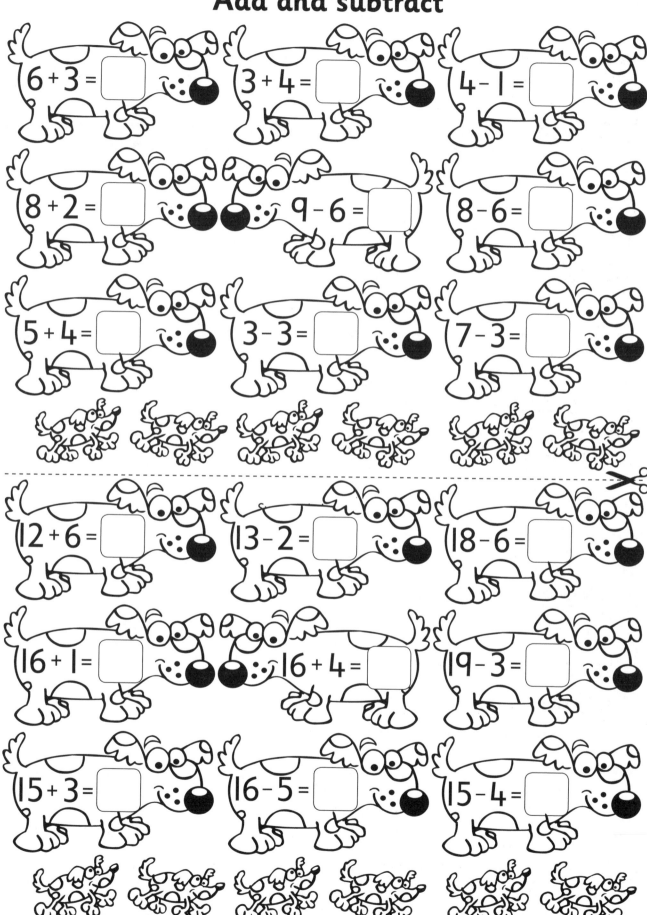

6 + 3 =

3 + 4 =

4 − 1 =

8 + 2 =

9 − 6 =

8 − 6 =

5 + 4 =

3 − 3 =

7 − 3 =

12 + 6 =

13 − 2 =

18 − 6 =

16 + 1 =

16 + 4 =

19 − 3 =

15 + 3 =

16 − 5 =

15 − 4 =

Solving problems and making decisions

Children total costs of two items, to up to 20p then calculate the change from 20p. This is extended to totalling the cost of more than two items. They make choices about the operations and mental strategies to solve problems in different contexts.

LEARNING OBJECTIVES

	Topics	Starter	Main teaching activities
Lesson 1	Problems involving 'real life', money or measures	● **Understand the operation of subtraction (as 'difference') and use the related vocabulary.**	● Recognise coins of different values. ● Find totals and change from up to 20p. ● Work out how to pay an exact sum using smaller coins.
Lesson 2	Problems involving 'real life', money or measures	As for Lesson 1.	As for Lesson 1.
Lesson 3	Problems involving 'real life', money or measures	As for Lesson 1.	As for Lesson 1.
Lesson 4	Problems involving 'real life', money or measures Making decisions	● Begin to know addition facts for all pairs of numbers with a total up to at least 10, and the corresponding subtraction facts.	● **Use mental strategies to solve simple problems** set in 'real life', money or measurement contexts, **using counting, addition, subtraction, doubling and halving, explaining methods and reasoning orally.** ● Choose and use appropriate number operations and mental strategies to solve problems.
Lesson 5	Problems involving 'real life', money or measures Making decisions	As for Lesson 4.	As for Lesson 4.

Lessons   overview

Preparation
Set up a class shop with some items for sale, priced from 1p to 20p. Include a till with some coins, and paper and pencils for writing shopping bills. Decide whether to include price labels to 30p, and some 50p coins, for more able children.

Learning objectives
Starter
● **Understand the operation of subtraction (as 'difference') and use the related vocabulary.**
Main teaching activities
● Recognise coins of different values.
● Find totals and change from up to 20p.
● Work out how to pay an exact sum using smaller coins.

Vocabulary
money, coin, penny, pence, price, cost, buy, sell, spend, spent, pay, change, dear, costs more, cheap, costs less, cheaper, costs the same as, how much…?, how many…?, total

You will need:
CD pages
'Price labels 1p–10p' and 'Price labels 11p–20p', for each pair, 'Price labels 21p–30p' for each pair of more able children and a 'Number fan' for each child (see General Resources).

Equipment
Items for a class shop (such as a grocer's, newsagent's or baker's shop); individual whiteboards and pens; a selection of coins (1p to 20p) for each pair.

Lesson ①

Starter

Explain to the children that you will be asking them some difference questions. Ask them to put up their hands to respond. Ask:

- *What is the difference between 8 and 3? How did you work that out?*
- *What is the difference between 9 and 4? 10 and 7? 12 and 10…?*
- *How many must I add to 7 to make 9?*
- *How many more is 8 than 4?*
- *How many fewer is 6 than 11?*

Continue in this way, keeping the largest number to no more than 12, and using a range of vocabulary.

Main teaching activities

Whole class: You will need some items from the class shop and some coins. Hold up an item that costs 10p and another one that costs 7p, and ask: *How much do these cost altogether? How did you work that out?* Encourage the children to use general facts such as the fact that adding a single digit to 10p does not alter the tens digit (for example, 10p + 7p = 17p).

Now say: *If I give the shopkeeper a 20p coin, how much change will I have? How did you work that out?* Encourage the children to use the 'shopkeeper method' of giving change, by counting on from the price to the coin value given: *17p and 1p is 18p, and 2p more is 20p. 1p + 2p is 3p. So there is 3p change.* Repeat this for another pair, such as 12p and 6p. Here the children should use the fact that if 2 + 6 = 8, then 12 + 6 = 18. Repeat this using other pairs of prices where the total does not cross over 10 or 20. Invite some children to take turns to act as shopkeeper, giving change and explaining how they worked it out.

Group work: Set up a circus of activities for the children to complete over the next three days, in rotation.

1. Ask a group of about four children to work in the class shop. They should take turns to be the customer and the shopkeeper. The customer chooses two items each time; the shopkeeper adds up the total and gives any change that is needed. If the children need further practice in counting out the correct coins for a given cost, the activity can be adapted for that purpose.
2. Ask the children to work in pairs. They will need price labels for 1p to 20p. Ask them to take turns to choose two price labels that add up to a total no more than 20p, and then to work out the change from 20p. The children write an addition sentence to show the total cost, and a subtraction sentence to show the change.
3. Provide each pair of children with price labels for 1p to 20p. Say: *You have 20p to spend. How many different ways can you find to do this?* Ask the children to write number sentences to record. They can combine two or three price labels to make their totals.

Differentiation

Less able: 1. Decide whether to limit the price range to 10p. Encourage the children to use rapid recall or mental methods for adding up and giving change, rather than just counting on or back in ones. **2.** Decide whether to limit the price range to 10p. The children may find it easier to work out the totals in one session, then find the change in another. If this option is taken, the children should use a third session both to find the totals and to work out the change. **3.** Decide whether to limit the total to 10p.

More able: 1. Decide whether to include price labels 21p–30p. The children can give change from 30p. For children who are very confident with money, include some 50p coins and talk about counting in tens to work out the change: *It cost 29p, so 29p and 1p is 30p and 10p more is 40p and 10p more is 50p. 1p + 10p + 10p is 21p, so the change is 21p.* **2.** Decide whether to include price labels 21p–30p. The children should make totals within 30p, such as: '25p + 4p…' **3.** Challenge the children to find ways to combine four prices each time to make a total of 20p.

Plenary & assessment

Repeat the adding up from the whole-class activity, inviting children from each ability group to be the shopkeeper and the customer. For each pair of children, give a maximum total of 10p for the less able, 20p for the average ability group and 30p for the more able. Invite the children who are watching to use their rapid recall and mental strategies to work out the totals and the change, so that they can check what is happening. Ask questions such as:

- *How much are these altogether? How did you add them up?*
- *Who did this another way?*
- *What is the change from …? How did you work that out?*

Lesson ②

Repeat the Starter from Lesson 1, this time encouraging the children to use counting on methods if they do not have rapid recall of the differences. Ask them to show you the answer on their number fans when you say: *Show me.* Review adding up and giving change, as in Lesson 1, during the whole-class activity. This time, include crossing the tens barrier. For example, the children can work out 8p + 6p by partitioning to make 10 and recombining: 8p + 2p + 4p = 10p + 4p = 14p. During the plenary, review adding up across the tens barrier. Ask: *How did you work that out?* Encourage the children to explain how they partitioned and recombined to find the total where they did not have rapid recall of it.

Lesson ③

Repeat the Starter from Lesson 1. This time, ask the children to write the answer on their whiteboards and hold them up when you say: *Show me.* In the whole-class activity, provide more examples of adding up and giving change; this time, include adding three amounts (within 20p). Use the options from Lesson 1 for the group activity. During the plenary, encourage the children to demonstrate the range of mental methods that can be used to work out totals and change: ask for totals that include crossing the tens boundary; adding 10p and a single digit; and adding a 'teen' number and a single digit (without crossing the 20 boundary). Ask: *How did you work that out? Who used a different method? Which method do you think is best? Why?*

Lessons   overview

Learning objectives

Starter
● Begin to know addition facts for all pairs of numbers with a total up to at least 10, and the corresponding subtraction facts.

Main teaching activities
● **Use mental strategies to solve simple problems** set in 'real' life, money or measurement contexts, **using counting, addition, subtraction, doubling and halving, explaining methods and reasoning orally.**
● Choose and use appropriate number operations and mental strategies to solve problems.

Vocabulary
answer, right, wrong, how did you work it out?, number sentence, sign, operation

You will need:

Photocopiable pages
'Two-step word problems' (see page 177), and 'Money problems' (see page 178), one for each child.

CD pages
'Two-step word problems', less able and more able versions, and 'Money problems', less able and more able versions (see Summer term, Unit 4); a teaching set of 'Add facts to 5', 'Add facts 6 to 10', 'Takeaway facts to 5' and 'Takeaway facts 6 to 10', a 'Number fan' for each child (see General Resources).

Equipment
A selection of coins (1p to 20p) for each pair; flip chart or board.

Lesson

Starter
Use the 'Add facts to 5' and 'Add facts 6 to 10' cards. Explain to the children that you will hold up a card with an addition question on. Ask them to hold up their number fans to show the answer when you say: *Show me.*

Main teaching activities
Whole class: Explain that today's work is about solving some problems that need two steps to work them out. Ask: *There were 5 toffees, 3 chews and 2 lollipops on the table. How many sweets were there altogether?* Invite answers from the children, then ask them to explain how they worked out the problem. They may have:
● counted on in ones from 5 to 8, then to 10
● known that 5 + 3 is 8 and 8 + 2 is 10.
Repeat this for other two-step problems, each time eliciting from the children the methods they used to solve it. Use problems such as the following (which can be adapted with different numbers):
● *Half of the oranges in this box of 12 are gone. How many are left?* (6)
● (Write the scores on the flip chart.) *Three children played a game with two rounds. Sara scored 5 and 2; Mark scored 6 and 4; Chang scored 7 and 1. How many more did Mark score than Chang?* (2)
● *Tomas had 6 marbles, Jack had 8 marbles and Pradesh had 4 marbles. How many did the three boys have altogether?* (18) *How many more marbles would they need to make a total of 20?* (2)
Individual work: Give each child a copy of the 'Two-step word problems' activity sheet. Read through the problems together. Ask the children to write the answers on the sheet.

Differentiation
Less able: Provide the version of the sheet with numbers to 10. Read the problems through with the children.
More able: Provide the version with numbers to 30.

Plenary & assessment

Review a problem from each version of the activity, and invite children from the appropriate group to explain how they solved the problem. Write the addition and subtraction sentences for their solutions on the board, so that everyone can see a possible way to solve the problem. Invite other children who have used different methods to explain how they solved the problem. Ask questions such as:

- *What do you need to find out?*
- *How do you know you need to add… subtract… double? What clues are there?*
- *What did you do in your head first? Then what did you do?*

Lesson ⑤

Starter

Explain to the children that the questions will all be to do with subtraction. Repeat the starter for Lesson 4, this time using 'Take away facts to 5' and 'Take away facts 6 to 10'.

Main teaching activities

Whole class: Explain that you will ask some money questions. Use problems such as the following (which can be adapted with different numbers):

- *Chews cost 5p each. What will two chews cost?* (10p)
- *Gemma had a 1p, 5p and a 10p coin. How much money did she have in total?* (16p) *She bought a toffee apple for 9p. How much money did she have then?* (7p)
- *Paul paid 12p for an apple. What three coins could he have used?* (5p, 5p, 2p or 10p, 1p, 1p)

Ask children to explain how they worked out the solutions. Invite them to write number sentences on the board to demonstrate their thinking.

Individual work: Provide a copy of the 'Money problems' activity sheet for each child to work on individually.

Differentiation

Less able: Provide the version of 'Money problems' with totals to 10p. The children may find it helpful to have coins in order to model the questions.

More able: Provide the version with totals to 30p.

Plenary & assessment

Ask questions such as:

- *What do you need to find out?*
- *How do you know you need to add/subtract? What clues are there?*
- *What did you do in your head first? Then what did you do?*

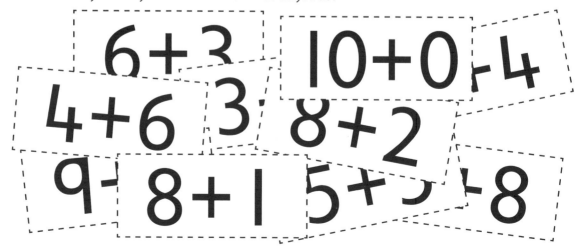

Name	Date

Two-step word problems

Write the answers to these problems.

Sara	4 + 4 + 3
Beena	5 + 4 + 5
Niall	3 + 5 + 4
Harry	6 + 5 + 6

1. Who had the lowest score? ☐

How many did they score? ☐

2. Who had the highest score? ☐

How many did they score? ☐

3. How many more did Harry score than Sara? ☐

4. How many more did Beena score than Niall? ☐

Name	Date

Money problems

Write the answers to these problems.

1. There are three coins in my pocket.
The coins make a total of 15p.

What coins do I have?

2. Tom buys some toffees for 12p.
He gives the shopkeeper 20p.

How much change does he get? ☐ p

3. Vicky has 20p to spend.
She buys a lolly for 9p and a
chocolate bar for 8p.

How much does she spend? ☐ p

How much change does she get? ☐ p

4. Mark buys a comic for 15p and three 1p chews.

How much does he spend? ☐ p

How much change will he get from 20p? ☐ p

Shape and space

Children fold paper shapes in half in order to make symmetrical shapes and patterns. They copy with construction materials a picture of a model made from solid shapes. They use shapes or tiles to make, describe and continue repeating patterns. They explore position, direction and movement through practical activities. They begin to understand about turns and half turns.

LEARNING OBJECTIVES

	Topics	Starter	Main teaching activities
Lesson 1	Shape and space	● **Order numbers to at least 20**, and position them on a number track.	● Fold shapes in half, then make them into symmetrical patterns. ● Begin to relate solid shapes to pictures of them. ● Use one or more shapes to make, describe and continue repeating patterns…
Lesson 2	Shape and space	As for Lesson 1.	As for Lesson 1.
Lesson 3	Shape and space	As for Lesson 1.	As for Lesson 1.
Lesson 4	Shape and space	● Know by heart addition doubles of all numbers with a total up to at least 5 (e.g. 4 + 4).	● Use everyday language to describe position, direction and movement. ● Talk about things that turn. ● Make whole turns and half turns.
Lesson 5	Shape and space	As for Lesson 4.	As for Lesson 4.

Lessons   overview

Preparation
Make four cards showing 2-D sketches of simple models (see Lesson 1).

Learning objectives
Starter
● **Order numbers to at least 20**, and position them on a number track.
Main teaching activities
● Fold shapes in half, then make them into symmetrical patterns.
● Begin to relate solid shapes to pictures of them.
● Use one or more shapes to make, describe and continue repeating patterns…

Vocabulary
size, bigger, larger, smaller, symmetrical, pattern, repeating pattern, match

You will need:
Equipment
Paint, paper, safety mirrors, pegs and pegboards, scissors, 2-D shape tiles, wooden building bricks, construction kits; pictures of buildings; an individual whiteboard and pen for each child.

Lesson ①

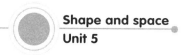

Starter

Write some numbers on the board, such as 4, 5, 8, 6 and 7. Say: *Which number has been moved?* Invite the children to say the numbers in their correct order, and to correct them on the board. Repeat this for other series of numbers between 0 and 20, such as: 7, 8, 10, 11, 12, 9; 12, 13, 15, 16, 17, 14.

Main teaching activities

Whole class: Fold a sheet of A4 paper in half, showing the children what you are doing. Explain that you will now cut out a design on the paper. Cut out a simple design, being careful not to cut away the fold. The design could be a mask.

Ask: *What picture do you think I will have when I open out the paper? Why do you think that?* Open out the paper and show the children the picture you have made. Discuss how its shape is symmetrical, pointing to the fold and to the matching features on either side.

Group work: Set up a circus of shape activities for today and the next two days. The children can be assigned to undertake a different activity each day, so that they have opportunities to explore symmetry, to revisit making patterns, and to make models from pictures.

1. Make symmetrical patterns by making and folding paint blots. Use a mirror to look at half,
   then all, of the pattern.

2. Fold a sheet of paper in half, then carefully cut out a design in order to make a symmetrical pattern. Use a mirror to look at half, then all, of the design.

3. Use pegs and pegboards to make a repeating pattern that is symmetrical about one axis only. Use mirrors to look at half, then all, of the design.

4. Use shape tiles to make a repeating pattern on the floor.

5. Provide four cards showing 2-D sketches of simple models made using 3-D shapes. The children should make the models from construction bricks, matching the shapes on the sheet to the correct bricks.

6. Make a model of a house, using a construction kit or building bricks. Encourage the children to draw the model as accurately as they can.

Differentiation

Less able: The children will enjoy activity 1. Discuss with them how their patterns are symmetrical. Encourage them to use the vocabulary of direction and position: *There is a circle on the left side of the fold. There is a matching one on the right...* Encourage the children to try activity 5, and to make these models as accurately as they can. Ask them to explain what they have done, and to describe the position of each piece used.

More able: Challenge the children to try activity 3, and to check carefully that their pattern is symmetrical. Activity 6 is also challenging, as the children will need to sketch their models accurately.

Plenary & assessment

Invite the children who have made symmetrical patterns or designs to show the class what they have done. Discuss the symmetry, and invite children from each group to point out the line of symmetry and to show how the pattern or design is balanced on either side of this line. It may help to demonstrate this for them with a large mirror. Say:
- *Tell me the pattern that you can see.*
- *How is this pattern the same here as it is there?* (Point to the two halves of the symmetrical pattern.)
- *Is this symmetrical? How can you tell?*

Lesson

Repeat the Starter from Lesson 1, this time writing sets of three numbers (not in order) and asking the children to write each set on their whiteboard in order (starting with the smallest number). For example, write 6, 1 and 8; 9, 4 and 3... During the whole-class activity, review making repeating patterns. For example, put a rectangle and circle together to make a tree, then a square and a triangle to make a house. Make this a repeating pattern: tree, house, tree, house. Discuss how the pattern repeats. Choose an activity for each group from the circus described in Lesson 1. During the plenary, invite children from each group to show their patterns. Ask questions such as:
- *What would come next in the pattern?*
- (of peg patterns) *Is this pattern symmetrical? How can you tell?*

Lesson

Repeat the Starter from Lesson 2, this time using sets of four numbers such as 2, 1, 9 and 7; 6, 2, 4 and 8... During the whole-class activity, review building models from pictures. Look together at the pictures of buildings and ask the children to name the shapes and their faces. Choose activities from the circus for each group. During the plenary, review some of the activities that have been completed, such as the models in activity 5. Ask the children to look carefully at each model made and the drawing it is based on: *How is this the same as the drawing? How is it different?*

Lessons   overview

Learning objectives

Starter
- Know by heart addition doubles of all numbers with a total up to at least 5 (e.g. 4 + 4).

Main teaching activities
- Use everyday language to describe position, direction and movement.
- Talk about things that turn.
- Make whole turns and half turns.

Vocabulary
left, right, turn, whole turn, half turn

You will need:

CD pages
A teaching set of 'Double facts to 5 + 5' cards, a 'Number fan' for each child (see General Resources).

Equipment
Scissors, glue; a Roamer; models (a dolls' house with furniture, a garage with cars, a farm with animals).

Lesson

Starter
Explain that you will hold up a card with a double fact on it. Ask the children to raise a hand if they can tell you the answer. Keep the pace sharp.

Main teaching activities
Whole class: Play 'I spy' with the whole class. Explain that you will say where something is, and the children should raise a hand to tell you what it is. Use the language of position and direction. For example: *I spy something on top of the cupboard, near to the window. I spy something blue in the left-hand room of the dolls' house…* When the children have played this game four or five times, ask them to stand up and follow your directions in a game of 'Simon says'. Decide whether to make this a forfeit game for those who respond to instructions without being told 'Simon says' (for example: *Simon says put your hands on your head. Simon says turn to your left. Simon says turn all the way round. Turn to the right!*)

Check that the children can follow your directions to identify the objects. Invite a child to give instructions for 'Simon says'.

Group work: Set up a circus of activities for today and tomorrow.
1. Ask the children to work in a group of three or four. They program a Roamer to move from one place in the classroom to another, making left and/or right turns on the way. They will find it helpful to record the Roamer's moves.
2. Ask the children to work in groups of three or four to arrange the furniture in a dolls' house according to agreed placements. This activity works best if an adult gives position, direction and movement instructions to the children as they work. Other groups can work on the same activity, using a model garage and cars, or a model farm and animals.

Differentiation
Less able: Activity 1 can be simplified by including just one left or right turn.
More able: Activity 1 can be made more challenging by asking the children to program for a route that involves a number of turns.

Plenary & assessment

Invite some children who have tried the Roamer activity to demonstrate what they have done. Invite the other children to describe the movements that they see. Encourage them to use words such as *left, right* and *turn* as they make their descriptions. Ask questions such as:

- *Which way did the Roamer turn?*
- *How can you make the Roamer turn left/right?*
- *How can you make the Roamer turn all the way round?*

Lesson 5

Repeat the Starter from Lesson 4, this time asking the children to use their number fans to show you the answer when you say: *Show me*. Keep a good, sharp pace, so that the children are encouraged to use rapid recall. During the whole-class session, play 'Simon Says' again (without the forfeits). Encourage the children to respond rapidly to directions and turns, and check that they know their left from their right. If they find this activity difficult, suggest that they keep a cube in their right hand. Choose from the circus of activities for each group. Review the dolls' house activity during the plenary. Invite children from different groups to place the furniture, following your instructions: *Put the bed in the room upstairs, on the left, and next to the window…* Ask questions such as:

- *Where is the …?*
- *What is next to the …?*
- *What is on the left/right of the …?*

Measures and investigating general statements

Children estimate and measure using uniform non-standard units. They identify 3-D and 2-D shapes from given properties in order to make a general statement about a specific shape.

LEARNING OBJECTIVES

	Topics	Starter	Main teaching activity
Lesson 1	Measures	● **Know by heart all pairs of numbers with a total of 10** (e.g. 3 + 7).	● Understand and use the vocabulary related to length, mass and capacity. ● **Compare two lengths, masses or capacities by direct comparison**; extend to more than two. ● Measure using uniform non-standard units (e.g. straws, wooden cubes, plastic weights, yogurt pots), or standard units (e.g. metre sticks, litre jugs).
Lesson 2	Measures	As for Lesson 1.	As for Lesson 1.
Lesson 3	Reasoning about numbers or shapes	● Read the time to the hour or half hour on analogue clocks.	● Investigate a general statement about familiar numbers or shapes by finding examples that satisfy it.

Lessons   overview

Preparation
Label each set of boxes A, B and C.

Learning objectives
Starter
● **Know by heart all pairs of numbers with a total of 10** (e.g. 3 + 7).
Main teaching activities
● Understand and use the vocabulary related to length, mass and capacity.
● **Compare two lengths, masses or capacities by direct comparison;** extend to more than two.
● Measure using uniform non-standard units (e.g. straws, wooden cubes, plastic weights, yogurt pots), or standard units (e.g. metre sticks, litre jugs).

Vocabulary
measure, size, compare, guess, estimate, about the same as, just over, just under

You will need:
Photocopiable pages
'Box measures' (see page 187) for each child.

CD pages
'Box measures', less able and more able versions (see Summer term, Unit 6); a teaching set of 'Complements of 10' cards and a 'Number fan' for each child (see General Resources).

Equipment
An individual whiteboard and pen for each child. For each group: three small or medium-sized boxes of different heights, weights and capacities; a balance; cubes; some extra boxes.

Lesson ①

Starter

Explain that you will hold up cards with number facts on them. Ask the children to show the answers using their number fans when you say: *Show me.* They should have rapid recall of these facts, so keep the pace sharp.

Main teaching activities

Whole class: Explain that today and tomorrow the children will be working with measures. Hold up an empty box and some cubes. Say: *How tall do you think this box would be if we measured it with cubes?* Invite estimates and write them on the board. Ask a child to measure the height of the box with cubes. Discuss how close the estimates were to the measure, using language such as *roughly, a bit over/under, nearly the same…* Now ask: *How much do you think this box would weigh if we measured it with cubes?* Repeat the process, with a child balancing the box with cubes. Ask: *How many cubes do you think this box would hold?* Repeat the process, with a child filling the box with cubes. Discuss how a container has length (height, width or depth), weight and capacity.

Group work: The children work in groups of four with three boxes. Ask them to estimate, then measure the height, weight and capacity of each box. They should then put the boxes in order of height, then weight, then capacity. They can record their results on the 'Box measures' activity sheet. This activity is likely to take up two group work sessions. Ask some groups to start with weight or capacity, so that the balances can be shared out among the groups over time. Emphasise that whichever measure the children are working with, they must complete that part of the work today.

Differentiation

Less able: The children can start by estimating and measuring the heights of the containers, then ordering them. If an adult works with this group, the children can make a group record of what they find. Ask the adult to encourage the children to use the vocabulary of length.

More able: The children can use five boxes (labelled A–E) with the appropriate version of the sheet.

Plenary & assessment

Ask each group to explain what they have found out. Encourage them to use the language of estimating, comparing and ordering. Ask questions such as: *Which did you think was the tallest/the heaviest/held the most? Which did you think was the shortest/lightest/held the least? How close was your estimate to your measure?*

Lesson ②

Repeat the Starter from Lesson 1, this time asking the children to record their answer on their whiteboard and hold it up when you say: *Show me.* Keep the pace sharp and encourage rapid recall. During the whole-class session, ask individuals to remind the other children of what they have done and what they still need to do. Encourage the children to move on swiftly to the group work, which continues that in Lesson 1. If some groups finish early, provide another box (labelled D) so that they can order four boxes. In the plenary, ask the children to discuss what they have found out, using the language of estimation, comparing and ordering. Make statements such as these: *The taller the box the more it holds. The heavier the box the taller it will be. The larger the box the heavier it will be.* Ask the children to find examples that show these statements to be wrong.

Lesson overview

Preparation
Put the shapes into boxes for each table group. Write six or seven descriptions of 3-D shapes and their names on the flip chart (see Lesson 3).

Learning objectives
Starter
- Read the time to the hour or half hour on analogue clocks.

Main teaching activities
- Investigate a general statement about familiar numbers or shapes by finding examples that satisfy it.

Vocabulary
shape, flat, curved, straight, round, corner, point, pointed, face, side, edge, end, sort, puzzle, answer, right, wrong, how did you work it out?

You will need:
Equipment
A teaching clock; for each table: a set of 3-D shapes (cube, cuboid, sphere, cone, cylinder, pyramid) in a box; a set of 2-D shape tiles (square, rectangle, triangle, circle) in a box; flip chart or board; paper and pencils.

Lesson

Starter
Explain that you will set the hands on the clock to show o'clock or half past times. Ask the children to put up their hands to answer. Set the hands to, for example: 6.30, 7.00, 9.30, 12.30, 1.00, 5.00…

Main teaching activities
Whole class: Explain that today the children will be looking carefully at shapes to identify their properties. Ask the children to sit at their tables and work as a group. You will say a shape riddle and they should put back into the box any shapes that do not fit what you say. Ask them to take out the shape tiles. Say, giving time after each statement for sorting: *I am thinking of a shape that has straight sides. My shape has opposite pairs of sides the same length. Next-door sides are not the same length.* The children should now have only the rectangle in front of them. Ask: *What is a rectangle? How can we tell it apart from the other shapes?* Repeat this for another shape, for example a triangle: *My shape has straight sides. It has less than four sides. How many sides does it have?*

Now repeat this with the 3-D shapes, for example a cube: *My shape has all flat faces. All the faces are the same size. All the faces are the same shape.*
Individual work: On the flip chart, write six or so descriptions of numbered 3-D shapes. For example: *I have no flat faces. I am round all over. What am I?* Draw the corresponding 3-D shapes and label these A to F. Ask the children to match the descriptions to the correct shapes and to record their answers on paper.

Differentiation
Less able: Work with this group, reading the statements together. Encourage the children to point to each property on the shape they think is correct.
More able: When the children have finished, challenge them to write their own description of another 3-D shape, such as a rectangular prism. Introduce the shape and tell the children its name.

Plenary & assessment
Look at the descriptions and shapes on the flip chart. Invite children from each group to say which statements apply to which shape. Ask questions such as: *What makes this shape different from that shape? How do you know that this shape is a …? Are all … shapes like this one?*

Name		Date

Box measures

You will need three boxes, some cubes and a balance.

Estimate, then measure, the height of each box with cubes.

Estimate, then weigh, how many cubes will balance each box.

Estimate, then find out, how many cubes will fit in each box.

Write down your estimates and your measures.

Height

Box	Estimate	Measure
A		
B		
C		

Box _____ is the tallest.   Box _____ is the shortest.

Weight

Box	Estimate	Measure
A		
B		
C		

Box _____ weighs the most.   Box _____ weighs the least.

Capacity

Box	Estimate	Measure
A		
B		
C		

Box _____ holds the most.   Box _____ holds the least.

Counting, investigating, general statements and explaining

Children count in threes from zero to 30. They identify the counting sequences in missing number puzzles for counting in threes. They investigate general statements about addition sentences and explain how they worked out their answers. They repeat this for general statements about 2-D shapes.

LEARNING OBJECTIVES

	Topics	Starter	Main teaching activities
Lesson 1	Counting, properties of numbers and number sequences	● **Count reliably at least 20 objects.**	● Describe and extend number sequences: begin to count on in steps of 3 from zero.
Lesson 2	Counting, properties of numbers and number sequences	As for Lesson 1.	As for Lesson 1.
Lesson 3	Reasoning about numbers or shapes	● **Read and write numerals from 0 to at least 20.**	● Investigate a general statement about familiar numbers or shapes by finding examples that satisfy it. ● Explain methods and reasoning orally.
Lesson 4	Reasoning about numbers or shapes	As for Lesson 3.	As for Lesson 3.
Lesson 5	Reasoning about numbers or shapes	As for Lesson 3.	As for Lesson 3.

Lessons   overview

Preparation
Copy 'Steps of 3' to A3 size and pin it to the flip chart.

Learning objectives
Starter
● **Count reliably at least 20 objects.**
Main teaching activities
● Describe and extend number sequences: begin to count on in steps of 3 from zero.

Vocabulary
number, zero, one, two, three… to twenty and beyond, count (up) to

You will need:
Photocopiable pages
'Steps of 3' (see page 193) for each child and an A3 copy.

CD pages
'Steps of 3', less able and more able versions (see Summer term, Unit 8).

Equipment
For each pair: at least 20 counters on a paper plate or in a container; board pens in two colours; flip chart or board; paper and pencils.

Lesson ①

Starter

Ask the children to work in pairs with at least 20 counters. Explain that you will say an amount to count out. The children take turns to count out the counters; their partner checks by counting again. Say, for example: *Count out 15 counters. Partners check the count. Now count out between 16 and 20 counters. Tell your partner how many you have counted. How many did you count? Who chose a different number?* Repeat this for various numbers and number ranges to 20.

Main teaching activities

Whole class: Ask the children to count together from zero to 30. Explain that you would like them to say all the numbers, but to gently slap their knees with their hands for every third number: *0, 1, 2, (slap) 3, 4, 5, (slap) 6…* When the children are confident with this, ask them to repeat the counting, this time clapping on every third number but not saying the number aloud: *0, 1, 2, clap, 4, 5, clap, 7, 8, clap…* Now ask the children to clap on all the numbers except for every third, which they say: *clap, clap, 3, clap, clap, 6, clap, clap, 9…*

On the flip chart, write the numbers 0, 1, 2, 3… As you write them, ask the children to clap each time you write a third number. Circle this number with a different-coloured pen, so that the number sequence 3, 6, 9… is circled. Say the circled numbers together, and explain to the children that these are the numbers they will say when they are counting in threes from zero.

Group work: Remove the numbers from the flip chart. Ask the children to work in pairs. They write the numbers from zero to 30 on paper, then circle every third number: 3, 6, 9…

Differentiation

Less able: Encourage the children to complete the task as far as they can. It may be appropriate to ask them to write the numbers to 15, 18 or 21, and then to circle every third number.

More able: Challenge the children to continue their number sequence, writing numbers to about 45 and continuing to circle every third number.

Plenary & assessment

Tell the children that they can use their number lists to help them. Now ask them to say every third number: 3, 6, 9… Continue to 30. Repeat this. Now ask the children to hide their sheets and do the same activity, using their memory. Repeat this several times. Now ask the more able children to continue the count beyond 30 (to about 45). Repeat this, and ask the other children to join in. Ask, for example: *If we count in threes, what comes next after 3, 6, 9? What comes next after 15, 18? What comes next after 21?*

Lesson ②

Starter

Repeat the Starter from Lesson 1, this time asking the children to count out amounts that are just beyond 20, such as 21, 22, 23…

Main teaching activities

Whole class: Ask the children to count together in threes from zero. Repeat this, counting around the class individually up to about 30 and then starting again at zero, so that each child has a turn. Repeat this several times, starting with a different child each time.

Group work: Provide the 'Steps of 3' activity sheet for each pair. Ask the children to complete this individually.

Differentiation

Less able: Decide whether to provide the version of 'Steps of 3' with numbers to 21.

More able: Decide whether to provide the version with numbers to 45.

Plenary & assessment

Ask the children to help you complete the enlarged copy of 'Steps of 3'. Work through the number tracks together. Invite children from each ability group to suggest solutions and write them on the enlarged sheet. Ask questions such as:

● *What comes next? How did you work that out?*
● *What would come next, and next… in this pattern of threes?*

Lessons   overview

Preparation

Photocopy the shape tiles on thin card and cut them out. Draw six regular 2-D shapes and write their names on the flip chart (see Lesson 5).

Learning objectives

Starter
● **Read and write numerals from 0 to at least 20.**

Main teaching activities
● Investigate a general statement about familiar numbers or shapes by finding examples that satisfy it.
● Explain methods and reasoning orally.

Vocabulary

pattern, puzzle, answer, how did you work it out?, number sentence, sign, operation

You will need:

CD pages
A teaching set of 'Numeral cards 0–9', 'Numeral cards 10–20' and Numeral cards 21–30', a set of 'Shape tiles 1' and 'Shape tiles 2' for each group of four (see General Resources).

Equipment
A set of coins (one 1p, two 2p and one 5p) for each pair; an individual whiteboard and pen for each child; flip chart or board.

Lesson

Starter

Using a shuffled set of numeral cards 0–20, explain to the children that you will hold up a card and would like them to say the number together. Ask, for example: *What number comes before/after …? How do you know that? What is one more/less than this number? What is ten more/less than this number?*

0 + 7 = 7
1 + 6 = 7
2 + 5 = 7
3 + 4 = 7
4 + 3 = 7
5 + 2 = 7
6 + 1 = 7
7 + 0 = 7

Main teaching activities

Whole class: Explain to the children that their work for the next three days will be about finding examples that match sentences about numbers or shapes. Start by saying: *I can make seven by adding two numbers. Can you think of some addition sentences that match this?* Write the children's suggestions on the flip chart. They will find it helpful if the sentences are ordered, so leave spaces as you write up the sentences to allow for all the possibilities in order:

Discuss with the children how each of these addition sentences matches what you said at the beginning: the two numbers add together to make seven.

Group work: Ask the children to work in pairs to find number sentences that match this statement: *I can make nine by adding two numbers.*

Differentiation

Less able: Decide whether to offer an addition statement with a lower total, such as: *I can make five by adding two numbers.*

More able: Decide whether to offer an addition statement with a higher total, such as: *I can make 12 by adding two numbers.*

Plenary & assessment

Start with the total of five, if you used this with the less able children. Ask individual children to suggest addition sentences. Write these on the flip chart so that all the answers appear in order, as above. Repeat this for the total of nine. If there is time, continue with the total of 12, encouraging all of the children to make suggestions. As they give suggestions, ask:

- *How do you know that these numbers have a total of …?*
- *What other numbers could we try?*
- *What if I said 'I can make two by subtracting one number from another number'? What subtraction sentences could we write?*

Lesson ④

Starter

Repeat the Starter from Lesson 3, this time including all the numeral cards to 30.

Main teaching activities

Whole class: Tell the children: *I can pay for anything from 1p to 5p if I have two 2p coins and one 1p coin.* Ask them to suggest how you could pay amounts of 1p, 2p, 3p, 4p and 5p. Write their suggestions on the board as single coin values or addition sentences, in order (see illustration).

```
1p
2p
3p = 1p + 2p
4p = 2p + 2p
5p = 2p + 2p + 1p
```

Group work: Ask the children to work in pairs. They write addition sentences for this statement: *I can pay for anything from 1p to 8p if I have two 2p coins, one 1p coin and a 5p coin.*

Differentiation

Less able: Decide whether to limit the children to making amounts to 6p with the same coins.

More able: Challenge the children to find other amounts that can be made with this selection of coins. They may find it helpful to model their answers using coins, then write the addition sentences.

Plenary & assessment

Invite children from each group to suggest coin values or addition sentences. Write these on the board, in order (see right):

Ask questions such as:

- *How did you work this out?*
- *(for 5p) Is there another way of making this amount?*
- *If you had another 1p coin, what other amounts could you make?*

```
        1p
        2p
    1p + 2p = 3p
    2p + 2p = 4p
5p or 5p = 2p + 2p + 1p
    6p = 5p + 1p
    7p = 5p + 2p
    8p = 5p + 2p + 1p
    9p = 5p + 2p + 2p
   10p = 5p + 2p + 2p + 1p
```

Lesson ⑤

Starter

Explain that you will say a number between zero and at least 20. Ask the children to write it in numerals on their whiteboard. When you say *Show me*, the children hold up their whiteboards for you to check. Say, for example:

- *Write the number 15. Show me.*
- *Write the number that is one more/less than …*
- *Write the number that is ten more/less than …*

Main teaching activities

Whole class: Explain that today, the children will think about some sentences that describe shapes. Provide each group of about four children with a set of 2-D shape tiles. Begin by saying: *All triangles have three sides.* Ask the children to work in their groups to sort through their shape tiles and find the triangles. Ask:

- *What shapes are not triangles? How do you know that?*
- *How many sides do rectangles/squares/pentagons/circles have?*

Repeat this with another statement, such as: *All pentagons have five points.*

Group work: On the flip chart, draw six regular 2-D shapes and number them 1 to 6. Also write appropriate descriptions for each shape and label these, randomly, A to F. Ask the children to match the descriptions to the shapes. Encourage them to discuss all the statements before they decide which shape matches which statement.

Differentiation

Less able: Work with the children in a group. If they need help with reading the statements, read them together. Ask them to decide which shape matches each statement, and to explain why.
More able: Challenge the children to work in pairs, writing their own general statement about a shape. For example, they might write: *All triangles have three points.*

Plenary & assessment

Look at the flip chart and read through the statements together. Ask children from each ability group to say which shape belongs to each statement. Ask:

- *Which sentence does this shape belong to? Why?*
- *How do you know that this shape belongs to this sentence?*

Invite the more able children to say their own general statements about shapes. The other children can use their shape tiles to provide examples of the statement.

Invite all of the children to think of a general statement. Ask:

- *How do you know this is true?*
- *Which shapes do not belong to this sentence?*

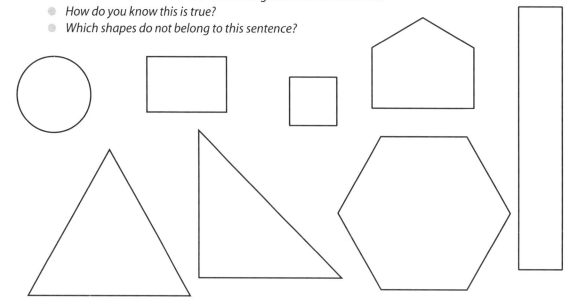

Name	Date

Steps of 3

Write in the missing numbers.

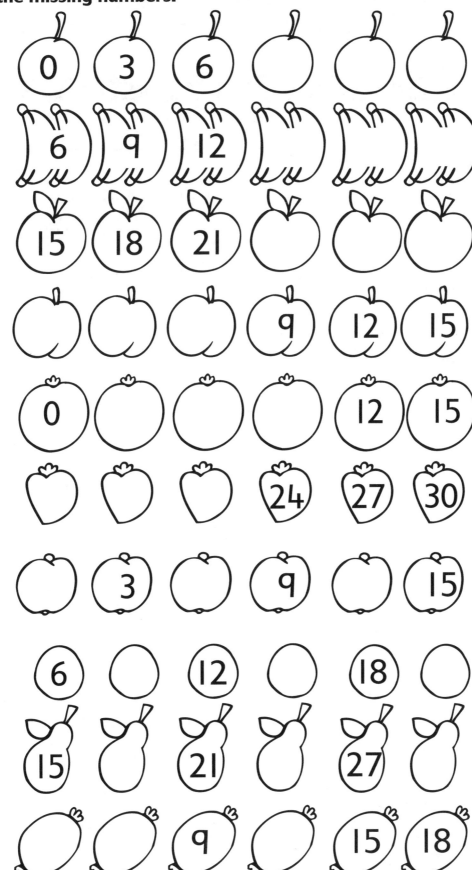

Place value, ordering and addition

Children order numbers to at least 20. They order a random set of numbers. They add three small numbers, using mental strategies that they already know to do this. They begin to realise that the order of adding numbers does not matter.

LEARNING OBJECTIVES

	Topics	Starter	Main teaching activities
Lesson 1	Place value and ordering	**Know by heart all pairs of numbers with a total of 10** (e.g. 3 + 7).	**Order numbers to at least 20**, and position them on a number track.
Lesson 2	Place value and ordering	As for Lesson 1.	As for Lesson 1.
Lesson 3	Understanding addition and subtraction	Begin to know addition facts for all pairs of numbers with a total up to at least 5, and the corresponding subtraction facts.	Begin to recognise that more than two numbers can be added together.
Lesson 4	Understanding addition and subtraction	As for Lesson 3.	As for Lesson 3.
Lesson 5	Understanding addition and subtraction	As for Lesson 3.	As for Lesson 3.

Lessons   overview

Preparation
Put up the washing line where the children will be able to see and reach it.

Learning objectives
Starter
- **Know by heart all pairs of numbers with a total of 10** (e.g. 3 + 7).
Main teaching activities
- **Order numbers to at least 20**, and position them on a number track.

Vocabulary
units, ones, tens, digit, 'teens' number, largest, smallest, compare, order, first, second, third… tenth, eleventh… twentieth, last, last but one, before, after, next, between, halfway between

You will need:
Photocopiable pages
'Ordering numbers' (see page 199) for each child.

CD pages
'Ordering numbers', less able and more able versions (see Summer term, Unit 9); sets of enlarged teaching cards from 'Complements of 10', 'Numeral cards 0–9' and 'Numeral cards 10–20', 'Numeral cards 21–30' for each pair of more able children (see General Resources).

Equipment
Individual whiteboards and pens; a washing line and pegs; flip chart or board.

Lesson

Starter

Use a teaching set of 'Complements of 10' cards. Explain that you will hold up a card with a number sentence on it. Ask the children to put up their hands to answer. Keep the pace sharp, and encourage rapid recall.

Main teaching activities

Whole class: Show the children the large numeral cards 1–20. These can be spread out in order on a table. Explain that you would like them to take turns to peg a card in its position on the number line. Start with the 1 card, then the 20 card, so that these positions are clear. Now ask a child to peg a card in the '10' position. Ask: *What comes next after 1? Before 20? Before/after 10?* Continue to ask children to place the cards on the line, now choosing the cards randomly. Ask: *Why have you put that card there? Which numbers will come before/after it?* When all the cards are on the line, invite individual children from each ability group to collect a card. Say, for example: *Meena, take the card that is between… and… Josh, take the card that is one before/after…*

When all the cards have been taken, ask the children who have cards to stand at the front of the class, in any order, holding up their cards. Ask the other children to help you sort out these children so that the numbers are in order again. For example: *Paul, you have 1, stand at the beginning of the line. Jane, you have 2, stand next to Paul. Mark, you have 20, stand at the end of the line…*

Group work: The children work in pairs with 1–20 numeral cards. Ask them to shuffle the cards, then take turns to take the top card. They place their card on the table where they think it will go in a number track. When all 20 cards are on the table, this should form a 1–20 number track. The children can repeat this by gathering the cards, shuffling them thoroughly and playing again.

Differentiation

Less able: If the children are still unsure about the order of numbers beyond 10, decide on a limit such as numbers to 15.

More able: Decide whether to include numbers beyond 20 by providing numeral cards 21–30.

Plenary & assessment

Put all the number cards back onto the washing line, but out of order. Invite children from each ability group to take the card that you say and place it in the correct position. Ask questions such as:

- *What is the first/last number in the line?*
- *What comes before/after …? How do you know that?*
- *What comes between … and …?*

Lesson

Starter

Repeat the starter from Lesson 1, this time asking the children to write the answers on their individual whiteboards and hold them up when you say: *Show me*. Keep the pace sharp.

Main teaching activities

Whole class: Write the numbers 6, 1, 9 and 5 on the flip chart. Say: *Put the smallest number first. Which number comes first? Which comes next…? How do you know that?* As the children give their responses, write these on the flip chart, so that the numbers are ordered from the smallest to the largest. Now say: *What if we started with the largest number? What would come first? And next…? How do you know that?* Repeat this for other sets of numbers to about 20, such as:

- 6, 1, 12, 19, 8, 5
- 13p, 10p, 8p, 19p, 22p, 14p

Individual work: Provide the 'Ordering numbers' activity sheet for each child to complete individually.

Differentiation

Less able: Decide whether to use the version of 'Ordering numbers' with numbers to 15. Read the sheet through together before the children begin.
More able: Decide whether to use the version with numbers to 30.

Plenary & assessment

Write 15, 3, 19, 12, 6 and 18 on the flip chart. Ask the children to help you order these numbers from the smallest to the largest, then from the largest to the smallest. Write what the children say on the flip chart. Ask questions such as:

- *Which number is first? How do you know?*
- *Which number goes between … and …? How do you know?*
- *What would come before/after …? How did you work that out?*

Lessons   overview

Preparation)

Make two A3-sized copies of 'Number line 0–20'. Pin one to the flip chart.

Learning objectives

Starter
- Begin to know addition facts for all pairs of numbers with a total up to at least 5, and the corresponding subtraction facts.

Main teaching activities
- Begin to recognise that more than two numbers can be added together.

Vocabulary

add, more, plus, make, sum, total, altogether, equals, sign, is the same as

You will need:

Photocopiable pages
'3-number total' (see page 200) for each child.

CD pages
'3-number total', less able and more able versions (see Summer term, Unit 9); a teaching set of cards from 'Add facts to 5' and 'Take away facts to 5' for each pair; 'Number line 0–20', two sets of 'Numeral cards 0–9' (use 1–5 only, and 1–6 for more able children) for each pair, an A3 copy of 'Number line 0–20 (see General Resources).

Equipment
Flip chart or board; pencils.

Lesson

Starter

Use the 'Add facts to 5' cards. Explain that you will hold up a card with an addition fact on it. Ask the children to put up their hands to answer. Keep the pace sharp. At this stage, the children should be using rapid recall of these facts.

Main teaching activities

Whole class: Explain that for the next three lessons, the children will be adding more than two numbers together. Start by pointing to the number line you have pinned to the flip chart and saying: *We can use a number line to help us add numbers.* Write 4 + 3 + 2 = on the flip chart. Put the flip chart pen on the 4, then say: *From 4, we can hop 3 to 7, and then 2 more to 9. So 4 + 3 + 2 = 9.* Repeat this for other examples, inviting individual children from each ability group to show the hops along the line.

Now ask the children to try this mentally. They close their eyes and make the hops along their mental number line as you say the number sentence. Say: *5 + 3 + 2. Start on 5, hop 3 to ... yes, 8. Now hop 2 to ... yes, 10. So 5 + 3 + 2 equals 10.* Repeat this for some more examples, keeping the total to about 10 (for example, 6 + 1 + 3).

Group work: Ask the children to work in pairs. They shuffle two sets of 1–5 numeral cards, then take turns to take the top three cards. They add the numbers together, then draw the 'hops' on a 0–20 number line and write an addition sentence next to it.

Differentiation

Less able: Decide whether to provide two sets of 1–3 or 1–4 numeral cards.
More able: Decide whether to provide two sets of 1–6 numeral cards.

Plenary & assessment

Invite children from each ability group to write one of their number sentences, without the total, onto a fresh A3-sized copy of the 0–20 number line. Invite another child to draw in the 'hops' on the line and write the total. Ask: *How did you add up these small numbers?* Praise those who used a mental number line or had rapid recall of the addition facts. Check which children need the number line as an aid: these children may need further experience of adding with a mental number line.

Lesson

Starter

Repeat the Starter from Lesson 3, using the 'Take away facts to 5' cards.

Main teaching activities

Whole class: Explain that you would like the children to think about different ways of making 10 by adding three numbers. Write two or three examples that the children suggest onto the A3 0–20 number line, showing the 'hops' along the line and writing the addition sentence (for example, 2 + 4 + 4 = 10). Remind the children that they can do this mentally by imagining a number line to hop along, and by using addition facts that they already know.

Group work: Ask the children to work in pairs, finding at least five different ways of making 10 by adding three numbers.

Differentiation

Less able: Decide whether to work with the children as a group, and to record their suggestions on an A3 copy of the 0–20 number line to make a group record.
More able: Challenge the children to find eight ways.

Plenary & assessment

Write up the children's suggestions. Encourage them to work mentally, using a number line or, preferably, using rapid recall. Ask:

- *How did you work that out?*
- *Who did this another way?*
- *Which way do you think is quicker?*

Lesson

Starter

Explain that you will say a number from 1 to 5. Ask the children to say which two numbers could add to make that total. Encourage lots of responses and write them on the flip chart. For example, a total of 4 could be made by: 0 + 4, 1 + 3, 2 + 2.

Main teaching activities

Whole class: Say some three-number additions, such as 3 + 1 + 4 and 2 + 3 + 2. Ask the children to add the numbers mentally and raise a hand to respond. Discuss how it does not matter in which order the numbers are added. For example, 3 + 1 + 4 gives the same answer as 3 + 4 + 1 and 4 + 1 + 3. Use the A3-sized 0–20 number line to demonstrate this.
Individual work: Provide copies of '3-number total'. Ask the children to complete the sheet, working individually.

Differentiation

Less able: Provide the version of '3-number total' with totals to 10. If the children find it difficult to add three numbers mentally, decide whether to provide number lines to help them.
More able: Provide the version of '3-number total' with totals to 15.

Plenary & assessment

Choose some examples from each differentiated version of the activity sheet and ask the children to complete these mentally. Target the questions according to ability. Ask questions such as:

- *How did you work this out?*
- *Which numbers did you add together first?*
- *Does it matter which order we add numbers in?*

Name	Date

Ordering numbers

Write these numbers in order. Start with the smallest number.

6 1 4 3

9 2 7 6

12 11 19 5

16 14 10 7

20 15 18 13

17 8 16 4

Write these numbers in order. Start with the largest number.

2 4 3 5

9 11 7 18

6 17 13 15

13 16 20 14

17 19 8 16

10 12 20 1

Name	Date

3-number total

Add up the 3 numbers.

Write the answer.

1 + 2 + 3 = ☐

3 + 4 + 5 = ☐

2 + 2 + 2 = ☐

7 + 1 + 2 = ☐

3 + 2 + 4 = ☐

8 + 2 + 2 = ☐

4 + 4 + 4 = ☐

2 + 1 + 9 = ☐

6 + 1 + 2 = ☐

2 + 4 + 6 = ☐

5 + 5 + 2 = ☐

3 + 6 + 3 = ☐

Mental strategies for addition and subtraction

Children use known number facts and place value in order to add or subtract a pair of numbers mentally, such as 17 – 5. They add a single-digit number to 10, then to 20, and observe the result. Then they subtract a single-digit number from 10, then 20, and again observe the result.

LEARNING OBJECTIVES

	Topics	Starter	Main teaching activities
Lesson 1	Mental calculation strategies (+ and –)	● **Understand the operation of subtraction (as 'difference') and use the related vocabulary.**	● Use known number facts and place value to add or subtract a pair of numbers mentally within the range 0 to at least 10, then 0 to at least 20.
Lesson 2	Mental calculation strategies (+ and –)	As for Lesson 1.	As for Lesson 1.
Lesson 3	Mental calculation strategies (+ and –)	As for Lesson 1.	As for Lesson 1.
Lesson 4	Mental calculation strategies (+ and –)	● Know by heart addition doubles of all numbers to at least 5 (e.g. 4 + 4).	As for Lesson 1.
Lesson 5	Mental calculation strategies (+ and –)	As for Lesson 4.	As for Lesson 1.

Lessons   overview

Preparation
Write the numerals on removable labels stuck onto the blank dice.

Learning objectives
Starter
● **Understand the operation of subtraction (as 'difference') and use the related vocabulary.**
Main teaching activities
● Use known number facts and place value to add or subtract a pair of numbers mentally within the range 0 to at least 10, then 0 to at least 20.

Vocabulary
add, more, plus, total, altogether, subtract, minus, leave, difference between, equals, sign, is the same as

You will need:
Photocopiable pages
'Addition and subtraction 1' (page 206) for each child.

CD pages
'Addition and subtraction 1', less able and more able versions (see Summer term, Unit 10); 'Numeral cards 0–9' for each pair (see General Resources).

Equipment
Two blank dice marked 2, 2, 3, 3, 4, 4 and 1, 2, 3, 4, 5, 5 for each pair; flip chart or board.

Lesson ①

Starter

Explain that you will say what the difference is between two numbers. Ask the children to think of a number sentence with that difference. For example, if you say 2, the children might respond with '4 – 2' or '8 – 6'. Write some of their responses on the flip chart. Keep the pace sharp, and encourage the children to think of as many examples as they can.

Main teaching activities

Whole class: Write 4 + 3 on the flip chart and ask: *What is 4 add 3?* Write the answer. Now write 14 + 3 and ask: *What is 14 add 3? How did you work that out? What do you notice about 4 + 3 and 14 + 3?* Discuss how the units are the same in both sums, because 14 + 3 is the same as 10 + 4 + 3. Discuss how rapid recall of addition facts like this can be used to work out facts that we do not know. Repeat this with, for example, 8 – 5 and 18 – 5.

Now write 5 + 3 and ask: *What is 5 add 3? So what is 15 add 3? What would 13 + 5 be? What do you notice?* Discuss again how rapid recall of a fact can help us to work out facts that we do not know.

Group work: Ask the children to work in pairs with a 2, 2, 3, 3, 4, 4 dice and a 1, 2, 3, 4, 5, 5 dice. They take turns to roll both dice, add the two scores and write an addition sentence (such as 4 + 5 = 9). Then they add 10 to one of their dice scores and write a new addition sentence (such as 14 + 5 = 19). They repeat this until they have rolled the two dice ten times.

Differentiation

Less able: Decide whether to use a 1, 1, 2, 2, 3, 3 dice and a 1, 2, 3, 4, 5, 5 dice.
More able: Challenge the children to write two different 'teens' addition sentences based on the same two dice throws. For example, they could use 4 and 5 to make 14 + 5 = 19 or 15 + 4 = 19.

Plenary & assessment

Ask children from each ability group to give examples of number sentences. Invite them to write their number sentences on the flip chart for the other children to solve. Ask questions such as:
- *How did you work that out?*
- *Who used a different way of working?*
- *How does knowing some addition facts help you to add 'teens' numbers?*

Finish by asking some oral questions, such as: *15 + 3, 17 + 2, 13 + 6.*

Lesson ②

Starter

Repeat the Starter for Lesson 1, using a different number – for example, asking the children to think of number sentences with a difference of 3.

Main teaching activities

Whole class: Explain that today, the children will be using subtraction facts that they already know to help them to find other facts that they do not know. Write 8 – 5 on the flip chart and ask: *What is 8 subtract 5? So what is 18 subtract 5? How did you work that out?* Discuss how these two subtractions involve the same change in the units and no change in the tens. Repeat this for further examples such as 9 – 3 and 8 – 4.

Group work: Ask the children to work in pairs. They shuffle a set of 1–9 numeral cards and take turns to take the top two cards (for example, 4 and 9). They arrange the numbers to make a subtraction sentence: 9 – 4 = ? They write this down, then write a 'teens' sentence: 19 – 4 = ? Finally, they write the answers to both sentences. Ask the children to write ten pairs of subtraction sentences in this way.

Differentiation
Less able: Decide whether to limit the children to the numeral cards 1–6.
More able: Challenge the children to write 15 pairs of subtraction sentences.

Plenary & assessment
Review the children's work by asking children from each ability group to write a set of subtraction sentences on the flip chart for the others to solve. Discuss how rapid recall of subtraction facts can be used to find other facts that are not known. Ask: *How did you work that out? Who did this a different way? How would you work out 19 take away 8?*

Lesson ③

Starter
Repeat the Starter for Lesson 1 with a different number – for example, asking the children to think of number sentences with a difference of 4.

Main teaching activities
Whole class: Review the main teaching activities from Lessons 1 and 2 by writing questions on the flip chart (see right). Ask the children to explain how they worked out each answer. Check that they are confident with the strategy of using known number facts and place value to work out unknown facts. If necessary, write and discuss further examples.

Group work: Provide a copy of 'Addition and subtraction 1' for each child. This sheet contains a mixture of addition and subtraction sentences for the children to complete. Encourage them to work quickly and efficiently, using number facts they know to work out unknown facts.

$$5 + 2 =$$
$$15 + 2 =$$
$$12 + 5 =$$

$$5 - 2 =$$
$$15 - 2 =$$

Differentiation
Less able: Decide whether to use the version of 'Addition and subtraction 1' that limits the range of units digits to 1–5.
More able: Decide whether to use the version that extends the children's understanding into working with twenties (for example, 22 + 5 and 28 – 4). Work with the children initially to check that they understand that the same strategy works for these numbers as for 'teens' numbers.

Plenary & assessment
Choose examples from each of the versions of 'Addition and subtraction 1'. Write the number sentences on the flip chart; encourage the children to answer swiftly and to explain how they worked out their answers. Ask questions such as:
- *How did you work that out?*
- *Who used a different way?*
- *What is 7 + 2? So what is 17 + 2? So what is 12 + 7?*
- *What is 7 – 2? So what is 17 – 2?*

Lessons ④ ⑤ overview

Learning objectives
Starter
- Know by heart addition doubles of all numbers to at least 5 (e.g. 4 + 4).

Main teaching activities
- Use known number facts and place value to add or subtract a pair of numbers mentally within the range 0 to at least 10, then 0 to at least 20.

Vocabulary
add, more, plus, total, altogether, subtract, minus, leave, difference between, equals, sign, is the same as

You will need:
Photocopiable pages
'Addition and subtraction 2' (see page 207) for each child.

CD pages
'Addition and subtraction 2', less able and more able versions (see Summer term, Unit 10); a teaching set of 'Double facts to 5 + 5' cards; 'Numeral cards 0–9' for each pair (see General Resources).

Equipment
An individual whiteboard and pen for each child; flip chart or board.

Lesson ④

Starter
Explain that you will hold up cards with double facts on them. Ask the children to try to remember the double facts, and to hold up their hands as soon as they have an answer. Use the 'Doubles to 5 + 5' cards. Keep the pace sharp.

Main teaching activities
Whole class: Explain that today the children will be adding a single digit (a number below 10) to 10, then to 20. They will also be taking a single digit away from 10, then 20. Write 10 + 4 on the flip chart and ask: *What is 10 add 4? How did you work that out?* Discuss how adding a single digit to 10 leaves the tens digit unchanged. Now write 20 + 4 on the flip chart and ask: *What is 20 add 4? How did you work that out?* Discuss how, when we add a single digit to 20, the tens digit stays the same. Provide further examples of this, such as 10 + 7 and 20 + 8.

Now explain that you will ask some take away questions. Write 10 – 6 on the flip chart and ask: *What is 10 take away 6? How did you work that out? So what is 20 take away 6?* Repeat this for other examples, such as 10 – 3 and 20 – 9.

$$10 + 4 = 14$$
$$20 + 4 = 24$$
$$10 - 4 = 6$$
$$20 - 4 = 16$$

Group work: Ask the children to work in pairs. They shuffle a set of numeral cards 1–9, then take turns to take a card and write four number sentences (with answers) for each card. For example, for the 4 card, they would write the examples shown left. Ask the children to write a set of number sentences like this for each of the cards.

Differentiation
Less able: Decide whether to limit this to addition and subtraction to/from 10 only.
More able: Decide whether to extend this to addition and subtraction of single digits to/from 30 and 40.

Plenary & assessment

Write the four questions shown right on the board. Ask the children to help you fill in the answers. Repeat this for 10 + 2… and so on to 10 + 9, ordering the number sentences in columns. Discuss the answers and how the children can use number facts that they already know to work out facts that they do not know. Ask questions such as:

- *What is 10 + 5? How do you know?*
  So what is 20 + 5?
- *What is 10 – 7? How do you know that? So what is 20 – 7?*

Challenge the more able children with questions such as 30 + 5 and 30 – 6.

$$10 + 1 =$$
$$20 + 1 =$$
$$10 - 1 =$$
$$20 - 1 =$$

Lesson

Starter

Repeat the Starter from Lesson 4, this time asking the children to write their answers on their whiteboards and hold them up when you say: *Show me.*

Main teaching activities

Whole class: Write 12 + 14 on the flip chart and ask: *What is 12 add 14? How could we work this out?* Children may suggest that they can use 10 + 10 + 2 + 4. Discuss how the two 10s can be added together and then the units. Repeat this for other examples, such as 13 + 16 and 15 + 11.

Group work: Provide copies of the 'Addition and subtraction 2' activity sheet. This requires addition and subtraction of a single digit to/from 10 or 20, and addition of two 'teens' numbers without crossing the tens boundary.

Differentiation

Less able: Decide whether to provide the version of 'Addition and subtraction 2' that requires only addition and subtraction of a single-digit number to/from 10.

More able: Decide whether to provide the version that includes addition totals to 40.

Plenary & assessment

Explain that you will ask some oral questions. Ask:

- *What is 16 + 11? How did you work that out?*
- *What is 15 + 13?*
- *Paul has 13 marbles and Tara has 12. How many do they have altogether? How did you work that out?*

Repeat this, asking similar questions.

Name   Date

Addition and subtraction 1

○ **Write the answers to these number sentences.**

5	–	2	=			

5 – 2 = ☐   3 + 6 = ☐

3 + 4 = ☐   2 + 6 = ☐

6 – 2 = ☐   5 – 4 = ☐

8 – 1 = ☐   3 + 5 = ☐

2 + 7 = ☐   6 – 1 = ☐

○ **Now try these.**

13 + 4 = ☐   13 + 5 = ☐

16 – 1 = ☐   12 + 6 = ☐

16 – 2 = ☐   18 – 1 = ☐

12 + 7 = ☐   13 + 6 = ☐

15 – 2 = ☐   15 – 4 = ☐

Name   Date

Addition and subtraction 2

Write the answers to these number sentences.

$10 + 4 = \boxed{}$	$20 + 5 = \boxed{}$
$10 + 7 = \boxed{}$	$20 + 3 = \boxed{}$
$10 + 8 = \boxed{}$	$20 - 4 = \boxed{}$
$10 - 6 = \boxed{}$	$20 - 8 = \boxed{}$
$10 - 9 = \boxed{}$	$20 + 7 = \boxed{}$

Now try these.

$13 + 16 = \boxed{}$	$15 + 14 = \boxed{}$
$15 + 12 = \boxed{}$	$16 + 13 = \boxed{}$
$18 + 11 = \boxed{}$	$12 + 14 = \boxed{}$
$16 + 13 = \boxed{}$	$13 + 12 = \boxed{}$
$12 + 17 = \boxed{}$	$11 + 17 = \boxed{}$

Mental calculation strategies, solving problems and making decisions

Children use the mental strategies that they have already learned in order to respond mentally to addition and subtraction questions. They add 9 by adding 10 then subtracting 1. They begin to bridge through 10, then 20, when adding a single-digit number. They solve word problems in different contexts using the mental strategies that they have learned, and explain how they worked out the answers.

LEARNING OBJECTIVES

	Topics	Starter	Main teaching activities
Lesson 1	Mental calculation strategies (+ and –)	Begin to know addition facts for all pairs of numbers with a total up to at least 10, and the corresponding subtraction facts.	Use known number facts and place value to add or subtract a pair of numbers mentally within the range 0 to at least 10, then 0 to at least 20.
Lesson 2	Mental calculation strategies (+ and –)	As for Lesson 1.	Add 9 to single-digit numbers by adding 10 then subtracting 1.
Lesson 3	Mental calculation strategies (+ and –)	As for Lesson 1.	Begin to bridge through 10, and later 20, when adding a single-digit number.
Lesson 4	Problems involving 'real life', money or measures Making decisions	**Order numbers to at least 20,** and position them on a number track.	**Use mental strategies to solve simple problems** set in 'real life', money or measurement contexts, **using counting, addition, subtraction, doubling and halving, explaining methods and reasoning orally.** Choose and use appropriate number operations and mental strategies to solve problems.
Lesson 5	Problems involving 'real life', money or measures Making decisions	As for Lesson 4.	As for Lesson 4.

Lessons   overview

Preparation
Make an A3-sized copy of 'Bridging' (core version) and pin it to the flip chart.

Learning objectives
Starter
Begin to know addition facts for all pairs of numbers with a total up to at least 10, and the corresponding subtraction facts.
Main teaching activities
Use known number facts and place value to add or subtract a pair of numbers mentally within the range 0 to at least 10, then 0 to at least 20 (Lesson 1).
Add 9 to single-digit numbers by adding 10 then subtracting 1 (Lesson 2).
Begin to bridge through 10, and later 20, when adding a single-digit number (Lesson3).

Vocabulary
add, more, plus, total, altogether, subtract, minus, leave, difference between, equals, sign, is the same as

You will need:

Photocopiable pages
'Bridging' (see page 213) for each child and an A3 copy.

CD pages
'Bridging', less able and more able versions (see Summer term, Unit 11); a teaching set of 'Add facts to 5', 'Add facts 6 to 10', 'Take away facts to 5' and 'Take away facts 6 to 10', 'Number fan' for each child, a set of 'Numeral cards 0–9' and a set of 'Numeral cards 10–20' for each pair (see General Resources).

Equipment
An individual whiteboard and pen for each child; flip chart or board.

Lesson ①

Starter

Use 'Add facts to 5' and 'Add facts 6 to 10'. Explain that you will hold up a card and ask the children to find the answer on their number fan, then hold it up when you say: *Show me*. Keep the pace of this sharp, and encourage the children to recall the addition facts from memory.

Main teaching activities

Whole class: Ask: *What is 5 add 10? How did you work that out?* Discuss how adding a single-digit number to 10 does not change the tens digit. Repeat this for other examples such as 6 + 10 and 9 + 10, writing them on the flip chart.

Now ask: *What is 15 subtract 10? How did you work that out?* Discuss how subtracting 10 from a teens number leaves only the units digit of the teens number. Repeat this for other examples, such as 18 – 10 and 12 –10.

Group work: Provide each pair with 1–19 numeral cards. Ask the children to sort the cards into three piles: 1–9, 10 and 11–19. Explain that you would like them first to write an addition sentence for each of the 1–9 cards added to 10: 1 + 10, 2 + 10 and so on. When they have finished this, ask them to write a subtraction sentence for each of the 11–19 cards with 10 taken away: 11 – 10, 12 – 10, and so on.

Differentiation

Less able: Decide whether to work with the children and carry out the two parts of the group work as a larger-group activity, with an adult recording. Encourage the children to work quickly and efficiently. By ordering the number sentences, they should be able to see the pattern that emerges when they add or subtract 10.

More able: Challenge the children to add single-digit numbers to 20, then subtract 10 from numbers between 20 and 29. Ask them to explain their results.

Plenary & assessment
Ask children from each ability group to say one of their addition sentences. Write these in order on the flip chart: 1 + 10, 2 + 10 and so on. Ask:
- *What do you notice about these addition sentences?*
- *What happens to a unit if 10 is added to it?*

Repeat this for the subtraction sentences, ordering them on the flip chart: 11 – 10, 12 – 10 and so on. Encourage the children to explain what is happening. Ask:
- *How might this pattern help you to answer other questions?*
- *Can you now work out 5 + 20? 5 + 30?*
- *And can you work out 25 – 10? 35 – 10?*

Help the children to see how they can use this to help them when they are working mentally to add or subtract a 'tens' number to/from a TU number.

Lesson

Starter

Repeat the Starter from Lesson 1, this time using 'Take away facts to 5' and 'Take away facts 6 to 10'. Again, keep the pace sharp to encourage rapid recall.

Main teaching activities

Whole class: Write 5 + 9 on the flip chart and say: *How can we work this out?* Children may recall the strategy of adding 9 by adding 10 and then subtracting 1. If this is not suggested, explain it and write the example shown below on the flip chart. Repeat for other examples, such as 7 + 9 and 4 + 9.

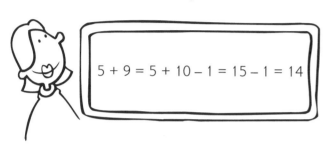

$$5 + 9 = 5 + 10 - 1 = 15 - 1 = 14$$

Group work: Provide each pair with a set of 1–9 numeral cards. Ask them to shuffle the cards and place the pack face down on the table. The children take turns to take a card and say an addition sentence for the card's number add 9. For example, with the 4 card, they would say '4 add 9 is…' and the answer. If their partner does not agree with the answer, their partner should write down the addition sentence and work out the answer by adding 10 and subtracting 1.

Differentiation

Less able: The children can work in a group with adult help. The adult shows the children each card, and all of them work out the answer. They can show the answer using their number fans. The adult should encourage individual children to explain the steps that they took to reach the answer.
More able: If the children finish the group activity quickly, challenge them to use the same strategy for adding 19 to each single-digit number.

Plenary & assessment

Provide each child with a number fan. Explain that you will ask them some 'add 9' questions. Ask the children to show you their answers with the number fans when you say: *Show me.* Keep the pace reasonably sharp, but give the children enough time to work mentally if this is still needed. Ask:
- *How did you work out the answer?*
- (For more able children) *Who can tell me how to work out 5 + 19?*

Lesson

Starter

Repeat the Starter from Lesson 1, using addition and subtraction facts from 'Add facts to 5', 'Add facts 6 to 10', 'Take away facts to 5' and 'Take away facts 6 to 10'. The children write their answers on their whiteboards. Keep the pace sharp.

Main teaching activities

Whole class: Write 6 + 7 on the flip chart. Ask: *How can we work this out?* Children may remember the strategy of bridging 10. Write: 6 + 4 + 3 = 10 + 3 = 13. Discuss the idea that we can make 10 by combining part of one digit with another digit. Repeat for other examples, such as 5 + 8 and 9 + 7. Each time, ask a child to explain how he or she worked out the answer; write the steps on the flip chart.

Now explain that this strategy can also be used for adding a single-digit number to a 'teens' number. Write 17 + 4 on the flip chart Ask: *How can we work this out?* Children may suggest splitting the 4 into a 3 and a 1: 17 + 3 + 1 = 20 + 1 = 21. Repeat for other examples, such as 18 + 6 and 16 + 7. Each time, ask a child to explain how they worked out the answer; write the steps on the flip chart. **Individual work:** Give each child a copy of the 'Bridging' activity sheet. Ask the children to complete the sheet, working individually.

Differentiation
Less able: Provide the version of 'Bridging' that involves crossing 10 only.
More able: Provide the version that involves crossing 30 as well as crossing 20.

Plenary & assessment
Using an A3 copy of 'Bridging' pinned to the board, invite children from each ability group to suggest answers and to explain how they worked them out. Encourage the children to explain the two steps in each addition. Write out what they say as addition sentences on the flip chart. For example, for 14 + 7 write: 14 + 7 = 14 + 6 + 1 = 20 + 1 = 21. Ask: *How did you work that out?* Ask more able children: *So how can I work out 24 + 8?*

Lessons   overview

Preparation
Make A3 copies of the 'At the zoo' and 'Money and measures problems' activity sheets (core versions) and pin them to the flip chart.

Learning objectives
Starter
● **Order numbers to at least 20**, and position them on a number track.
Main teaching activities
● **Use mental strategies to solve simple problems** set in 'real life', money or measurement contexts, **using counting, addition, subtraction, doubling and halving, explaining methods and reasoning orally.**
● Choose and use appropriate number operations and mental strategies to solve problems.

Vocabulary
half, halve, answer, right, wrong, what could we try next?, how did you work it out?, number sentence, sign, operation

You will need:
Photocopiable pages
'At the zoo' (see page 214) and 'Money and measures problems' (see page 215) for each child.

CD pages
'At the zoo' and 'Money and measures problems', less able and more able versions of both (see Summer term, Unit 11).

Equipment
Individual whiteboards and pens; flip chart or board

Lesson

Starter
Explain that you will write some numbers on the flip chart, out of order. Ask the children to write the numbers on their whiteboards in order, starting with the smallest number. Ask them to hold up their boards when you say: *Show me.* Encourage them to work quickly and efficiently. Ask questions such as: *Which is the smallest/largest number? What comes 1 before/after …? What comes 10 before/after …?* Numbers to use could include: 6, 1, 2, 8; 9, 2, 4, 1; 19, 15, 18, 12.

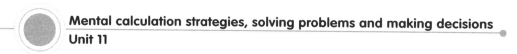
Main teaching activities

Whole class: Explain to the children that today and tomorrow, they will be solving word problems using the mental strategies that they have learned. Begin with an oral problem such as: *6 people get on a bus. At the next stop another 8 people get on the bus. How many are on the bus altogether?* Encourage the children to explain the strategies that they use. For example, in this problem they could bridge 10: $6 + 8 = 6 + 4 + 4 = 14$.

Repeat this for another problem, such as: *There are 4 cakes in a box. If I buy 2 boxes, how many cakes will I have?* Discuss how this problem involves doubling.

Individual work: Give each child a copy of the 'At the zoo' activity sheet, which contains problems in a real-life context. Read through the problems together before the children start, so that they are clear about the vocabulary used.

Differentiation

Less able: Decide whether to use the version of 'At the zoo' that involves totals to 10.
More able: Decide whether to use the version that involves totals to 32.

Plenary & assessment

Using an A3 copy of 'At the zoo' pinned to the flip chart, invite individual children from each ability group to suggest how they would solve each problem. Discuss the strategies that the children would use. Ask:

- *What do you need to find out?*
- *How do you know that you need to add… subtract… double… halve?*
- *How did you work out the answer?*

Lesson

Starter

Repeat the Starter for Lesson 4. This time, ask the children to write the numbers in order from the largest to the smallest.

Main teaching activities

Whole class: Explain that today the children will be working on money and measurement problems. Say, for example: *I bought two apples for 12p. How much would one apple cost?* Discuss how they can solve this by using a double fact they know (double 6 is 12) to find a half: half of 12p is 6p.
Individual work: Provide each child with a copy of the 'Money and measures problems' activity sheet.

Differentiation

Less able: Provide the version of 'Money and measures problems' that involves numbers to 12.
More able: Provide the version that involves numbers to 30.

Plenary & assessment

Using an A3 copy of 'Money and measures problems' pinned to the flip chart, ask individual children from each ability group to suggest appropriate strategies and solutions. Ask:

- *How do you know what to do? What clues are there in the problem?*
- *What did you do in your head first?*

Name	Date

Bridging

Write the answers to these number sentences.

8 + 5 = ☐   7 + ☐ = 15

6 + 9 = ☐   9 + ☐ = 17

7 + 8 = ☐   7 + ☐ = 11

9 + 8 = ☐   ☐ + 5 = 13

7 + 4 = ☐   ☐ + 9 = 15

8 + ☐ = 13   ☐ + 8 = 15

6 + ☐ = 15   ☐ + 8 = 17

                   ☐ + 4 = 11

Now try these.

14 + 7 = ☐   17 + 5 = ☐

16 + 8 = ☐   19 + 5 = ☐

13 + 9 = ☐   12 + 9 = ☐

18 + 5 = ☐   14 + 5 = ☐

15 + 6 = ☐   18 + 9 = ☐

Name	Date

At the zoo

1. Tom looks at the animals.

He can see 8 elephants and 6 giraffes.

How many animals can he see altogether?

2. Dileep counts the birds.

He counts 16 hawks.

He counts 4 fewer owls than hawks.

How many owls are there?

3. Voica likes the big cats.

She sees 4 lions and 4 tigers.

How many big cats does she see?

4. There are 12 hippos.

There are half as many rhinos as hippos.

How many rhinos are there?

Name	Date

Money and measures problems

Write the answers to these problems.

1. Iqbal buys 2 books for 4p each.

How much does he spend?

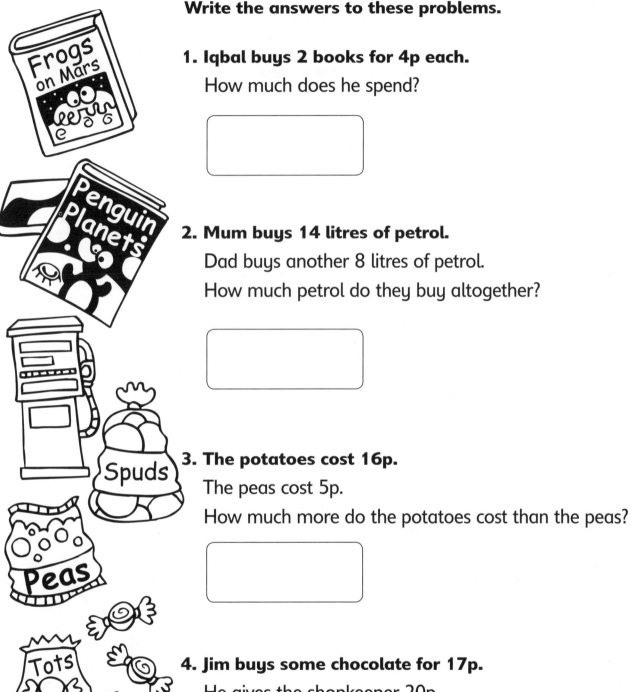

2. Mum buys 14 litres of petrol.

Dad buys another 8 litres of petrol.

How much petrol do they buy altogether?

3. The potatoes cost 16p.

The peas cost 5p.

How much more do the potatoes cost than the peas?

4. Jim buys some chocolate for 17p.

He gives the shopkeeper 20p.

How much change does he have?

Measures

Children suggest suitable units for measuring and explain why they have chosen those units. They make estimates then check these by measuring, recording their results.

LEARNING OBJECTIVES

	Topics	Starter	Main teaching activities
Lesson 1	Measures	● Describe and extend number sequences: begin to count on in steps of 3 from zero.	● **Suggest suitable standard or uniform non-standard units and measuring equipment to estimate, then measure, a length, mass or capacity**, recording estimates and measurements as 'about 3 beakers full' or 'about as heavy as 20 cubes'.
Lesson 2	Measures	As for Lesson 1.	As for Lesson 1.
Lesson 3	Measures	As for Lesson 1.	As for Lesson 1.
Lesson 4	Measures	● Know by heart addition doubles of all numbers to at least 5 (e.g. 4 + 4).	As for Lesson 1.
Lesson 5	Measures	As for Lesson 4.	As for Lesson 1.

Lessons   overview

Preparation
On a large sheet of sugar paper, draw four or five thick 'wiggly' lines. These could be curves or zigzags. The lines must be different lengths, so that the children can order them. Label the lines A, B, C…

Learning objectives
Starter
● Describe and extend number sequences: begin to count on in steps of 3 from zero.
Main teaching activities
● **Suggest suitable standard or uniform non-standard units and measuring equipment to estimate, then measure, a length, mass or capacity**, recording estimates and measurements as 'about 3 beakers full' or 'about as heavy as 20 cubes'.

Vocabulary
measure, size, compare, guess, estimate, enough, not enough, too much, too little, too many, too few, nearly, roughly, close to, about the same as, just over, just under

You will need:
CD pages
'Estimate and measure' and 'Measures chart 2' for each pair (see General Resources).

Equipment
Items for measurement such as: a beaker, scoops, spoons, egg cups, cups, dried peas, pasta, sand, balances, parcels, cubes, rods, straws, string, weights, scissors, a wiggly lines sheet (see Preparation), ribbons of different lengths; flip chart or board; pencils.

Lesson ①

Starter

Ask the children to count with you in threes by saying all the numbers from 0 to 30 and clapping on 3, 6, 9… Repeat this several times. Keep the pace sharp.

Main teaching activities

Whole class: Explain to the children that the lessons for this week are about measuring. Review the use of some non-standard units. Show the children a beaker and then some spoons, scoops and egg cups. Ask: *Which unit would be best for filling this beaker? Why do you think that?* Invite estimates of how many of the preferred unit will fill the beaker, and write them on the flip chart. Agree on a sensible estimate. Ask a child to fill the beaker while the other children count the units used. Write how many were used on the flip chart. Ask: *Did we make a good estimate? Was our estimate nearly the same? Was it a bit over/under the measure?*

Now repeat this with a parcel: let the children pass it around and 'feel' the weight with their hands. Ask them to decide which unit would be best to measure the weight. Ask them to estimate how many of these units the parcel weighs. They could choose from, for example, cubes, scoops of sand, scoops of dried peas or pasta pieces. Write the estimate on the flip chart, then measure the weight by comparing with the chosen unit using a balance. Ask: *Did we estimate too much/too little? Was our estimate just over/just under?*

Show the children a length of ribbon, and some units of length such as cubes, rods and straws. Ask: *What units should we use to estimate and measure this?* Invite suggestions for the best unit, then invite estimates of how many units will match the length of the ribbon. Write these on the flip chart and agree on a sensible estimate. Invite a child to check by measuring. Ask the children to compare their estimate with the measure, and ask: *Did you make a good guess? What could you use to estimate and then measure the width of this ribbon?*

Group work: Choose from the selection below and set up a circus of activities. Explain that the children will be trying a different measuring activity each day of this week.

1. Put out a selection of items to be estimated and measured, and a range of units for length. Ask the children to work in pairs. They decide for each item which will be the best unit and why, then estimate and measure. They can record this on the 'Estimate and measure' sheet.

2. Put out a selection of parcels to be estimated and measured, and a range of units for weight. Ask the children to work in pairs. They decide for each parcel which will be the best unit and why, then estimate and measure. They can record this on the 'Estimate and measure' sheet.

3. Put out a selection of containers and a range of units for capacity. Ask the children to work in pairs. They decide for each container which will be the best unit and why, then estimate and measure. They can record this on the 'Estimate and measure' sheet.

4. Provide some clear containers of different shapes and heights. Put out some filling material, such as sand, already measured into a margarine tub. There should be just enough sand to fill the smallest of the containers. Ask the children to estimate where the sand will reach in a chosen container. They draw their container and mark their estimate. They then check by pouring, again drawing the level. They repeat this for different containers.

5. Put an elastic band onto a clear container with straight sides, such as a plastic beaker. Ask the children to estimate how many scoops of sand will be needed to reach the band. The children estimate, then check. They can record this on paper. Ask them to move the band to a different position and repeat. This activity should help the children to improve the accuracy of their estimation of capacity.

6. Provide a 200g weight, some sand, and some plastic bags and ties. Ask the children to estimate how much sand they will need to balance the 200g weight, and then to measure it accurately. They put the measured sand into a bag and tie the top firmly. Now they try to find items in the classroom that they estimate weigh about 200g – then check by balancing with the bag of sand. They can record this on the 'Measures chart 2' sheet.

7. Ask the children to list the wiggly lines on the prepared sheet in order of length, from shortest to longest. They can record the order by listing the letters. They should estimate the order first, then use string to check. They should write the measured order next to the estimated order. Ask: *How good was your estimate?*

Differentiation

All of the children can tackle the above activities.

Less able: The children will benefit from opportunities to discuss what they are doing with an adult, so that they can experience hearing and using the vocabulary of measurement. They may also need more help with recording, such as a fuller explanation (with examples) of what is expected.

More able: In activity 6, challenge the children to make different sand weights such as 50g, 100g and 300g. They should then find items in the classroom that they estimate weigh about the same as each of these.

Plenary & assessment

Review one of the activities that has been tackled. Ask individual children to explain what they did and their results. Ask questions such as: *Which of these was a sensible choice for measuring? Which was the longest/shortest… heaviest/lightest… held the most/least? How did you find out?*

Lesson

Repeat the Starter for Lesson 1, this time asking the children to count just the 3, 6, 9… pattern and to clap for the other numbers. Starting on 1, the count will go: 'Clap, clap, 3, clap, clap, 6…' Repeat this several times. Reverse the pattern so that the children say '1, 2, clap, 4, 5, clap…' Keep the pace sharp.

For the whole-class teaching activity, show the children four ribbons of different lengths and invite them to order these. Encourage them to use the language of ordering lengths: 'longer/shorter' and 'longest/shortest'. Choose from the circus of activities for each group.

During the plenary, review another of the group activities with the whole class, inviting the group who carried out this activity to explain what they did and why. Ask the class, for example: *Would this be a good unit to measure this with? Why/why not?*

Lesson

For the Starter, ask the children to count with you, in ones, from zero to 30. On each three (3, 6, 9…) they say the number accompanied by a quiet clap. Repeat this several times, keeping the pace sharp. Now ask the children to count again, this time just saying the threes: 0, 3, 6, 9… Again, repeat this several times. Finally, ask the children to count from zero to 30, this time not saying the threes numbers, instead nodding their heads.

For the whole-class teaching activity, ask the children to explain what an estimate is. Discuss what makes a good estimate: being reasonably accurate. Choose from the circus of activities for each group.

During the plenary, review another of the group activities with the whole class, inviting the group who carried out this activity to explain what they did and why. Ask the class, for example: *Before you measure, what are the important things to remember about measuring?*

Lessons   overview

Learning objectives

Starter
● Know by heart addition doubles of all numbers to at least 5 (e.g. 4 + 4).

Main teaching activities
● **Suggest suitable standard or uniform non-standard units and measuring equipment to estimate, then measure, a length, mass or capacity**, recording estimates and measurements as 'about 3 beakers full' or 'about as heavy as 20 cubes'.

Vocabulary

measure, size, compare, guess, estimate, enough, not enough, too much, too little, too many, too few, nearly, roughly, close to, about the same as, just over, just under

You will need:

CD pages
A teaching set of 'Double facts to 5 + 5' cards and a 'Number fan' for each child (see General Resources).

Equipment
Individual whiteboards and pens; containers such as beakers, jugs, boxes and plastic bottles; filling materials; measuring units such as cubes, metre sticks, rods and strips of paper; balances; marbles; spoons; paper and pencils.

Lesson

Starter

Explain that you will hold up a double fact card and that you want the children to show you the answer with their number fans when you say: *Show me.* Use the 'Double facts to 5 + 5' cards. Keep the pace sharp to encourage rapid recall.

Main teaching activities

Whole class: Explain that today you would like the children to estimate and measure some things in the classroom. Say: *Which units would you choose to measure the length/width of the classroom? Why would you choose these?*

Repeat this for the height and length of a table, a chair, the cupboard, the bookcase and so on. Check that the children are suggesting sensible units by inviting a child to choose a unit and measure with it. Discuss the appropriateness of the unit chosen. Where a unit is far too small (for example, using cubes to measure the length of a carpet) or far too large (for example, using a metre stick to measure an eraser), ask the children to suggest a more realistic unit and check again by measuring.

Group work: Provide pairs with four different units for measuring. Ask them to choose an appropriate unit to measure the length and width of the classroom, the height of their chair and the width of their table. They should estimate first and record both the estimate and the actual measurement.

Differentiation

Less able: Work with this group and provide support for counting how many of the chosen unit are needed for each measure. Support them in recording their results.

More able: Challenge the children to suggest other classroom items that they could measure, and then to estimate and measure these items.

Plenary & assessment

Review the children's choices of units for estimating and measuring the items. Ask some children to explain their choices. Discuss how good their estimates were. Ask:
● *Which was the longest/shortest thing you measured?*
● *What units did you choose? Was this a good choice? Why?*

Lesson ⑤

Starter

Repeat the Starter from Lesson 4, this time asking the children to respond by writing the answer on their whiteboards and holding these up when you say: *Show me.*

Main teaching activities

Whole class: Hold up a clear container and discuss how its height, weight and capacity could be found. Ask the children to suggest what units could be used for each measurement.

Group work: Suggest to the group, five or six different units for measuring and provide a container. Ask them to choose appropriate units to measure the height, weight and capacity of the container. They should estimate first and then record both the estimate and the actual measurement.

Differentiation

Less able: Work with this group and provide support for counting how many of the chosen unit are needed for each measure. Support them in recording their results.

More able: Challenge the children to compare two containers and to write which container is heavier, which is taller and which holds more.

Plenary & assessment

Ask the children to report back on what they found out. Invite contributions from each ability group. Say:

- *The taller the container, the more it holds. Is this true? Why not?*
- *The larger the container, the heavier it is. Is this true? Why not?*

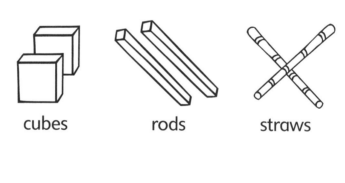

cubes   rods   straws

scoops   spoon   marbles

Time, and organising and using data

Children respond to analogue clocks set to o'clock and half past times. They solve simple time-based problems explaining how they worked out their answer. They find the solution to a problem by collecting, sorting and organising data, and deciding how to record it. They make graphs using stacked cubes. They interrogate the data to answer questions about it.

LEARNING OBJECTIVES

		Topics	Starter	Main teaching activities
Lesson	1	Measures	● **Know by heart all pairs of numbers with a total of 10** (e.g. 3 + 7).	● Read the time to the hour or half hour on analogue clocks.
Lesson	2	Measures	As for Lesson 1.	As for Lesson 1.
Lesson	3	Organising and using data	● **Read and write numerals from 0 to at least 20.**	● Solve a given problem by sorting, classifying and organising information in simple ways, such as: using objects or pictures; in a list or simple table. ● Discuss and explain results.
Lesson	4	Organising and using data	As for Lesson 3.	As for Lesson 3.
Lesson	5	Organising and using data	As for Lesson 3.	As for Lesson 3.

Lessons   overview

Preparation
Draw six clock faces on the flip chart (see Lesson 2).

Learning objectives
Starter
● **Know by heart all pairs of numbers with a total of 10** (e.g. 3 + 7).
Main teaching activity
● Read the time to the hour or half hour on analogue clocks.

Vocabulary
time, hour, o'clock, half past, clock, watch, hands, how long ago?, how long will it be to…?, how long will it take to…?, how often?, always, never, often, sometimes, usually

You will need:
CD pages
A teaching set of 'Complements of 10' cards, a 'Number fan' and 'Clock face' for each child (see General Resources).

Equipment
Individual whiteboards and pens; scissors and glue for each child or group; a geared teaching clock; ready-cut squares of paper, all the same size.

Lesson

Starter
Explain that you will hold up a card with a number sentence on it. Ask the children to use their number fans to show you the answer when you say: *Show me*. Use the 'Complements of 10' cards. Keep the pace sharp, encouraging the children to use rapid recall.

Main teaching activities

Whole class: Explain that you will show the children some times on the teaching clock. Ask them to put up their hands to say the time. Choose, over the session, children from each ability group to say the time. Include a range of o'clock and half past times. Ask: *What time is this? How do you know that? What does the hour hand show? What does the minute hand show?*

When the children are confident with this, ask some time questions, such as:

● *How long is it between getting up at 7 o'clock and eating lunch at 12 o'clock?*
● *My favourite television programme begins at half past 7 and ends at 9 o'clock. How long does it last?*

For each question, invite a child to explain how he or she worked out the answer. Less able children may benefit from having individual clock faces to help them with these questions.

Group work: Ask the children to work in pairs. They take turns to say a time, and their partner sets the clock to show that time. Ask the children to say 'o'clock' and 'half past' times.

Differentiation

Less able: Decide whether to work with these children as a group. Encourage the children to say the time and to use other time vocabulary.

More able: Challenge the children to include 'quarter past' times.

Plenary & assessment

Ask more time questions, such as:

● *At 3 o'clock James goes his gran's. He comes back home at 6 o'clock. How long is he out for?*
● *Sarah watches her favourite TV programme. The programme starts at 4 o'clock and finishes at half past 4. How long does it last?*
● *Maisie leaves home to go to her grandma's at half past 2. She comes home at 7 o'clock. How long was she away from home?*

For each question, invite the children to explain how they worked out the answer.

Lesson ②

Starter

Repeat the Starter from Lesson 1. This time, ask the children to use their individual whiteboards and pens to show you their answers.

Main teaching activities

Whole class: Ask more time questions involving whole and half hours, such as: *I went to the shops at 2 o'clock and came home at half past 4. How long was I out?*

Individual activity: Draw, on the flip chart, six clock faces showing different times of the day, for example, 6 o'clock, 4 o'clock, half past 3, 8 o'clock, 7 o'clock, 11 o'clock. Ask the children to draw an appropriate activity for each time, such as have breakfast for 8 o'clock. Before the children begin, you might want to discuss whether the times are morning or afternoon.

Differentiation

Less able: The children may find it helpful to set an individual clock face to the times shown on the activity sheet. Alternatively, less able children could complete this activity as a group, with an adult helping them to read and say the times.

More able: Challenge the more able children to think of more things that they do during the day, and to say at what times these happen.

Plenary & assessment

Review the activity together, using the clocks on the flip chart. Ask, for example: *What time do you get up? What time do you go to school? So how long do you take to get ready for school?*

Lessons   overview

Learning objectives

Starter
- **Read and write numerals from 0 to at least 20.**

Main teaching activities
- Solve a given problem by sorting, classifying and organising information in simple ways, such as: using objects or pictures; in a list or simple table.
- Discuss and explain results.

Vocabulary
count, sort, vote, list, group, set, table

You will need:
Equipment
Individual whiteboards and pens; a computer with graphing software; small squares of white paper and of coloured gummed paper; glue; sugar paper; marker pens; flip chart or board.

Lesson

Starter
Explain that you will say a number, and you would like the children to write the number on their whiteboard and hold it up when you say: *Show me.* Say, for example: *Write 12; 15; 20… Write the number that is one more/ less than 2, 6, 12… Write the number that is ten more/less than …* Keep the number range between 0 and 20.

Main teaching activities
Whole class: Explain that for the next three lessons, the children will be collecting and sorting data and making simple lists and graphs. It is a good idea to have a linking theme for these three days' work; the theme used in this lesson plan is 'Ourselves'.

Ask the children to listen carefully to the question and then put themselves into groups according to how they answer it. Ask: *Who has a brother?* All the children who have a brother can stand in one area. Ask one child to count how many children have a brother and write this on the flip chart. Write how many children there are in total on the flip chart. Repeat this for: *Who has a sister?* Ask questions such as:
- *Are there more people with sisters or with brothers?*
- *How many people do not have a brother/a sister?*
- *How else could we record all this information?*

Suggestions could include making a chart or making a simple block graph to show how many children have brothers and how many have sisters.

Group work: Choose from the list of activities for collecting and organising data (see below). The children can work in groups of four to eight to carry out these activities over the three days.

You may want to carry out two or more of the activities during a lesson. You could set the first task for the children, give them a limited time to carry it out and then come together as a class to record class data. This can be an opportunity for the children to collect data in their group and make a list or simple table, before a class chart is made. The second task can then be carried out in the same way.

Where the children are sticking squares of paper onto a graph, remind them to make sure that all their squares are placed edge to edge so that the rows and columns are equally spread. The data gathered could be recorded using computer software that produces pictograms or block graphs.

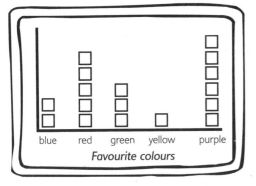

Favourite colours

1. The children record how many brothers and sisters they each have by making a graph, using identical-sized squares of paper. They draw a picture of each brother or sister on a square and stick this carefully onto the graph.
2. The children find out about pet ownership in their group. They decide how to gather the data and then how to produce a graph.
3. The group find out how old each person is. They make a simple graph showing 5 years and 6 years. This can be combined with other groups' data to produce a whole class graph.
4. Each child can draw his or her eyes on a square of paper, which is stuck onto a class chart.
5. Hair colour can be recorded as in activity 4 above.
6. At this age, children begin to lose their milk teeth. They can draw a picture of a tooth on a square of paper, and repeat this for each tooth they have lost. This can be used to make a group graph. The data from the group graphs can be transferred onto a class graph to show how many children have lost 0, 1, 2… teeth.
7. The children can work in their group to list their favourite colours. Group data can then be combined to produce a whole-class chart showing how many children prefer blue, green and so on. The data can be displayed as squares of colour, stuck evenly onto a chart.

Differentiation
Less able: The children can attempt any of the above activities. They will benefit from adult supervision to check that they understand how to construct a list or a graph.
More able: Challenge the children to suggest other topics for collecting data and making graphs; then ask them to collect and record data for one of their suggested topics.

Plenary & assessment
Review the graphs that have been made. Ask questions such as: *How many children like red? How many more children like blue than like red?* Adapt these questions for other tasks.

Lesson

Repeat the Starter for Lesson 3, this time writing numbers in words on the flip chart for the children to write as numerals on their whiteboards: *ten, four, fifteen…*

During the whole-class teaching activity, ask the children to choose their favourite fruit from a list. Make a class graph of the results by asking each child to stack a cube in their favourite fruit column. The cubes can be stacked on the ledge under the flip chart, with the names of the fruits written on the flip chart. Ask questions as in the plenary for Lesson 3. For the group work, choose from the list of activities in Lesson 3.

During the plenary, ask questions about one of the activities covered in the group work.

Lesson

Combine the Starters for Lessons 3 and 4, so that the children write (in numerals) the numbers that you say or write on the flip chart (in words).

During the whole-class teaching activity, ask the children to write a number from 1 to 20 on their whiteboards. Make a class graph of the numbers chosen, using cubes (as in Lesson 4). Ask questions such as: *Which number was chosen most often? How many more/fewer chose … than …?* Choose from the list of activities in Lesson 3 for the group work.

During the plenary, ask questions such as: *How many more … than … are there? How can you work this out? Which has the most? How can you tell by looking at the graph?*